Reading the World with Picture Books

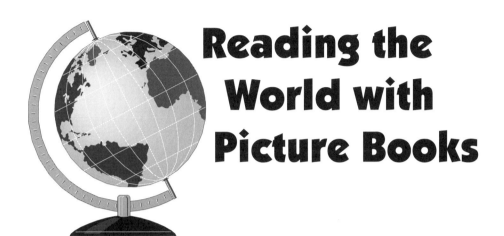

Reading the World with Picture Books

Nancy J. Polette

LIBRARIES UNLIMITED

AN IMPRINT OF ABC-CLIO, LLC
Santa Barbara, California • Denver, Colorado • Oxford, England

Library of Congress Cataloging-in-Publication Data

Polette, Nancy.
    Reading the world with picture books / Nancy J. Polette.
       p. cm.
    Includes bibliographical references and index.
    ISBN 978-1-59884-587-7 (pbk. : acid-free paper) — ISBN 978-1-59884-588-4 (ebook)
  1. Reading (Elementary) 2. Reading (Elementary)—Activity programs. 3. World history—Study and teaching (Elementary)—Activity programs. 4. Geography—Study and teaching (Elementary)—Activity programs. 5. Picture books for children. 6. Children—Books and reading. I. Title.
  LB1573.P648 2010
  372.46'5—dc22   2010021569

ISBN: 978-1-59884-587-7
EISBN: 978-1-59884-588-4

14 13 12 11 10   1 2 3 4 5

This book is also available on the World Wide Web as an eBook.
Visit www.abc-clio.com for details.

Libraries Unlimited
An Imprint of ABC-CLIO, LLC

ABC-CLIO, LLC
130 Cremona Drive, P.O. Box 1911
Santa Barbara, California 93116-1911

This book is printed on acid-free paper ∞
Manufactured in the United States of America

Contents

Part Three:
Europe

Part Four:
North and Central America

Part Five:
South America

Part Six:
Antarctica

Part Seven:
Australia/Oceania

Part Eight:
Asia and the Middle East

Introduction

Take your students on a world tour with picture books! Discover the people and places that make up the diverse cultures of the world and the many ways in which people provide for the basic needs of all who share the planet Earth.

At the beginning of each part of this book is a list of the countries in that continent as well as basic information about the continent. The sources of the information on the continents and individual countries are *Encyclopedia Britannica 2007 Deluxe DVD*; Software Mackievs, *World Book 2009 Edition* (DVD); and C. Allan, ed., *World Almanac for Kids* (World Almanac Books, 2007).

Reading the World with Picture Books offers booktalks for picture books set in the major countries of each continent, along with activities for sharing books, set in each country. In some cases where picture books could not be found for a particular country, an exciting read-aloud chapter book was substituted. Grade levels are provided for each book. Activities range from those for the beginning researcher/writer to the more experienced researcher/writer. All call for high-level thinking, and most allow students to respond in creative ways. In addition, many activities require the student to

> interpret information related to historical or geographical concepts;
>
> use problem-solving and decision-making skills as they apply to social studies data;
>
> demonstrate an understanding of how people adapt to their environment; and
>
> understand and use the following thinking processes: analyze, classify, compare, contrast, create, determine, distinguish, evaluate, identify, interpret, forecast, problem solve, sequence, and summarize.

The activities are keyed to selected National Standards in Language Arts and Social Studies (see p. xiii); the applicable standards are identified with each activity.

Reading the World with Picture Books will add a whole new dimension to the social studies program by emphasizing both the distinct cultures and commonalities of Earth's people.

Selected National Standards in Language Arts and Social Studies

1. Recognize and investigate problems; formulate and propose solutions supported by reason and evidence.

2. Express and interpret information and ideas.

3. Learn and contribute productively as individuals and as members of groups.

4. Recognize and apply connections of important information and ideas within and among learning areas.

5. Sequence, order, and classify information.

6. Form definitions based on observations and infer; generalize and predict outcomes.

7. Identify a problem; formulate and evaluate alternative solutions.

8. Draw conclusions about processes or outcomes and relate or apply knowledge gained.

9. Apply word analysis and vocabulary skills to comprehend selections.

10. Apply reading strategies to improve understanding and fluency.

11. Comprehend a broad range of reading materials.

12. Understand how literary elements are used to convey meaning.

13. Read and interpret a variety of nonfiction works.

14. Use correct grammar, spelling, punctuation, capitalization, and structure.

15. Compose well-organized and coherent writing for specific purposes and audiences.

16. Communicate ideas in writing to accomplish a variety of purposes.

17. Listen effectively in formal and informal situations.

18. Speak effectively using language appropriate to the situation and audience.

19. Locate, organize, and use information from a variety of sources to answer questions, solve problems, and communicate ideas.

20. Analyze and evaluate information from a variety of sources.

21. Apply acquired information, concepts, and ideas to communicate in a variety of formats.

Part One

Introducing the Seven Continents

Mnemonics: Remembering the Seven Continents (a Mostly True Story)

In 1889 Nellie Bly, a reporter for the *New York Times*, read a book by Jules Verne, *Around the World in Eighty Days*. "I can beat that record," she said, and she set sail from New York Harbor to do just that. Her first stops were in Europe, where she visited Jules Verne in France. She moved on to Italy and from there she set sail for Africa. She continued her journey on Egyptian camels, then traveled by boat up the Suez Canal. It's a fact that Nellie moved through Africa faster than a flea can sneeze.

"Amazing," people said. "She is tireless. How can a mere woman move so fast from one time zone to another and not collapse from exhaustion?" Nellie had a secret that she never told anyone. Because of her secret, she paid no attention to those who thought women were the weaker sex. She left Africa and made stops in six Asian countries. She stepped over a cobra in Sir Lanka, clung to a ship's mast in a monsoon off Hong Kong, and celebrated Christmas in China. Having no fondness for penguins or kangaroos, she skipped Antarctica and Australia, but she adopted a monkey in Singapore. Setting sail from Yokohama, she bypassed South America on her way to San Francisco. Nellie moved like a whirlwind. She beat the record! Because she never stopped to rest even though she experienced many sleepless nights, she made her trip around the world in 72 days!

Nellie never told anyone the secret of how she maintained such a high energy level. It is revealed here for the first time. To be a world traveler who never tires:

E–at	A-n	A-pple	A-fter	A	S-leepless	N-ight.
u	f	s	n	u	o	o
r	r	i	t	s	u	r
o	i	a	a	t	t	t
p	c		r	r	h	h
e	a		c	a		
			t	l	A	A
			i	i	m	m
			c	a	e	e
			a		r	r
					i	i
					c	c
					a	a

3

SCRAMBLED SENTENCE DEFINITIONS

Standards: 4, 5, 6

This activity can be used to describe any continent or country. The example here describes one of the seven continents.

Directions: Use marking pens to write each word in a sentence that describes a continent or country on separate pieces of cardboard or paper. Mix up the words.

Challenge students to arrange the words so that they correctly describe and name the continent or country.

ISLANDS	A	OF	1840	ESTABLISHED
IN	A	AND	IT	CONTINENT
GROUP	WAS	THIS		
WAS	NOT	THAT		

Answer key: In 1840 it was established that this was a continent and not a group of islands: ANTARCTICA

From *Reading the World with Picture Books* by Nancy J. Polette.
Santa Barbara, CA: Libraries Unlimited. Copyright © 2010.

VISITING THE CONTINENTS

Standards: 11, 13

Once there was a very large giant who wanted to capture the earth. The very large giant had a very large bag to hold all seven continents. On the side of his bag were the letters N,S, and E and four As to remind him to pick up North and South America, Europe, and the four continents whose names begin with the letter A.

Reaching down with his giant-sized hand, he picked up North and South America and dropped them in his bag. He took one VERY big step across the Atlantic Ocean, picked up Europe, and into his bag it went. Now he needed to find the four As. Africa and Asia were easy because they were so large. Then it was time to head south. The giant did not like the cold, so he spent very little time at the South Pole. He snatched up icy Antarctica, and into the bag it went!

By now the giant's bag was bursting with North and South America, Europe, Asia, Africa, and Antarctica. Would there be room for the one last continent? What continent does he not have? _____

Play the X Game!

Select the name of a familiar country to write on the chalkboard. However, rather than letters, use Xs for all but one or two of the letters in the name.

Example: X X O X X X X D tells those who are guessing that there are eight letters in this country's name. The third letter is O and the last letter is D.

Students take turns guessing a letter. For example: a student might guess (correctly) that the first letter is S. This X is then erased, and the letter S is put in its place. If the student cannot then guess the country, another student takes a turn guessing another letter. A student can only guess the name of a country if a letter is guessed correctly. The student should then identify the continent in which the country is found.

★ **Answer key:** The giant does not have Australia.

From *Reading the World with Picture Books* by Nancy J. Polette.
Santa Barbara, CA: Libraries Unlimited. Copyright © 2010.

AROUND THE WORLD WITH PIRATES!

Standards: 11, 13

Pirates, by David Harrison. Illustrated by Dan Burr. Wordsong (Boyds Mill), 2008. (Grades 2–5)

There are famous pirates, and then there are the rest of the pirates. All were a bunch of misfits, thugs, and ne'er-do-wells who spent most of their time bored, waiting for a few moments of excitement that could very well get them wounded and killed or captured, and executed. Eager to get under sail, they traveled the world. But to most of those who swore the oath of the Brotherhood, it was just a job. Still, a pirate's life was chosen by many, and this collection of poetry describes and depicts the high points, the low points, and everything in between.

Suppose a pirate ship landed on the shore of each of these continents. Which animal or animals would the pirates see? Match each animal with the continent on which it is found.

1. Africa	2. Antarctica	3. North America
4. Asia	5. Australia	6. South America

A. _____ elephants   B. _____ llamas

C. _____ grizzly bear   D. _____ lions

E. _____ camels   F. _____ toucan

G. _____ cobras   H. _____ penguins

I. _____ dingoes   J. _____ koala bears

✎ **Answer key:** A-1, 4; B-6; C-3; D-1; E-1; F-6; G-4; H-2; I-5; J-5

COUNTRY BINGO

Standards: 3, 10, 17, 20

Create Bingo boards with the names of nine countries found on one continent.

List below one fact for each country. The caller reads a fact, and players who know the answer can cover up that country. The first player to get three across or down is the winner.

FACT   COUNTRY

1. _____

2. _____

3. _____

4. _____

5. _____

6. _____

7. _____

8. _____

9. _____

SHARE

What's Inside? Fascinating Structures Around the World, writtten and illustrated by Giles Laroche. Houghton-Mifflin, 2009.

Tour the world and see some of the most beautiful, puzzling, and fascinating structures ever built.

GO TO	SEE
Egypt	King Tut's Tomb
Greece	the Parthenon
Mexico	Temple of Kukulcan
China	the Wooden Pagoda
Spain	The Gate of the Sun
Spain	Alcazar (castle) of Segovia
United States	Independence Hall
United States	Guggenheim Museum
Australia	Sydney Opera House
Malaysia	Petronas Twin Towers

From *Reading the World with Picture Books* by Nancy J. Polette.
Santa Barbara, CA: Libraries Unlimited. Copyright © 2010.

A FUN BOOK TO SHARE

Standards: 2, 4, 14

Rhymes Around the World, by Kay Chorao. Dutton, 2009. (Grades 1–4)

Poetry is a worldwide event in this collection of poems from many countries.

Form two teams. As a poem from a particular country is shared, one member from each team will try to find the country on a large "pull down" world map located in the front of the room. The first person to do so gets a point for his or her team.

Follow the pattern below and add more verses.

Take a trip to Pakistan. Come home with a feather fan.

Take a trip to Cameroon. Come home with a pet baboon

Take a trip to London town. Come home with an evening gown.

Take a trip to Paris, France. Come home with some purple pants

Take a trip to _____. Come home with _____.

Take a trip to _____. Come home with _____.

Take a trip to _____. Come home with _____.

Take a trip to _____. Come home with _____.

Part Two

Africa

Facts about Africa

Africa is the world's second largest and second most populous continent, after Asia. The continent covers 11,668,545 square miles, including adjacent islands, which is 20 percent of the earth's total land area. With more than 900 million people in 61 territories, it accounts for about 14 percent of the world's human population. The continent is surrounded by the Mediterranean Sea to the north, the Suez Canal and the Red Sea to the northeast, the Indian Ocean to the southeast, and the Atlantic Ocean to the west. Although the continent is rich in natural resources, many Africans are illiterate and live in poverty.

COUNTRIES OF AFRICA

Booktalks have been provided for the countries in boldface.

Algeria	Malawi
Angola	**Mali**
Benin	Mauritania
Botswana	Mauritius
Burkina Faso	**Morocco**
Burundi	**Mozambique**
Cameroon	**Namibia**
Cape Verde	Niger
Central African Republic	**Nigeria**
Chad	Reunion
Congo	**Rwanda**
Djibouti	Sâo Tomé and Principe
Egypt	**Senegal**
Equatorial Guinea	Seychelles
Eritrea	Sierra Leone
Ethiopia	**Somalia**
Gabon	**South Africa**
Gambia	Sudan
Ghana	Swaziland
Guinea	**Tanzania**
Guinea Bissau	Togo
Ivory Coast	Tunisia
Kenya	**Uganda**
Lesotho	**Zaire**
Liberia	Zambia
Libya	Zanzibar
Madagascar	**Zimbabwe**

Standards: 11, 13

1. Play the X Game (see page 5) using countries of Africa.

2. Create a word search using ten of the largest African countries.

3. Group the countries under these headings:

    Desert   Coastal   Savanna   Jungle

AFRICAN FOLKTALES
BY VERNA AARDEMA

Standards: 4, 6, 10, 11

These picture books introduce African animals in their natural settings and provide excellent predictive reading experiences. Match the title with the description of each book. (Grades K–3)

1. *Bimwili and the Zimwi* _____

2. *Bringing the Rain to Kapiti Plain* _____

3. *Oh, Kojo, How Could You!* _____

4. *Princess Gorilla and a New Kind of Water* _____

5. *Vingananee and the Tree Toad*

6. *What's So Funny Ketu?* _____

7. *Who's in Rabbit's House?* _____

8. *Why Mosquitoes Buzz in People's Ears* _____

    A. Mosquito tells a tall tale, which results in the sun not rising.

    B. Rabbit has a problem: someone is inside her house and won't let her in.

    C. For saving the life of a snake, Ketu is rewarded by being allowed to hear animals think.

    D. A strange animal called the Vingananee beats up all the other animals and eats their stew, until tiny Tree Toad offers to fight him.

    E. King Gorilla decrees that no one may marry his daughter until a suitor strong enough to consume a barrel of strange, smelly water can be found.

    F. Each time Kojo is sent to buy something, he is tricked out of his money by Ananse, until with the help of a cat he finally tricks the trickster

    G. This is a cumulative tale about animals of the grasslands and the need for rain.

    H. A Swahili girl is abducted by a Zimwi and told to be the voice inside his singing drum.

Answer key: 1-H; 2-G; 3-F;-4-E; 5-D; 6-C; 7-B; 8-A

From *Reading the World with Picture Books* by Nancy J. Polette. Santa Barbara, CA: Libraries Unlimited. Copyright © 2010.

CREATE A COUNTRY RELAY GAME

Standards: 2, 4, 5

Select two countries from Africa and write 20 statements that apply to one or both countries.

Example: KENYA AND SOMALIA

1. Is located on the continent of Africa. (both)
2. Exports coffee and tea. (Kenya)
3. Its average wage is barely enough to feed a family. (Somalia)
4. Part of the coast is on the Indian Ocean. (both)
5. Its chief economic activity is livestock raising. (Somalia)
6. It has a pleasant and sunny climate. (Kenya)
7. It has reserves to protect wild animals. (both)
8. It has only 1,800 miles of roads. (Somalia)
9. Its people use mainly wood for cooking. (both)
10. Joy Adamson worked with chimpanzees here. (Kenya)
11. Most of its rural towns cut off in the rainy season. (Somalia)
12. It has a long history of clan wars. (Somalia)
13. Lions, leopards, and elephants are found here. (Both
14. Storytelling is major entertainment. (Somalia)
15. Its has a high incidence of malaria. (Kenya)
16. The United Nations tried to stop its wars. (Somalia)
17. Its has a National Art Museum. (both)
18. It has four public universities. (Kenya)
19. Medical care not available to most of its people. (Somalia)
20. It is a popular tourist destination. (Kenya)

HOW TO PLAY

- Divide students into two teams. Give each team three small cards, one for each country and one reading "both."

- The leader reads a statement. The team decides whether the statement belongs to one country or to both and places the correct card face down on the table.

- Both teams turn up their cards, and the leader reads the correct answer. If a team is correct it receives one point for each correct answer.

- After all 20 statements have been read, the team with the most points is the winner.

From *Reading the World with Picture Books* by Nancy J. Polette.
Santa Barbara, CA: Libraries Unlimited. Copyright © 2010.

Botswana

This part-desert country covers more than 1.5 million square miles and is home to 1,600,000 people. It is a very poor country, with an average life expectancy of only 34 years. The official language is English, and the capital is Gaborone.

Bashi, Elephant Baby, by Theresa Radcliffe. Viking, 1997. (Grades K–2)

Little Bashi is full of milk and wants to go right to sleep, but he has to keep on walking to keep up with the herd. After a while the elephants reach a watering hole, where Bashi plays and gets stuck in the mud. Suddenly two fearsome lionesses appear. Bashi's mother and grandmother have to fight to protect him. Bashi is very frightened, but he knows his family is there to keep him safe. Lush, glowing illustrations beautifully depict the African plains.

THE DATA BANK

Standards: 2, 4, 13, 16, 21

A data bank is a source of information. You can make a data bank about any animal, like the one on this page about elephants.

THE AFRICAN ELEPHANT:			
EATS	LIVES	HAS	DOES
grasses	Africa	long trunk	grows 12 feet tall
leaves	tropical forests	ivory tusks	bathes in dust
495 lbs. per day	river valleys	only four teeth	pulls down trees
		wrinkled skin	lives 60–70 years

Insert the information from the data bank in the blank spaces below. Then sing the song to the tune of "London Bridge."

Elephants have

_____ and _____

_____ and _____

_____ and _____

Elephants eat

_____ and _____

And they _____

From *Reading the World with Picture Books* by Nancy J. Polette.
Santa Barbara, CA: Libraries Unlimited. Copyright © 2010.

Cameroon

Cameroon is home to 18 million people and covers an area of 183,500 square miles. The languages spoken are French and English, because at one time the country was controlled by France and Great Britain. The capital is Yaoundé.

The Fortune Tellers, by Lloyd Alexander. Illustrated by Trina Schart Hyman. Dutton, 1992. (Grades 3–5)

Imagine a fortune-teller who makes these predictions: "Rich you will surely be, if you earn large sums of money." Moreover, "You shall wed your true love . . . if you find her and she agrees. And you shall be happy as any in the world if you can avoid being miserable." This is the fortune given to a poor carpenter, who leaves the fortune-teller feeling that he has a rosy future indeed. On his way home he thinks of another question he has for the fortune-teller, who seems to have vanished. The villagers, however, think that the fortune-teller has turned himself into the young man, and the youth becomes the village fortune-teller, starting a whole new career.

BE A FORTUNE-TELLER

Standards: 5, 6, 12

Pretend you are the fortune-teller the young carpenter came to see. Pick five or six letters of the alphabet and write a fortune for the young man using the letters in ABC order.

Example:

C   arpenters

D   eserve

E   very

F   ine

G   ift

Congo

The Democratic Republic of the Congo covers about 905,500 square miles and has a population of 64.5 million people. The official language is French, although many different African languages are spoken there as well. The country originally was named Zaire. The capital is Kinshasa.

Looking for Miza: The True Story of the Mountain Gorilla Family Who Rescued One of Their Own, by Craig Hatkoff, Juliana Hatkoff, and Isabella Hatkoff. Scholastic, 2008. (Grades 2–5)

In a magical place called the Congo, in the beautiful forests and jungles of Virunga National Park, lives a young female mountain gorilla named Miza. She was just like any other baby gorilla, riding on her mother's back, playing, and taking naps. Then, one day, when Miza and her mother were out searching for food, Miza's mother disappeared, leaving her baby alone and frightened. Miza's father, a fierce silverback named Kabirizi and the leader of Virunga's largest family of mountain gorillas, set out to find Miza. The Congolese rangers, who dedicate their lives to protecting the gorillas, were searching for Miza, too. Everyone was worried about her. Then something amazing happened: Kabirizi found Miza and brought her back to live with her family.

Virunga is home to roughly 380 mountain gorillas, just over half of the planet's remaining mountain gorilla population. Miza and other mountain gorillas face an especially uncertain future. They are an endangered species, disappearing at an alarming speed. Without help, they could vanish completely.

Monkey for Sale, by Sanna Stanley. Frances Foster Books, 2002. (Grades K–3)

It is market day in the Congo, where colorful vendors open their stalls to sell everything from clothing to food. Luzolo has a coin to spend and debates with her friend, Kiese, about what she should spend it. Then she spies an old woman who has a monkey for sale. The monkey should never be someone's pet, Luzolo believes, but her coin is not enough to buy it and set it free. How can she free the monkey and let it return to its natural home?

RESEARCH ACTIVITY

Standards: 13, 14, 16, 19

Find information about an African monkey.

One thing it eats: _____

One place it lives: _____

One thing it has: _____

One thing it does: _____

Use the information in this pattern:

I am a _____

I live _____

I have _____

My color is _____

I am a _____.

From *Reading the World with Picture Books* by Nancy J. Polette.
Santa Barbara, CA: Libraries Unlimited. Copyright © 2010.

Egypt

The land of the Pyramids, the Sphinx, and the Valley of the Kings covers 386,660 square miles and is home to more than 80 million people. Egypt is mostly desert, except for some growing areas around the Nile. The language spoken is Arabic and the capital is Cairo.

Andy Shane and the Queen of Egypt, by Jennifer Richard Jacobson. Illustrated by Abby Carter. Candlewick Press, 2008. (Grades 3–5)

Andy Shane selects Egypt as the topic of his first-ever Culture Fair project. Granny Webb gives him a scarab necklace for his African-country assignment. When he announces that he has chosen Egypt, bossy Dolores, wearing elaborate, self-made Egyptian accessories, proclaims herself "Queen of Egypt" and tells Andy that he can't have it. She builds a pyramid out of pineapple chunks, and at T-ball, she distracts him with Egyptian dance in the stands, causing him to miss a catch and lose the game. The next day, Dolores shows her support during class presentations, and they agree to be partners on their assignment.

Bill and Pete Go Down the Nile, by Tomie dePaola. Penguin Group, 1996. (Grades K–2)

Little William Everett Crocodile and his friend Pete are excited. The whole class is going on a field trip to the Royal Museum in Cairo. This is after a week-long study of Egypt, in which they have learned about the Sphinx, pharaohs, burial chambers and pyramids, and the Sacred Eye of Isis. But who's that trying to steal the Sacred Eye? Will Bill and Pete catch the jewel thief and save the day once more?

Clever Ali, by Nancy Farmer. Illustrated by Gail De Marcken. Orchard Books, 2006. (Grades 2–4)

When seven-year-old Ali's greedy pet steals cherries from the wicked sultan for whom his father keeps carrier pigeons, Ali is given three days to find 600 new cherries, or his father will be thrown into the deep, dark oubliette. Includes facts about carrier pigeons and the sultan on whom this story is based, as well as an excerpt from "In Praise of Books" by al-Jahiz.

Day of Ahmed's Secret, by Florence Parry Heide and Judith Heide Gilliland. Illustrated by Ted Lewin. HarperCollins, 1995. (Grades 2–4)

Young Ahmed is making his daily rounds on a donkey cart through the busy streets of Cairo, delivering large canisters of butane gas. Through his eyes and ears one can see the busy marketplace, hear the cry of vendors, and feel the heat rising from the streets. On this particular day, Ahmed carries a secret with him (he has learned to write his name in Arabic), one children will enjoy trying to guess.

The Egyptian Cinderella, by Shirley Climo. HarperCollins, 1989. (Grades 2–4)

Rhodopes is a Greek maiden, captured by Egyptians and sold as a slave. Rhodopes is scorned by the Egyptian house servants and takes pleasure only in her rose-red gold slippers. When a falcon swoops down and snatches a slipper away as she washes clothes in a stream, Rhodopes is heartbroken. How is she to know that the falcon has delivered the slipper to the great Pharaoh himself? She cannot guess that the Pharaoh will search all of Egypt to find the owner of the tiny shoe and make her his queen.

How the Amazon Queen Fought the Prince of Egypt, by Tamara Bower. Atheneum Books for Young Readers, 2005. (Grades 3–5)

Queen Serpot rules the Land of Women, where the Amazon women live free, without men, and hunt and fight their own battles. But one day their peace is broken. An army of Egyptian soldiers is approaching their land, led by their prince, Pedikhons. Pedikhons has heard stories about these warrior women. Now he has come to see them with his own eyes, and to challenge them to combat. But the brave Serpot and her women are full of surprises. Can women truly equal men in strength and courage? This story of love and war is based on an actual Egyptian scroll from the Greco-Roman period.

Muti's Necklace: The Oldest Story in the World, by Louise Hawes. Illustrated by Rebecca Guay. Houghton Mifflin, Harcourt, 2006. (Grades 3–5)

Thousands of years ago in Egypt, a girl named Muti receives a beautiful necklace from her father. He has carved it himself—from "turquoise as blue as a dragonfly's wing, and carnelian, as red as the inside of a pomegranate." Muti wears it every day as she grows from a small child into an independent young woman. When at the age of 13 she is sent to work for King Snefru, the mighty Pharaoh of Egypt, Muti finds out just how precious her necklace really is. And in the process, she learns the value of standing up for what she treasures most.

The Pharaoh's Boat, by David Weitzman. Houghton Mifflin, 2009. (Grades 2–4)

In the shadow of the Great Pyramid at Giza, the most skilled shipwrights in all of Egypt are building an enormous vessel that will transport Cheops, the mighty Pharaoh, across the winding waterway and into a new world. Pharaoh's boat will be a wonder to behold, and well prepared for the voyage ahead. But no one, not even the Egyptian king himself, could have imagined just where the journey of the Pharaoh's boat would ultimately lead.

Scarab's Secret, by Nick Would. Illustrated by Christina Balit. Walker & Co., 2006. (Grades 2–4)

The tiniest of creatures can change the fate of a great Pharaoh. The chance meeting of Khepri, the small scarab beetle, and the powerful Pharaoh turns out to be a life-altering experience for both and ultimately shapes the fate of the young leader. After the scarab uncovers a mysterious plot to murder the Pharaoh, he is determined to put an end to it. When the Pharaoh is told by three armed guards to walk down a certain path, he chooses to follow the beetle instead. The tiny scarab with a big heart helps the Pharaoh avert danger and saves the life of his precious ruler.

Skippyjon Jones in Mummy Trouble, by Judy Schachner. Dutton Children's Books, 2006. (Grades K–3)

Skippyjon Jones, a Siamese kitten who thinks he's a Chihuahua, dreams of traveling to ancient Egypt with his gang of Chihuahua amigos. His doggy pals want to visit the Under Mundo—the underworld—where mummitos rest in peace. But they need El Skippito's brains and courage to answer the riddle of the Finx and enter the mummy's tomb. Our hero is up to the task, and he's in for another whirlwind adventure.

We're Sailing Down the Nile: A Journey Through Egypt, by Laurie Krebs. Illustrated by Anne Wilson. Barefoot Books, 2007. (Grades 3–5)

As the riverboat sails down the Nile River, remnants of Egypt's long history and aspects of its present culture are revealed on its banks. There is so much in store on this incredible, journey including enormous statues and temples, the legendary Sphinx, tombs and mummies, and of course the Great Pyramids. With seven exciting destinations, a god or goddess on each page, and informative notes at the end, you will be an Egypt expert in no time!

Zarafa, by Judith St. George. Illustrated by Britt Spencer. Philomel Books, 2009. (Grades 2–4)

The ruler of Egypt offers Zafara, a gentile giraffe, as a gift to the king of France. She travels by camel in deepest Africa, sails down the Nile by felucca, crosses the sea by brigantine, and walks the last 500 miles to Paris. The king of France is so delighted that he places her in his royal garden, where all the citizens of Paris can come to visit her.

SIGHTSEEING

Standards: 13, 14, 16, 19

What sights would visitors to Egypt see? Report on these sights using the following pattern. You may write more than one verse.

Tune: Mary Had a Little Lamb

Let's go visit Egypt Land
Where we will see, we will see
The very awesome _____ (name a sight)
A sight for all to see.

Let's go climb the Pyramids
Where we will touch, we will touch
The very awesome _____ (name something to touch)
To touch with both our hands.

Let's go down the River Nile
Where we will hear, we will hear
The very awesome _____ (name a sound)
A sound for all to hear.

Let's go to the olive groves
Where we can taste, we can taste
The very awesome _____ (name something to taste)
A food for all to taste.

Ethiopia

Some 76.5 million people share 500,000 square miles of land in Ethiopia. Many people speak more than one language. English and Amharuc are common. The capital is Addis Ababa.

Cool Time Song, by Carole Lexa Schaefer. Illustrated by Pierr Morgan. Viking, 2005. (Grades K–3)

On the sunbaked earth of the savanna, kudus and zebras, giraffes and lions move slowly through the hot African day, looking for shade, leaves to nibble, or a resting place. Everything is quiet. But when the sun sets, a cool time settles on the savanna and the song begins. "Puh-tuh, Puh-tuh, Puh-tuh," drum the zebras with their hooves. "Vroo-oot, Vroo-oot, Vroo-eet!" trumpet the elephants. And the lions roar "Grr-mrow-ool!" Like heat, their cool time song rises and spreads, sifting down to people's ears in words.

Faraway Home, edited by Ann Curtis. Illustrated by Earl Lewis. Harcourt Children's Books, 2000. (Grades 2–4)

As her father prepares for a trip back to his childhood home in Ethiopia, Desta begins to worry. Where does her father truly belong—in the village of his youth, or here in America with her? What was growing up in Ethiopia like? And will her father's love for his family be enough to bridge these two worlds and bring him back to her? Desta's father, who needs to return briefly to his Ethiopian homeland, describes what it was like for him to grow up there.

Honey, Honey—Lion!: A Story from Africa, by Jan Brett. G.P. Putnam's Sons, 2005. (Grades K–3)

For as long as anyone can remember, the honeyguide bird and the African honey badger have been partners when it comes to honey. Honeyguide finds the honeycomb, Badger breaks it open, and they share the sweetness inside. But this day, Badger keeps all the honey for himself. Foolish Badger!

In no time, Honeyguide leads Badger on a fast chase. Badger thinks it's for honey, but Honeyguide has a surprise waiting for her greedy friend. As they swim across a pond, push through a thicket of reeds, and leap over a huge anthill, a menagerie of exotic animals passes the news along in a kind of animal Bush Telegraph. Finally Badger faces a lift-the-flap page, revealing the twist that teaches Badger a lesson. Can you guess who's under that flap?

Pulling the Lion's Tail, by Jane Kurtz. Illustrated by Floyd Cooper. Simon & Schuster, 1995. (Grades 2–4)

Almaz hates to wait for anything. It has been a year since her mother died, and she wants her father's new wife to love her right away. Her wise grandfather promises to tell her how to win her stepmother's affection, if she will bring him a handful of hair from the tail of a lion. As she gains the trust of the lion, she also becomes close to her new stepmother, one step at a time. Her grandfather finds a clever way to help an impatient young Ethiopian girl get to know her father's new wife.

ETHIOPIA POEM

Standards: 15, 16, 21

After sharing a picture book about Ethiopia, complete the pattern that follows.

Line 1

_____

One word for the place

_____

Line 2

_____

Two words to describe the place

_____

Line 3

_____

Three animals found there

_____

Line 4

_____

One thing that happens there

_____

Line 5

_____

What the place reminds you of (one word)

_____

Illustrate your Ethiopia poem.

Gabon

Over 1.5 million people live in Gabon's 103,300 square miles. More than seven African languages are spoken there, although French is the official language. Gabon is a poor country, where the average life expectancy is slightly over 50 years.

Omar Bongo Ondimba has been president of Gabon for more than 40 years. The capital is Libreville.

Albert Schweitzer: An Adventurer for Humanity, by Harold E. Robles. Preface by Rhena Schweitzer Miller. Millbrook, 1994. (Grades 4–6)

Who could imagine the impact on the world that a little boy born in Alsace would ultimately have! Albert Schweitzer was a brilliant scholar, an exceptionally talented musician and could have had a life of ease using his many talents. Instead, he studies medicine, became a physician and devoted his life to caring for thousands at his river mission at Lambar, Africa. He faced and overcame many problems during two world wars, made a trip to the United States to raise money for his Mission and won the 1952 Nobel Peace Prize for his humanitarian work. He donated the prize money to his hospital for lepers. This is the true story of one man's dedication to human and animal rights, world peace and the protection of the environment.

BIOGRAPHICAL POEM

Standards: 4, 6, 11, 12, 14, 16

Fill in the lines to create a biographical poem about this amazing man.

I AM _____ Albert Schweitzer _____

I WONDER _____

I HEAR _____

I SEE _____

I WANT _____

I TOUCH _____

I FEEL _____

I SAY _____

I TRY _____

I GIVE _____

I AM _____ Albert Schweitzer _____

Ghana

Ghana covers an area of 902,500 square miles and has a population of nearly 23 million people live. It is a poor country, with an average life expectancy of about 56 years. English is the official language, and the capital is Accra. Ghana was once ruled by the British and was named the Gold Coast.

Home Now, by Lesley Beake. Illustrated by Karin Littlewood. Charlesbridge, 2007. (Grades 2–4)

When she arrives at her Aunty's home, Sieta is both sad and lonely. Her parents have died, and the child has trouble adapting to her new surroundings. The people are friendly, but this is not enough to make up for her loss. Then something very special happens. Sieta's class visits an elephant park where orphan elephants are cared for. The young elephant, Satara, seems in special need of a friend, and Sieta returns to the park to visit. Both her friendship with the elephant and her visits to the park ease the sadness and loneliness and help the girl to adapt to her new home.

Jamari's Drum, by Eboni Bynum and Roland Jackson. Illustrated by Baba Wagué Diakité. Groundwood Books, 2004. (Grades K–3)

Little Jamari loves the sound of the great village drum and often sits at drummer Baba's feet. "Why do you play every day?" he asks. "The drum is the keeper of peace in the village," Baba replies. Time passes, and many of the village elders pass on. One day Jamari agrees to take over the beating of the drum, to keep the peace. But little by little he forgets his promise, until disaster looms and he learns a lesson about duty and the greater good.

Pretty Salma: A Little Red Riding Hood Story from Africa, by Niki Daly. Clarion Books, 2007. (Grades K–3)

In this version of *Little Red Riding Hood* set in Ghana, Granny asks Pretty Salma to go to the market one day and warns her not to talk to strangers. But Salma fails to heed Granny's warning when she meets cunning Mr. Dog, who tricks Salma, and before she knows it, he's wearing her pretty white beads and her yellow sandals. And he's on his way to Granny's house! What do you suppose will happen when he gets there? What will Salma find when she returns from the market?

COMPARING CHARACTERS

Standards: 4, 11, 12, 20

Sosu's Call, by Meshack Asare. Kane/Miller Book Publishers, 2002. (Grades K–3)

Sosu, an African boy, is unable to walk. The villagers consider him to be bad luck, so he must remain at home with only his dog for a companion. When a great storm threatens the village, the boy knows he must warn the villagers by sounding an alarm, which, with the help of his dog, he is able to do.

Use the chart to compare characters from two Ghana tales.

Names		
Setting		
Task		
Meets?		
How the trickster is defeated		

Kenya

Kenya covers about 225,000 square miles and is home to 37 million people. Many people go to Kenya to visit the wild game preserves. The official language is English, and the capital is Nairobi.

Akimbo and the Lions, by Alexander McCall Smith. Illustrated by LeUyen Pham. Bloomsbury, 2007. (Grades 2–4)

Ten-year-old Akimbo lives on a game preserve in Africa. His father is the head ranger, and Akimbo is eager to help him whenever he can—even if it means getting into some pretty dangerous situations. In this tale Akimbo helps his father set a trap for a lioness that has been attacking cattle on nearby farms. But when the lion they catch turns out to be a cub, Akimbo must find a way to care for the young lion until it's old enough to be released in the wild.

First Come the Zebra, by Lynne Barasch. Lee & Low, 2009. (Grades 2–4)

One day when Abaani, a Maasai boy, takes his family's cattle out to graze, he is surprised to see a Kikuyu boy, Haki, tending a new fruit and vegetable stall alongside the road. The boys know of traditional conflicts between the Maasai and the Kikuyu. They take an immediate dislike to each other.

A short while later, as customers surround Haki's stall, a dangerous situation suddenly arises. Abaani calls to Haki, and together they act quickly. Little do the boys know that they have taken the first step in overcoming their differences and forging a path to friendship.

Daddy, There's a Hippo in the Grapes, by Lucy M. Dobkins. Illustrated by Kirk Botero. Pelican, 2008. (Grades 2–4)

The story follows the successes and failures of a Kenyan boy named Ibrahim Ngobe, providing young readers with a personal perspective on his family, their farm, their society, and their relationship with the environment and nature. Set in the hills of Kenya, it tells the story of young Ibrahim and his rather special problem: his father's harvest of grapes has suddenly become a delicacy to the local hippos. Ibrahim has difficulty convincing his family that hippos are invading their vineyard, and once they finally believe him, he must face the task of ridding the vineyards of the hippos and the other animals who have come to dine there.

The First Bear in Africa!, by Satomi Ichikawa. Philomel Books, 2001. (Grades K–3)

It's a race to the finish as young Meto chases a motorcar through the African savanna. A girl is in that car, and she has forgotten her little bear. Meto must get it back to her! Taking a shortcut through the marshes, he comes upon his friends, Hippopotamus, Lion, Elephant, and Giraffe. Can they help Meto return this strange little animal in time, before the girl flies off and leaves Africa forever?

For You Are a Kenyan Child, by Kelly Cunnane. Illustrated by Ana Juan. Simon & Schuster, 2006. (Grades K–3)

Imagine you live in a small Kenyan village, where the sun rises over tall trees filled with doves. You wake to the sound of a rooster's crow instead of an alarm clock and the school bus. Your afternoon snack is a tasty bug plucked from the sky instead of an apple. And rather than kicking a soccer ball across a field, you kick a homemade ball of rags down a dusty road. But despite this, things aren't that different for a Kenyan child than they would be for an American kid, are they? With so much going on around you, it's just as easy to forget what your mama asked you to do.

Kidogo, by Anik McGrory. Bloomsbury Children's Books, 2005. (Grades K–3)

Kidogo is sure he's the tiniest creature on earth. All the other animals are so much bigger than he is. Kidogo sets out on a journey—through the woodlands, over the plains, down to the river—to see if he can find an animal smaller than he is. Is it possible that Kidogo is exactly the right size after all? Heartwarming illustrations and a gentle story will inspire and reassure young children who are just starting to find their own way in a big world.

Mama Panya's Pancakes: A Village Tale from Kenya, by Mary Chamberlin and Rich Chamberlin. Illustrated by Julia Cairns. Barefoot Books, 2005. (Grades K–3)

Mama Panya and her son, Adika, are on their way to market. Mama Panya has saved a few coins to buy ingredients for pancakes. She plans to make pancakes for supper, not realizing that Adika has invited all their friends and neighbors to eat with them. Mama knows she can't possibly cook enough pancakes for everyone, but when the friends and neighbors arrive, each brings a gift. When all the gifts (or ingredients) are used, there is enough food for everyone.

ENDANGERED ANIMAL POEM PATTERN

Standards: 2, 4, 5, 13

Choose an endangered animal to write about. Find out where it lives, what it looks like, and how it moves. Use the information in the pattern poem below.

Example:

Animal name:	Elephant
How it moves:	Lumbering, Plodding
Where:	In Asian teak forests
Where:	In the African grasslands
Describe:	Gray Giant!

Animal name: _____

How it moves: _____, _____

Where: _____

Where: _____

Describe: _____

Madagascar

Madagascar covers 226,600 square miles and has a population of 19.5 million people. The languages spoken are Malagasy and French. Many animals, such as the ring-tailed lemur, are found in Madagascar and nowhere else in the world.

Adventures of Riley—Mission to Madagascar, by Amanda Lumry. Eaglemont Press, 2005. (Grades 4–6)

Not really a picture book, but one of the few books on Madagascar. You can learn about how animals are tracked and captured as you enjoy a fictional tale about a family that travels to this country. You will see the sights of Madagascar through their eyes.

Lemur Landing: A Story of A Madagascan Tropical Dry Forest, by Deborah Dennard. Illustrated by Kristin Kest. Soundprints, 2001. (Grades 3–5)

In the tropical dry forest of Southern Madagascar, a baby ring-tailed lemur and his mother follow their troop of lemurs through their forest home in search of food and water. Giant birds, a radiated tortoise, brown lemurs, shifakas, a harrier hawk, and a chameleon are introduced. They sunbathe, drink rainwater from empty snail shells, groom one another, eat sweet tamarind pods, play with each other, have a stink fight for territory, and search for a place to bed down for the night in the rain forest.

Madagascar: Born to Be Wild, by Erica David. Scholastic, 2005. (Grades 2–4)

Marty the zebra has lived in the zoo his entire life, but staring at a mural of a grass-covered plain isn't enough anymore. So he escapes and heads off for the "wild" of Connecticut, only things don't go as planned, and he ends up shipwrecked on Madagascar with his friends. Can this city zebra survive and thrive in the wild? Or will he start to miss the bright lights of the big city?

RAIN FOREST TRIP

Standards: 2, 5, 11, 12

Pretend you have stepped into the rain forest. Complete the following lines about your experience.

Into the tropical rain forest

Over _____

Under _____

Above _____

Between _____

Lives a _____

Mali

Mali covers nearly 500,000 square miles and is home to 12 million people. The official language is French, although many African languages are spoken there. Fewer than half of the people can read, and fewer than half live longer than 50 years.

Mali was once home to the great ancient city of Timbuktu. The capital is Bamako.

I Lost My Tooth in Africa, by Penda Diakite. Illustrated by Baba Wague Diakit. Scholastic, 2006. (Grades K–3)

More than anything, Amina wants to lose her loose tooth while visiting her family in Mali, West Africa. Only then can she put it under a gourd for the African tooth fairy, who will exchange it for two chickens! Happily this happens, and even better, the chickens lay eggs. But will the eggs hatch before it's time to return home to America? In this fresh, spontaneous story that is infused with close family warmth, Penda June Diakite joins forces with her award-winning author/artist father to give a charming peek at everyday life in Mali.

My Baby, by Jeanette Winter. Frances Foster Books, 2001. (Grades K–3)

Much African cloth is hand-made or woven on a loom. In this beautiful picture book a young mother is making a cloth for her baby, who will soon arrive. But there are dangers in Mali that she must face, including drought, which will leave the village hungry if the crops do not grow, and scorpions, whose bite can make one very ill. The young mother meets all the problems that arise and becomes one of the best cloth makers in the village.

RESEARCH PROJECT

Standards: 3, 17

Visit this Web site to learn more about African cloth: Outreach World (www. outreachworld.org/resource.asp?curriculumid=237). It provides step-by-step instructions for craft activities that can be used to enhance other teachings about Africa. The activities include:

Making galimotos

Tie-dying

African cloth: fabric-binding techniques

Morocco

Morocco covers 172,400 square miles and has a population of more than 33.5 million people. The official language is Arabic, although many people speak either French or Spanish. The average life expectancy is more than 70 years. The world's oldest university is found in Morocco, and the capital is Rabat.

Ibrahim, by Frances Sales. Illustrated by Eulalia Sariola. Lippincott, 1989. (Grades 2–4)

What young boy wouldn't rather be playing or seeking out an adventure rather than working in his father's market stall? Ibrahim is such a boy. Although he cannot actually enjoy the freedom he longs for, he sees that freedom can come in dreams and stories. As an adult Ibrahim, who works in his own stall, tells stories of dreams.

My Father's Shop, by Satomi Ichikawa. Kane Miller, 2008. (Grades K–3)

There is a rug in his father's shop that Mustafa loves. (It has a hole in it, so he can put it over his head and still see out.) No one else wants the rug, though lots of tourists visit the shop. His father always welcomes them—"Bienvenue"—and offers them tea—"O cha wa ikaga desu ka?" Mustafa's father would like him to know some words in other languages, too, and he tells Mustafa that he may have the rug if he agrees to learn. But after the first lesson, Mustafa is so bored he runs out of the shop (with the carpet on his head). Ending up at the market, he finds a very different way of learning foreign languages . . . and of getting tourists to visit his father's shop.

The Nightingale, by Hans Christian Andersen. Illustrated by Jerry Pinkney. Dial, 2002. (Grades 2–4)

The Nightingale is the story of a plain little bird whose beautiful songs bring her great fame, even winning her an esteemed place in the king's court. Eventually, however, after saving the life of the king, the modest nightingale chooses to return to her peaceful life in the forest. Although the original tale is set in China, Jerry Pinkney decided to add a unique twist to his own adaptation by moving the setting to Morocco!

Zorah's Magic Carpet, written and illustrated by Stefan Czernecki. Hyperion, 1995. (Grades 2–4)

An old woman visits the marketplace, and the many goods displayed there from many different countries instill in her a desire to travel. When she rescues a sheep, she uses its wool to weave a magic carpet that includes designs from the many counties she has seen over the years. To her surprise, the carpet really is magic, and it takes her in the sky from country to country.

MAKING USEFUL THINGS

Standards: 1, 2, 4, 14

The old woman in *Zorah's Magic Carpet* used the wool from the sheep to make a magic carpet. Use your imagination! Think of some useful things you could make using plants, rocks, or trees.

I could use _____

to make _____, and

I would use it for _____.

I could use _____

to make _____, and

I would use it for _____.

Mozambique

Mozambique covers 309,484 square miles and has a population of more than 21 million people. The official language is Portuguese, although many people speak the Bantu language. In this very poor country, the average life expectancy is 40 years. Less than half of the people can read. The capital is Mputo.

The Village That Vanished, by Ann Grifalconi. Illustrated by Kadir Nelson. Dial Books for Young Readers, 2002. (Grades 2–4)

In southeastern Africa, a young Yao girl and her mother find a way for their fellow villagers to escape approaching slave traders. Young Abikanile and all of the villagers of Yao feel safe hidden deep within the African jungle. But word has come that the slavers are on their way! Abikanile looks to her mother and her grandmother for strength and guidance. These two brave women come up with a plan to fool the slavers and protect their tribe. But as the villagers retreat into the forest, Abikanile finds that she too has the courage to help her people stay safe and free.

ENCOURAGING READERS

Standards: 4, 7, 14

Complete the pattern to tell what you might do to help more people of Mozambique become readers.

If I were in charge of Mozambique

I would _____

And I'd _____

But I wouldn't _____

Because that wouldn't help at all.

Instead I would _____

And _____

_____

Namibia

Namibia was once part of South Africa but is now an independent nation of 318,700 square miles and 2 million people. The people speak Afrikaans, German, and English. The great majority can read and write, and the capital is Windhoek.

Sand and Fog: Adventures in Southern Africa, by Jim Brandenburg. Edited by JoAnn Bren. Guernsey Walker, 1994. (Grades 4–6)

During a trip to Namibia, a wildlife photographer traveled to the Namib Desert on the coast and to the Etosha Pan National Park, a game reserve in the north of the country. He took photographs of the stark but beautiful desert and its array of animals, including the oryx (or gemsbok), flamingos, giraffes, ostriches against the rising sun, and elephants around a water hole. There are other photographs of diamonds from a diamond mine, a religious ceremony, and seals at play on the coast.

DESERT ANIMALS

Standards: 1, 2, 4, 14

Choose one of the desert animals pictured in the book. Use the pattern below to write about the animal. Use factual information in your writing.

Example:

In the hot Namib desert

By Etosha Pan National Park

Between flat sandy rocks

Are the eggs of an ostrich named Oma.

Your Turn:

In the _____

By the _____

Between _____

Lives a _____ named _____.

Nigeria

Amadi's Snowman, by Katia Saint-Lot. Illustrated by Dimitria Tokunbo. Tilbury House, 2008. (Grades 2–4)

Amadi is a young Ibo man of Nigeria who wants to be a trader of goods. He knows his numbers, which he feels are important in trading, but sees little use in learning to read. His mother insists, however, that he must learn to read and arranges for a teacher. Before the teacher arrives, Amadi escapes to the marketplace, where he finds a friend, Chima, reading a book with intriguing pictures. He has never seen a snowman and wants to learn all about this strange creature. Perhaps learning to read could be useful after all.

Bikes for Rent, by Isaac Olayleye. Illustrated by Chris Damarest. Orchard, 2001. (Grades 2–4)

Lateef, "a determined and hardworking lad" who lives in western Nigeria, gathers firewood and mushrooms to sell at the village market so he can afford to rent a bike from Babatunde. Despite his friends' taunts, Lateef finally learns to ride sufficiently well that Babatunde agrees to rent him a big, new bike rather than the usual small, older model. After the boy succumbs to his peers' dare to ride downhill without holding onto the handlebars, he predictably crashes. Lateef asks Babatunde for a job to work off his debt and, after having done so, stays on the job to earn his own bicycle.

Catch That Goat!, by Polly Alakija. Barefoot Books, 2002. (Grades K–3)

Ayoka has been left in charge of the family goat, but within minutes it has vanished! As Ayoka searches the streets of town, she sees how much trouble a runaway goat can cause among the market stalls. One thing after another disappears, and when Ayoka finally catches up with the goat, she finds more than she had bargained for.

In the Rainfield, Who Is the Greatest?, by Isaac Olaleye. Illustrated by Ann Gifalconi. Blue Sky Press, 2000. (Grades K–3)

In this Nigerian folktale Wind, Fire, and Rain, taking the form of two men and a woman, meet in the land of the Yoruba to decide which of them is the greatest. They squabble over who is greatest and finally hold a contest to determine the mightiest of all. Wind howls, Fire rages, but Rain wins, vanquishing her rivals with a downpour that demonstrates her credo, "The greatest must be the gentlest."

Lake of the Big Snake: An African Rain Forest Adventure, by Isaac Olaleye. Illustrated by Claudia Shepard. Boyds Mill, 1998. (Grades 2–4)

Their mothers have made it clear that Ade and Tayo are not supposed to leave the village while their mothers are out, but they can't resist the mysterious allure of Lake of the Big Snake. There they find tasty berries, but also encounter a huge snake that blocks their way back across the lake. The boys can't decide which fate is worse, meeting the snake or being confronted by their angry mothers.

RAIN FOREST ANIMALS

Standards: 2, 4, 11, 12, 16

BABOONS
hurrying, swinging
from one arm to another
through leaves and limbs
Troop-Group

Use this pattern to write about other animals that live in the Nigerian rain forest.

_____

(animal)

_____   _____

(verb) (verb)

_____

(prepositional phrase)

_____

(prepositional phrase)

_____   _____

(two rhyming words)

Rwanda

Rwanda is a small but crowded country of about 10,000 square miles, with a population of almost 10 million people. The average life expectancy is less than 50 years. The official languages are French and English, and the capital is Kigali.

Gorilla Rescue, by Jill Bailey. Illustrated by Alan Baker. Steck-Vaughn, 1990. (Grades 4–6)

If efforts are not made to protect wildlife in Rwanda, it will one day disappear. That is the purpose of the National Park of Rwanda, and in pictures and text we are taken on a journey to track gorillas and see how other animals are cared for and protected in their natural environment.

ABOUT CAMOUFLAGE

Standards: 13, 15

Gorillas are sometimes difficult to see because their dark fur blends in with the bark of the trees where they make their homes. A rhino, not being a camouflaged animal, would find it difficult to hide.

Visit the library to find books about camouflage animals.

Compile a simple scrapbook titled "Animals That Use Camouflage":

Staple three sheets of manila paper between two sheets of construction paper.

Find pictures of camouflaged mammals, reptiles, and amphibians in magazines, especially conservation and nature magazines, to clip and glue onto your sheets.

Senegal

Senegal covers 75,700 square miles and has a population of 12.5 million people. French is the official language, and the capital is Dakar. Crocodiles are found in the rivers of Senegal, and bands of monkeys are numerous in the river valleys.

Sofie and the City, by Karima Grant. Illustrated by Janet Montecalvo. Boyds Mill, 2006. (Grades 2–4)

When Sofie calls her grandmother in Senegal each week, she complains that her new home in the United States is ugly and crowded. Mame advises her to make it pretty, but the youngster would rather move back to her homeland. She feels sure that no one would miss her: her mother works days as a hairstylist, and her father drives a taxi at night. The children she meets make fun of her flip-flops, which were perfect for the sand but not for hard gray sidewalks. Then Sofie meets Kenya, a girl who is decorating the sidewalk with colorful pictures of the neighborhood. Sharing Kenya's chalk, Sofie draws Senegal's shore with its warm sand and fishing boats.

VISITING SENEGAL

Standards: 19, 20

Suppose Sofie's parents in *Sofie and the City* allowed her to visit her grandmother in Senegal.

Answer these questions.

1. Best way to travel _____. Total time _____.

2. Lowest cost means of travel _____. Total time _____.

3. Cost of the trip:

    Transportation _____

    Lodging _____

    Food _____

    Other _____

4. Problems to prepare for:

    _____

    _____

    _____

Somalia

Somalia covers 246,000 square miles and is home to 9 million people, who speak Arabic, English, and Italian. The lack of plant life means that much wildlife has disappeared from the country. Elephants have mostly disappeared, slaughtered by ivory poachers. The capital of Somalia is Mogadishu.

The Color of Home, by Mary Hoffman. Illustrated by Karin Littlewood. Phyllis Fogelman Books, 2002. (Grades 2–4)

Hassan has only recently arrived in the United States after he and his family were forced to flee war-torn Somalia, and he deeply misses the colorful landscape of his former home in Africa. But with the help of his parents, an understanding teacher, and a school art project, Hassan finds that by painting two pictures, one of his old home that shares his story of being forced to flee Somalia, and the other of his new home and his hopes for a better life there, his homesickness and the trauma of leaving a war-torn country are lessened. And he finds that there are many things to like about his new home in America.

DISAPPEARING ELEPHANTS

Standards: 2, 5, 13

Use the information in this data bank to write a song about Somalia's disappearing elephants.

THE AFRICAN ELEPHANT:			
EATS	LIVES	HAS	DOES
grasses	Africa	long trunk	grows 12 feet tall
leaves	tropical forests	ivory tusks	bathes in dust
495 lbs. per day	river valleys	only four teeth	pulls down trees
		wrinkled skin	lives 60–70 years

Use the information from the data bank in the blank spaces below. Sing the song to the tune of "London Bridge."

Elephants have

_____ and _____

_____ and _____

_____ and _____

Elephants eat

_____ and _____

And they _____

South Africa

South Africa covers 471,000 square miles and has a population of nearly 44 million people live. It has two capitals, Pretoria and Cape Town, and 11 official languages. The literacy rate is high, at 86 percent. More gold comes from South Africa than from any other country.

Abiyoyo, by Pete Seeger. Illustrated by Michael Hayes. Simon & Schuster, 2001. (Grades 2–4)

Once there was a little boy who played the ukulele. Wherever he'd go he'd play, Clink, clunk, clonk. His father was a magician. Wherever he'd go, he'd make things disappear, Zoop! Zoop! Soon the townspeople grew tired of the boy's noise and his father's tricks and banished both of them to the edge of town. There they lived, until one day the terrible giant, Abiyoyo, appeared. He was as tall as a tree, and it was said that he could eat people up. Everyone was terrified, except the boy and his father, and they came up with a plan to save the town.

The Day Gogo Went to Vote, by Eleanor Batezat Sisul. Illustrated by Sharon Wilson. Little, Brown, 1999. (Grades 2–4)

Thembi and her beloved 100-year-old great-grandmother, Gogo, who has not left the house for many years, go together to vote on the momentous day when black South Africans are allowed to vote for the first time, in the 1994 elections. Gogo becomes somewhat of a celebrity when she emerges from the voting booth as the oldest person to vote in the election.

Home Now, by Lesley Beake. Illustrated by Karin Littlewood. Charlesbridge, 2007. (Grades 2–4)

"This is your home now," everyone tells Sieta, but Sieta can't help feeling sad when she thinks back to her previous home over the mountains, before her mother and father died of illness and she came to live with Aunty. One day Sieta's teacher takes the children to see the orphan elephants in a nearby elephant park. The moment Sieta sees the baby elephant Satara, and he looks soulfully at her, each recognizes the sadness in the other. How Satara helps Sieta to forget her sadness and start living life afresh is sensitively told and warmly illustrated in a book children will love both for its emotional impact and its endearing portrayal of elephants.

The Song of Six Birds, by Rene Deetlefs. Illustrated by Lyn Gilbert. Dutton Children's Books, 2000. (Grades 1–3)

Wishing to make beautiful music, Lindiwe captures the songs of six birds in her new flute. Lindiwe asks six birds—a crowned crane, hornbill, rainbird, hoopoe, Paradise flycatcher, and wood owl—to "share" their sounds with her. As the winged creatures followed her home, the child played her flute and the birds "all made music while she ran."

A South African Night, by Rachel Isadora. Greenwillow Books, 1998. (Grades 1–3)

Twilight in Johannesburg, South Africa, finds the bustle of the city beginning to subside. Work is over, and it is time for rest. But in Kruger National Park the setting sun beckons the animals and their young from the bush. On the darkened plain it is time to hunt, graze, and cool off in the night air. Lionesses and leopards hunt, elephants and others visit water holes, and a black mamba surveys the landscape from his watery home. When the night is over the animals lie down in the shade as the people of the city begin their day.

TRAVELS IN SOUTH AFRICA

Sightseeing

Standards: 2, 5

List four sights one would see in touring South Africa. Insert the four sights on the lines below to create a song. Sing it to the tune of "This Land Is Your Land."

Example:

As I was walking through South Africa
I saw Cape Town and the Roggeveld Mountains
I saw Pretoria and the Indian Ocean
Sights that everyone should see.

As I was walking through South Africa

I saw _____ and _____

I saw _____ and _____

Sights that everyone should see.

Make a Travel Brochure

Standards: 14, 15

Fold an 11-by-14-inch paper in thirds. On the cover write your name and "Places in Africa I'd Like To Visit." Cut pictures from old travel brochures or magazines inside to complete the brochure. Add captions to each picture.

Pack Your Bags Game

Standards: 5

This word game will stretch one's imagination. It can be played singly or as a group. To begin, pretend that you are moving to a country in Africa. What would you pack in your trunk? Name one item, then add a second item that begins with the last letter of the first item. Continue to add items until you run out of things to add. Remember, each item must begin with the last letter of the last item added. For example, jeans, socks, sweater, raincoat, etc.

Tanzania

Tanzania covers an area of 365,000 square miles and has a population of 38 million people. The languages spoken are Swahili and English. Many people visit this country to climb the highest mountain in Africa, Mount Kilimanjaro. The capital is Dar es Salaam

True Friends: A Tale from Tanzania, by John Kilaka. Groundwood Books, 2006. (Grades K–3)

Only Rat knows how to make fire, and he generously provides it to all the other animals. When his best friend, Elephant, suggests that Rat store his food in Elephant's solid house, Rat agrees. But when the drought comes and food is scarce, Elephant refuses to share the stored food. "You are tiny, and you don't need much," he says. "So go away." When the other animals return to fetch their fire, Rat is gone, and Elephant is worried. What will his betrayed friend do? Elephant sets out to find Rat and is injured on his journey. Returning home, he realizes how much his friend means to him.

ENDANGERED PLACES

Standards: 1, 2, 7

If the animals don't get the warmth that fire brings, they will all die.

      Said the creatures of the jungle:

      Three minutes ago Elephant and Rat were friends.

      Two minutes ago Elephant refused to share.

      One minute ago saw Rat disappear.

      Now the jungle animals tremble in fear.

Write about another place you know that could be in danger. It might be a building in your neighborhood or a park being destroyed to make room for homes You can rhyme line 3 with line 5 if you choose.

Take time now to care about YOUR world.

_____

Three minutes ago _____

Two minutes ago _____

One minute ago _____

Now _____

Uganda

Uganda covers 91,000 square miles and is home to 30 million people. Mountain gorillas are found in the west and elephants and zebras in the north. Many animals are protected in ten national parks. The capital is Kampala.

Beatrice's Goat, by Page McBrier. Illustrated by Lori Lohstoeter. Atheneum, 2001. (Grades 2–4)

> To go to school in Uganda, each child must have a uniform and books paid for by his or her parents. Beatrice lives in a small village where there is no money to send children to school. But all this changes when a real organization, the Heifer Project International, provides Beatrice with a goat. "Fat and sleek as a ripe mango, Mugisa (which means "luck") gives milk that Beatrice can sell." With Mugisa's help, it looks as if Beatrice's dream may come true after all.

Mogo, the Third Warthog, by Donna Jo Napoli. Illustrated by Lita Judge. Hyperion Books for Children, 2008. (Grades 2–4)

> Mogo may be the runt of the litter, but he's determined to make it in the tough African savanna. When he and his two brothers are cast out of their burrow to make space for a new litter, it's time for each of them to venture out and build a new home and a new life. But the savanna is full of dangerous predators, and Mogo's bossy and lazy older brothers may not have what it takes to survive. On his own, Mogo must learn to battle not just lions, cheetahs, and wild dogs, but also fear and loneliness. Luckily, the friendship of a young baboon, who has also been cast out of his own community, helps Mogo find what he's been looking for: a life not just based on survival, but one that relishes the joy of friendship and love.

UGANDAN CRAFTS AND ACTIVITIES

Standards: 3, 17

Check out the following Web site for activities and crafts children in Uganda might make at school: Learning (www.enchantedlearning.com/crafts/africa/):

A coloring book of African countries to print

A string of African flags

A Good Luck Hand

African geography: maps, quizzes, and more

African countries: Label Me Printout

African spelling words questions

Zaire

Some 43,775,000 people live in Zaire, not counting the 1.5 million refugees from Rwanda who came to Zaire to escape the fighting in their country. Zaire covers a region of 2,345,000 square miles, with part of the country rich in minerals, especially diamonds. The capital of Zaire is Kinshasa.

The Rains Are Coming, by Sanna Stanley. Greenwillow, 1993. (Grades K–3)

Aimee is newly arrived in Zaire with her missionary family and is excited because she will have her first birthday party in Africa. As she invites each of her new friends to her birthday party, each one tells her in the native language, Kikongo, "Zimvula zeti kwiza." Aimee comes to understand that this means "the rains are coming," and on the day of the party the rains do come, but do not dampen the festivities.

ZAIRE CRAFTS

Standards: 3, 8

Check this Web site for crafts the children might have made at the party in *The Rains Are Coming*: African Crafts On Line (www.dltk-kids.com/world/africa/mdrum.htm):

Detailed directions for making: an African drum, an African wall mask, and an African spear

Replicate ancient African Cave Drawings

Egypt and Camel coloring pages

Egypt bookmarks

Egyptian Pharaoh Mask

Paper Pyramid

Paper Camel Silhouettes

Write your name in Hieroglyphics

Cat crafts and the cat coloring pages

Ideas for making an Egyptian costume and jewelry

Zimbabwe

Twelve million people live in Zimbabwe's 150,000 square miles. It is a very poor country, with a life expectancy of only 37 years. Its tropical grasslands allow for farming, and it contains a 5,000-square-mile national park to protect wild animals. The capital is Harare.

Gugu's House, by Catherine Stock. Clarion Books, 2001. (Grades K–3)

This is a tale set in the grassy plains of Zimbabwe. Gugu's house is like no other, for Gugu is an artist. Kukamba loves to visit her grandmother, Gugu, to see the beautiful house decorated with paintings and clay animals, all made by Gugu herself. Best of all, when Kukamba visits, she gets to help shape and paint some of the wonderful zebras, elephants, and birds that Gugu is always adding to the house. When the heavy rains come and her grandmother's showpieces are destroyed, Kukamba is crushed. But the Gugu helps her see that there are new colors to enjoy after the rains.

Mufaro's Beautiful Daughters, by John Steptoe. HarperCollins, 1987. (Grades 2–5)

Mufaro has two beautiful daughters. Nyasha is kind and considerate, but Manyara is selfish and spoiled. When the king decides to choose a bride, both girls travel to the capital city, meeting someone who needs help along the way. The selfish daughter sees a terrible sight in the throne room, but Nyasha, who has responded to a cry for help, is chosen to marry the king.

COMPARING CHARACTERS

Standards: 10, 11

List four ways *Mufaro's Beautiful Daughters* and *Cinderella* are alike.

1. _____

2. _____

3. _____

4. _____

Part Three

Europe

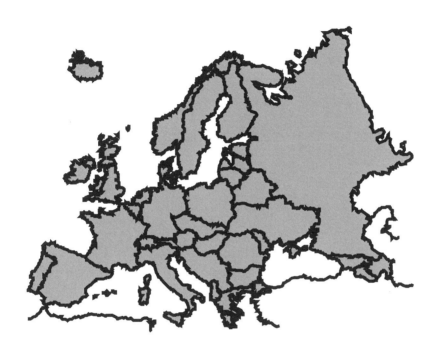

Facts about Europe

Europe is the world's second-smallest continent by surface area, covering about 4 million square miles or 2 percent of the earth's surface and about 6.8 percent of its land area. It is home to about 12 percent of the world's population. Russia is the largest of Europe's countries in both area and population.

Europe's climate is milder in comparison to other areas of the same latitude around the globe due to the influence of the Gulf Stream. The Gulf Stream is nicknamed "Europe's central heating," because it makes Europe's climate warmer and wetter than it would otherwise be.

COUNTRIES OF EUROPE

Booktalks have been provided for the countries in boldface.

Albania	Luxembourg
Andorra	Macedonia
Austria	Malta
Belarus	Moldova
Belgium	**Monaco**
Bulgaria	Montenegro
Czech Republic	**The Netherlands**
Denmark	**Norway**
England	**Poland**
Estonia	**Portugal**
Finland	Romania
France	**Russia**
Germany	San Marino
Greece Scotland	Serbia
Hungary	Slovakia
Iceland	Slovenia
Ireland	**Spain**
Italy	**Sweden**
Kosovo	**Switzerland**
Latvia	**Ukraine**
Liechtenstein	**Wales**
Lithuania	

Austria

Austria covers about 32,000 square miles and has a population of about 8 million people. Most of Austria is covered by the Alps. The language spoken is German. The capital is Vienna, a city of great beauty.

Silent Night: The Song and Its Story, by Margaret Hodges. Eerdman's Books, 1997. (Grades 2–4)

Tells how the well-known Christmas carol "Silent Night" first came to be written and performed in Austria in the early 1800s. It seems that when the people arrived for Christmas Eve service they rightly expected to hear beautiful music from the church organ, but alas, the organ was broken, There would be no music. What could the young priest do to ensure a memorable Christmas Eve? Would a poem take the place of the organ? He hoped so. The words he wrote were the words to one of the most beloved Christmas hymns, "Silent Night."

Young Mozart, by Rachel Isadora. Viking, 1997. (Grades 2–4)

This is the story of the exceptional child who could write music before the age of five and was performing for kings at the age of seven. His childhood had no time for play with others. His father made sure he practiced and practiced to perform well.

MOZART PLATES

Standards: 3, 17

There are many recordings of music by Mozart. Give each child two sturdy paper plates (not plastic) and ask the children to decorate the plates with their names.

Play a Mozart piece and let children keep time with the rhythm by tapping their plates together back to back. Designate different children to be leaders and others followers, tapping their plates above and below their heads, in front and behind, and/or any other movement they want to do with the plates.

Belarus

Belarus covers abut 80,000 square miles and has a population of nearly 10 million people. The territory that is now Belarus has changed hands repeatedly over the centuries. It was once a part of the Soviet Union and became independent in 1991. The language spoken is Belarusian, and the capital is Minsk.

How Mama Brought the Spring, by Fran Manushkin. Illustrated by Holly Berry. Dutton, 2004. (Grades K–3)

One wintry morning, Rosy is reluctant to leave her warm bed. "If you get up," says her mother, "I'll tell you how your Grandma Beatrice brought spring to Minsk." How can Rosy resist? It all happens in a Minsk kitchen as eggs, flour, milk, and sugar are mixed together, and then the batter goes into the pan. Pour, swirl, sizzle, flip. Anything can happen when Grandma Beatrice wields her clever spatula. Soon she has cooked up a delicious dish and also found the recipe for spring as her sweet surprise melts away the winter snow.

SPRING CHANT

Create a spring chant. On the lines below list 13 things related to spring. None can be more than three syllables.

Signs of Spring

1. Budding trees

2. _____

3. _____

4. _____

5. _____

6. _____

AND SKY SO BLUE

Belgium

Belgium covers almost 12,000 square miles and has a population of 10 million people. The people speak Dutch, French, and German. Belgium is a coal-mining country with many sea ports. The capital is Brussels.

Willy and Max: A Holocaust Story, by Amy Littlesugar. Illustrated by William Low. Philomel Books, 2006. (Grades 3–5)

A Jewish father and his son, Max, purchase a painting of a beautiful lady in an antique shop. The owner of the shop has a son named Willy, and Willy and Max become good friends. The friendship is short lived however, as Jewish people, including the Professor and Max, must flee Belgium as the country is invaded by the Germans during World War II and the Nazis are sending Jews to concentration camps. The painting of the lady is given back to Willy, who tries to hide it from the Germans. He rolls it up and hides it in the basement. However, the painting is found and becomes one of the many artworks stolen by the Nazis during the war.

POEMS AND PAINTINGS

Standard: 2

Visit the library. Find a book of poems and choose a favorite poem. Then find a book of paintings and find a painting that goes with your poem. Read the poem and show the painting to your class.

Example:

Match: Winslow Homer's famous painting *By the Seaside*

with: the Mother Goose rhyme "Bobby Shaftoe Went to Sea"

List your match here.

Painting _____

Poem _____

Found in _____

From *Reading the World with Picture Books* by Nancy J. Polette.
Santa Barbara, CA: Libraries Unlimited. Copyright © 2010.

Bulgaria

Bulgaria covers about 48,000 square miles and has a population of 10 million people. It was a communist country until 1991. Its rugged mountains and Black Sea Resorts make this a favorite tourist destination. The language spoken is Bulgarian, and the capital is Sofia.

My Name Was Hussein, by Khristo Kyuchukov. Illustrated by Allan Eitzen. Boyd Mills Press, 2004. (Grades 3–5)

A name is a very important thing and should never be taken away, but this is what happens to a young Muslim boy when his village is invaded by the Communists. Hussain's village is a blend of many civilizations. Not only are Muslim religious ceremonies important, but the boy has an Arabic name that has been in family for many years past. When the Communists take over the village, not only are all ceremonies and celebrations stopped, but everyone must suffer great indignities by being forced to adopt different names.

NAME CARDS

Standards: 14, 16

Make name cards for your desk. Fold an 8½-by-11-inch paper in half lengthwise. Decorate each side with your name. Be creative in forming your letters and adding other drawings that will help your name stand out.

Keep your name card in a safe place. If a substitute teacher is needed for a day, get out your name card and place it on your desk. That way the new teacher can quickly know who you are.

Czech Republic

The Czech Republic covers about 30,000 square miles and has a population of 10 million people. It is a landlocked country with many mountains and woodlands. The language spoken is Czech, and the literacy rate is 100 percent. The capital is Prague.

Built by Angels: The Story of the Old-New Synagogue, by Mark Podwal. Harcourt, 2009. (Grades 3–5)

In the city of Prague there is a synagogue that has stood for many, many years without a single stone being removed. At least this is what the citizens of Prague say, for they will tell visitors that this particular synagogue was built with many different kinds of stones by angels and that as long as no stone is removed, the synagogue will stand.

CZECH GAMES

Standard: 3

Visit the library to find books about games children around the world play. Teach the class a game that Czech children play.

Here are some books you might look for:

- *Play with Us: 100 Games from Around the World,* by Oriol Ripoll. Chicago Review Press, 2005. Paperback.

- *Sidewalk Games Around the World,* by Arlene Erlbach. Millbrook Press, 1998.

- *Games Around the World.* Teacher Created Materials, 2008.

- *Kids Around the World Play!: The Best Fun and Games from Many Lands,* by Arlette N. Braman. Wiley, 2002.

Denmark

Denmark covers almost 17,000 square miles and has a population of 5.5 million people. It is surrounded by almost 400 islands. Languages spoken are Danish and German. The literacy rate is 100 percent. The capital is Copenhagen.

The Classic Treasury of Hans Christian Andersen, by Hans Christian Andersen. Illustrated by Christian Birmingham. Running Kids Press, 2002. (Grades 3–5)

These beautifully illustrated tales are included: "The Princess and the Pea," "The Little Mermaid," "The Ugly Duckling," "Thumbelina," "The Steadfast Tin Soldier," "The Emperor's New Clothes," "The Nightingale," and "The Little Match Girl."

Grandfather's Gold Watch, by Louise Garff Hubbard. Deseret Book Co., 1997. (Grades 2–4)

Traveling long ago from Denmark to Salt Lake City in the United States was a difficult and dangerous journey. Before leaving home Peter, a young boy, is given both a name and a gold watch by his grandfather, with instructions to use both well. The sea voyage is difficult, but not as hard as the journey by covered wagon during which Peter's father dies. The boy does work hard, matures, and becomes a man with a family of his own. Many years later, at a state celebration, Peter is reunited with the watch, which he passes on to his grandson.

The Little Match Girl, by Hans Christian Andersen. Illustrated by Rachel Isadora. G. P. Putnam's Sons, 2001. (Grades 3–5)

The classic tale of the little orphan who tries to sell matches outside the palace gates on a freezing winter's night. The little girl dies, unnoticed by the passersby, but she sees her grandmother coming from Heaven to welcome her with loving arms.

The Little Old Lady and the Hungry Cat, by Nancy Polette. Illustrated by Frank Modell. Greenwillow, 1991. (Grades K–3)

A little old lady bakes cupcakes and tells her cat to leave them alone while she goes to mend the mayor's clothes. The cat eats the cupcakes and then goes for a walk, where he meets and swallows down a one-legged man and his squealing pig, a wedding party, and finally the old woman when she returns home. She uses her scissors to cut a hole in the cat's side, from which all emerge and celebrate except for the cat, who must spend the whole day sewing up its side.

The Yellow Star: The Legend of King Christian X of Denmark, by Carmen Agra
Deedy. Illustrated by Henry Sorenson. Peachtree, 2000. (Grades 2–4)

    Many legends have their beginning in truth, and it is true that King Christian X rode
daily through the streets of Copenhagen after the Germans had invaded his small country
during World War II. He rode alone without military or police guards to show courage to his
people and his belief in them. When the Germans decreed that all Jewish people must wear
the Yellow Star of David, the king wore a yellow star, and many of the Danish people followed his lead, showing that they were all united as one people.

MYSTERY TITLES

Standards: 2, 9, 11, 12

Guess the real titles of these Hans Christian Andersen tales as each title is read aloud.

1. "The Fighter Made of Tin Who Wouldn't Quit"

2. "The Tiny Girl Who Sold Fire on a Stick"

3. "The King's New Garments"

4. "The King's Daughter and a Small Green Vegetable"

5. "An Unsightly Water Fowl"

Create more mystery titles for others to solve!

Answer key: 1. The Steadfast Tin Soldier 2. The Little Match Girl 3. The Emperor's New Clothes 4. The Princess and the Pea 5. The Ugly Duckling

From *Reading the World with Picture Books* by Nancy J. Polette.
Santa Barbara, CA: Libraries Unlimited. Copyright © 2010.

England

England is part of the United Kingdom, which is made up of England, Scotland, Wales, and Northern Ireland. The total area of the United Kingdom is 94,525 square miles, and the total population is about 61 million people. Languages spokes are English, Welsh, and Scots Gaelic. The capital of England and the United Kingdom is London.

Barkus, Sly and the Golden Egg, by Angela McAllister. Illustrated by Sally Anne Lambert. Bloomsbury Children's Books, 2002. (Grades K–3)

> This timeless fable relates the story of three chickens hen-napped by two bad (and not very clever) foxes. With a bit of luck and a lot of pluck, these not-so-chicken chickens devise a plan to escape by tricking the foxes into believing that one of them has laid a golden egg. The two greedy foxes fight over the possession of the egg, leaving the clever chickens free to make their escape.

The Biggest Bed in the World, by Lindsay Camp. Illustrated by Jonathan Langley. HarperCollins, 2000. (Grades K–3)

> Mom and Dad and one small baby fit just fine in the family bed. When more children arrive, including twins and triplets, the bed gets smaller and smaller, As a last resort, Dad bans all the children from the bed and gets ready for a quiet, restful sleep. But something is not quite right. Until, that is, the bed fills up once again with children.

Bridget Fidget and the Most Perfect Pet!, by Joe Berger. Dial Books for Young Readers, 2009. (Grades K–3)

> When a big box arrives one morning, Bridget Fidget leaps out of bed and spins down the stairs. She knows what's inside—a unicorn! After all, she's always wanted a pet unicorn, so it must be a pet unicorn. But inside the box is just another . . . smaller . . . box. And it's buzzing. This is no unicorn. But could it possibly be something even better?

The Cat Lady, by Dick King-Smith. Knopf, 2006. (Grades 2–4)

> Not only does Miss Ponsonby have many, many cats, but she is quite sure that some had once been her parents and Queen Victoria. When a young orphan named Mary arrives at her door, Miss Ponsonby welcomes her, and Mary and a local girl help to take care of the house and the cats. Miss Ponsonby dies and leaves her fortune and home to the Royal Society for

the Protection of Cats, with young Mary in charge. Several months later Mary is sure a newly arrived cat is the former Miss Ponsonby.

The Christmas of the Reddle Moon, by J. Patrick Lewis. Illustrated by Gary Kelley. Dial, 1994. (Grades 3–5)

On a cold Christmas Eve, Will and Liddy set out along Puddletown Road to visit their cousins and exchange gifts. But on their way back home, a shortcut across the dark and forbidding heath leads them into danger. There, in a sudden blizzard, in the midst of swirling veils of snow, they become hopelessly lost. In the next instant they fall into a deep hole. When the children look up, all they can see peering down at them are the eyes of an enormous cat.

They have stumbled into a reddle pit, named for the red clay farmers once used to mark their sheep. This one belongs to Wee Mary Fever, a strange old woman. What happens to Will and Liddy, with the help of Wee Mary Fever and her cat, makes this a magical Christmas story.

Comus, adapted by Margaret Hodges. Illustrated by Trina Schart Hyman. Holiday House, 1996. (Grades 3–5)

Three children go for a walk in the woods near the castle where they live. As night falls, it becomes an enchanted forest, home of Comus, the evil magician. He captures Alice and takes her to his hidden kingdom, and it falls to her younger brothers, John and Thomas, with the help of the good spirits of the forest, to rescue her from his terrible spell.

The Fish Who Could Wish, by John Bush and Korky Paul. Kane-Miller, 1991. (Grades K–3)

This fish is most unusual. Whatever it wishes for, it gets, whether it be fancy clothing, a castle, musical instruments, or a sports car. Even seemingly impossible wishes come true, like wishing to ski and the snow suddenly appears. But one day the fish, without thinking of the consequences, makes his last wish when he decides that he wants to be just like all the other fish in the sea.

Good Night, Good Knight, by Shelley Moore Thomas. Illustrated by Jennifer Plecas. Dutton, 2000. (Grades K–3)

Three little dragons in a far-off cave can't sleep. Someone needs to tuck them in! Luckily a Good Knight keeps watch and hears their lonely ROAR. The Good Knight (because he is a good knight) helps by bringing them glasses of water, reading stories, singing songs, and dispensing kisses in multiple trips down his tower and through the dark forest. Young readers will fall in love with the agreeable Good Knight and the dragons with their sweet but repetitive requests. The repetition—though it tires the Good Knight—will help beginning readers build confidence.

In My Pocket, by M. Gerald Siam. Illustrated by Dorrith Fitzgerald. Harcourt Brace, 1996. (Grades 3–5)

In 1939 conditions in Germany were such that Jewish children were not safe. Jewish families were sent to concentration camps. Kindertransport was a rescue operation for the purpose of taking the Jewish children out of Germany for the duration of World War II. This is the story of one seven-year-old child who went to live with a family in England. During her long time away from home she receives one letter from her parents, which she treasures and keeps safe in her pocket until they can once again be reunited.

Little Kit, by Emily Arnold McCully. Dial, 1995. (Grades 2–4)

Little Kit lives in an alleyway and sells flowers from dawn to dusk just to get by. One day Professor Malefetta barges into the alley looking for a helper. He mistakes Little Kit for a boy and sets her to work looking after his trained fleas. She is miserable working for the professor and longs to escape. But where can she go?

Lucy Dove, by Janice Del Negro. Illustrated by Leonid Gore. DK Publishing, 1998. (Grades 2–4)

Lucy Dove is a brave lady indeed! She takes up the offer of a wealthy lord to sew him a pair of trousers in St. Andrew's graveyard under a full moon. The lord believes that if he owns such a pair of pants, he will have good luck for life. Lucy Dove waits for the full moon, enters the graveyard, and begins to sew the pants. A terrible ghost emerges from a nearby tomb to frighten Lucy away, but the stubborn seamstress is determined to finish sewing the pants and get the gold that is offered. Which will win the ghostly skirmish, Lucy or the ghost? Why Lucy, of course, who grabs on to her courage and uses her wits.

Mrs. Armitage and the Big Wave, by Quentin Blake. Harcourt, 1997. (Grades K–3)

It is possible to spend more time getting ready for an outing than the time actually spent at the outing. Mrs. Armitage arrives at the beach with her little dog but makes one trip after another from the water to the shore, to gather a spear, a horn, flags, a float, a sun hat, an umbrella, and dig biscuits. Amid all the stuff she spies a child caught by a wave and rescues her.

My Dad's a Birdman, by David Almond. Illustrated by Polly Dunbar. Candlewick Press, 2008. (Grades K–3)

Join a father and daughter as they find their wings together and take to the skies in this funny, tender tale. Lizzie and Dad live in a rainy town in the north of England. It's just the two of them, and Auntie Doreen, who pops round to check Lizzie's spellings and tell Dad he's daft—and make them nice hot dumplings. But today there's something unusual going on: Why is Dad building himself a pair of wings and studying the birds to see how they fly? For the Great Human Bird Competition, of course.

The Pirate Meets the Queen, by Matt Faulkner. Philomel Books, 2005. (Grades 2–4)

What do you get when you mix a fiery, red-headed girl with the high seas? Granny O'Malley. Would she rather raid ships than learn the ways of a woman? Yes. And though a woman, would she become captain of her own crew and take to pirating and plundering every English merchant ship that dares sail by? Indeed. But Red Liz, the Queen of England, isn't going to take Granny O'Malley's filching without a fight. When she imprisons Granny's son, the pirate and the Queen come face to face—and neither feisty female is prepared for what happens next!

Saint George and the Dragon: A Golden Legend, adapted by Margaret Hodges. Illustrated by Trina Schart Hyman. Little, Brown, 1984. (Grades 3–5)

Retells the segment from Spenser's *The Faerie Queene* in which George, the Red Cross Knight, slays the dreadful dragon that has been terrorizing the countryside for years, bringing peace and joy to the land. The illustrations show evidence of careful research as Saint George appears on his horse in all his splendor. Master storyteller Margaret Hodges brings this magical time in folklore history to life.

Tattercoats, edited by Joseph Jacobs. Illustrated by Margot Tomes. G. P. Putnam's Sons, 1989. (Grades 2–4)

In a Palace by the sea an old lord sat day after day. He was all alone except for servants and a granddaughter he hated bitterly, for her mother, his only daughter, had died at her birth. So the child was given only scraps from the kitchen and clothes from the rag bag. But when she grew sad she had only to find the gooseherd boy, who would play on his pipes and cheer her up and wipe away her tears. They had other magic as well. And at the King's ball there will be some surprises as Tattercoats and the stranger meet once again.

Twelfth Night, by Bruce Coville. Illustrated by Tim Raglin. Dial, 2003. (Grades 3–5)

This is a lively interpretation of one of Shakespeare's most beloved comedies. In this boisterous tale of hidden identities and misplaced love, Coville once again weaves his own lyrical prose together with pivotal lines from *Twelfth Night.*

The Well at the End of the World, by Daniel San Souci. Illustrated by Rebecca Walsh. Chronicle, 2004. (Grades 2–4)

The king is very ill, and his daughter, Princess Rosamond, goes on a journey to find the magic water that will bring him back to health. On her journey she does three kind deeds and receives the healing water. In addition, jewels and flowers fall out of her mouth when she speaks. Here stepsister, wanting the same rewards, undertakes the journey but is unsuccessful, because she does not stop to help those in need.

Will's Quill or, How a Goose Saved Shakespeare, by Don Freeman. Viking Press, 2004. (Grades 2–4)

Will's Quill tells the story of Willoughby Waddles, a goose in Shakespearean London who longs to be useful. When he befriends a young playwright named Will, Willoughby may have found the perfect way to help out by giving up some goose feathers. Could these feathers and this friendship be just what the playwright needs? It is possible the world might never have heard of William Shakespeare if not for the two Wills working together.

DEWEY DECIMAL GAME

Standards: 2, 4, 19

These are tales from England with Dewey Decimal numbers in place of words. Find the number on the library shelves. What topic does each number represent? That will be the missing word in each title.

1. "The Story of the Three Little 636.4 ________________________________"
2. "The Little Red 636.5____"
3. "Minnie's Midnight 808.81 ____________________________________"
4. "The 636.8 ____ Lady"
5. "The Christmas of the Reddle 523.3 ______________________________"
6. "My Dad's a 598 ____ Man"

Answer key: 1-Pigs; 2-Hen; 3-Dragon; 4-Cat; 5-Moon; 5-Bird

France

France covers 211,000 square miles and has a population of 61 million people. Its two mountain chains, the Alps and the Pyrenees, form natural borders. The language spoken is French. More tourists visit France than any other country. The capital is Paris.

Belinda in Paris, by Amy Young. Viking, 2005. (Grades 1–3)

All of Paris was abuzz with the news: Belinda the ballerina was coming to town! But when Belinda's extra-large ballet shoes wind up in Pago Pago by mistake, she and a young ballerina must hit the streets to look for a new pair. Along the way, Belinda befriends a trio of Parisians, each with his or her own problem. Can Belinda save the day and still find ballet shoes before her performance that night? New and old fans alike will cheer *magnifique!* for Amy Young's big-footed (and big-hearted) ballerina, as she wins over the City of Lights.

The Butterfly, by Patricia Polacco. Puffin Books, 2009. (Grades 2–4)

Ever since the Nazis marched into Monique's small French village, terrorizing it, nothing surprises her, until the night Monique encounters "the little ghost" sitting at the end of her bed. She turns out to be a girl named Sevrine, who has been hiding from the Nazis in Monique's basement. Playing after dark, the two become friends, until, in a terrifying moment, they are discovered, sending both of their families into a nighttime flight.

Come Fly with Me, by Satomi Ichikawa. Philomel Books, 2008. (Grades K–2)

When Woggy, the stuffed dog, and Cosmos, the wooden airplane, decide it is time to get away from the toy box and go somewhere, they figure the only way to go is to fly, and the only way to fly is together. So in a grand adventure, out and up they swoop, Satomi-style, whirling up stairs, past sleepy apartment windows, and over enchanting rooftops. Until they meet the Cloud Monster . . . and the surprise at the end of the book will take your breath away. It did theirs!

The Day We Danced in Underpants, by Sarah Wilson. Illustrated by Catherine Stock. Tricycle Press, 2008. (Grades 1–3)

One of the funniest words in a first grader's vocabulary is "underpants." This is sure to be a hit with six-year-olds. A young boy and his father arrive at the king's picnic with three aunts and two dogs. Father dances so energetically that his pants split, and other nobles end up dancing in their underwear as well. This will have great appeal to youngsters who have a love for the absurd.

Doggie in the Window, by Elaine Arsenault. Illustrated by Fanny. Groundwood Books, 2005. (Grades K–3)

Doggie sits in the window of Monsieur Albert's pet shop watching the world pass by and wishing someone would come and take him home. Along the street comes a ravishing woman, ribbons fluttering, many-colored buttons wobbling as she runs along in her bright green shoes. It is Mademoiselle Madeleine, the seamstress from next door. Doggie decides then and there that he must persuade Mademoiselle Madeleine to adopt him and devises fantastic schemes to gain her attention. But she is looking for help with her sewing, so Doggie must prove that he can be the tailor she needs. Eventually his ingenuity with a needle wins the day. Beautifully illustrated by Fanny, this warm and witty book is bound to appeal to readers big and small with its originality and the charm of its hero, Doggie.

The Grand Mosque of Paris, by Karen Gray Ruelle and Deborah Durland DeSaix. Holiday House, 2009. (Grades 3–5)

During the Nazi occupation of Paris, many Jews found refuge in an unlikely place, the sprawling complex of the Grand Mosque of Paris. It was an ideal temporary hiding place for escaped prisoners of war and Jews of all ages, including children. This true story tells how French Muslims saved the lives of many Jews.

Madeline and the Bad Hat, by Ludwig Bemelmans. Viking Press, [2008], 1984. (Grades K–3)

One day the Spanish ambassador moves into the Parisian house next door to Miss Clavel, Madeline, and her 11 classmates. And His Excellency has a boy! Pepito, as he is named, is not just any boy; according to Madeline, he is a "bad hat." For starters, he's equipped with an irksome slingshot, he "ghosts," and he boasts. And when Miss Clavel gives him a box of tools to function as an "outlet for his energy," he makes a guillotine for the cook's chickens. ("He ate them ROASTED, GRILLED, AND FRITO! Oh what a horror was PEPITO.") What will Madeline do to rebuff this noisy neighbor?

Madeline and the Gypsies, by Ludwig Bemelmans. Viking, 2000. (Grades K–3)

Madeline and Pepito have run off to join the carnival with a band of traveling gypsies! At first they're having the time of their lives, but then they get homesick. Leave it to clever Miss Clavel to find Madeline and Pepito and bring them home.

Madeline in London, by Ludwig Bemelmans. Viking, 2000. (Grades K–3)

Pepito has moved to England. To help celebrate his birthday, Miss Clavel and the girls pay him a visit. When his mother won't let Pepito keep one of his birthday presents—a horse—Madeline is more than willing to help out.

Madeline's Christmas, by Ludwig Bemelmans. Viking, 2000. (Grades K–3)

It's the night before Christmas, and everyone is sick in bed. All except brave Madeline, who is up and about and feeling just fine. Taking care of 11 little girls and Miss Clavel is hard work, but Madeline finds help from a magical merchant peddling flying carpets door-to-door. Now the girls are going on a Christmas journey that will surely make them forget their sniffles and sneezes.

Madeline's Rescue, by Ludwig Bemelmans. Viking Press, reissue 2000. (Grades K–3)

When Madeline falls into the river Seine and nearly drowns, a courageous canine comes to her rescue. Now Genevieve the dog is Madeline's cherished pet, and the envy of all the other girls. However, Lord Cucuface issues a ruling that no dogs are allowed in the orphanage and sends the dog, Genevieve, out into the Paris streets to fend for herself. Of course Madeline and the other little girls search high and low for Genevieve and find more than they expected!

The Miraculous Tale of the Two Maries, by Rosemary Wells. Illustrated by Petra Mathers. Viking, 2006. (Grades 2–4)

In the south of France there is a tiny town called Saintes Maries de la Mer. Inside the town church is a wooden boat . . . with two wooden ladies—one in a rose dress and one in blue. Both are called Marie. Traveling in their modest wooden boat, the mysterious two Saint Maries are said to have performed 40 miracles during the nineteenth century. But who were these two saints? Inspired by this question, Rosemary Wells crafts a vivid portrayal of the saints as 16-year-old friends drifting through the skies in their boat, meeting with God himself, and swooping down to Earth to perform loving good deeds

Moi and Marie Antoinette, by Lynn Cullen. Illustrated by Amy Young. Bloomsbury Children's Books, 2006. (Grades 1–3)

The Moi in this story is not only a dog but the favorite pet of Marie Antoinette, who became queen of France. The dog begins his story as her pet when Marie is 13. Later she becomes not only the Queen of France but a mother as well.

Life in the French court is not a happy one for Marie Antoinette, and the pug dog is un-happy as well because he receives little attention from his mistress. It is then that the pug dog and six-year-old Therese, the queen's daughter, find each other and show the queen the im-portance of love and family.

Mr. Satie and the Great Art Contest, by Tomie dePaola. Puffin Books, 2007. (Grades 1–3)

Rosalie and Conrad love it when Uncle Satie comes to visit, because he always has ex-citing stories to tell about his adventures abroad. This year he went to Paris, where he found himself at the center of an art dispute. It all began one Sunday evening when his friends in-vited him to an art show. The famous painter Pablo was to show his work, when, unexpect-edly, the famous artist Henri arrived from Nice with his new paintings. Soon the two began to argue about who was the better artist—and it was up to Mr. Satie to help end the argument so the painters could become friends.

Where's Our Mama?, written and illustrated by Diane Goode. Dutton, 1991. (Grades K–2)

The illustrator has created a 1920s Paris setting in which a harried mother carrying a baby and herding two very young children through a train station has her hat blown away. The preschoolers, who have been told not to move until she finds her hat, get worried when she does not return. They ask the help of a gendarme to find their mother, and he takes the children on a tour of Paris, during which they assure him that none of the women he points out is their mother. At last the children remember mother's instructions to stay put, and they return to the train station, where mother and children are reunited.

ABOUT FRANCE

Standards: 4, 9, 10, 11

Cover up the poem at the bottom of the page. Work with a friend to guess yes or no to each fact about France. Then read the poem to support or deny your guesses.

1. The capital of France is Paris. _____

2. To say "hello" in French you say "bon jour." _____

3. A very famous French King was Louis XIV. _____

4. The highest place in France is the Himalayas. _____

5. French people like to eat snails. _____

6. A famous French bicycle race is called the Tour de France. _____

Support or refute your guesses by reading the poem below.

HAIL TO FRANCE!
I see Paris
Capital of France
I'd go there if I had the chance.
I've heard of Mont Blanc
The highest place,
The Tour de France is a famous bike race.
"Bon Jour," says the waiter,
"Will you have some escargot?"
He said, "Hello" and offered you some slimy snails to go.
Louis XIV was a famous French king.
The flag is red and white and blue
As Hail to France we sing.

Answer key: Number 4 is the only incorrect statement.

From *Reading the World with Picture Books* by Nancy J. Polette.
Santa Barbara, CA: Libraries Unlimited. Copyright © 2010.

Germany

Germany covers 132,000 square miles and has a population of almost 83 million people. The language spoken is German. From 1949 to 1990, Germany was divided into two countries, East and West Germany. The Black Forest is the setting for many fairy tales. The capital of Germany today is Berlin.

As Luck Would Have It: From the Brothers Grimm, by Robert D. San Souci. August House Little Folk, 2008. (Grades 2–4)

Jonas and Juniper are the twin sons of the bear family and are more often than not into mischief. Adapted from an old tale by the Grimm Brothers, this story tells of the twins' misadventures when left alone at home by their parents. All turns out well, however, when they encounter and overcome thieves.

Doctor All-Knowing, retold by Doris Orgel. Illustrated by Alexandra Boiger. Simon & Schuster, 2008. (Grades 2–4)

Crayfish is a woodcutter, too poor to feed his daughter, Maggie. But with the advice of a local physician, the destitute man does as he's told and gets himself an alphabet book, a suit, and a sign and starts claiming to be Doctor All-Knowing. With Maggie's help he soon solves the mystery of who's been stealing money from the town's richest man, and rewards follow.

The Frog Prince by the Brothers Grimm, as retold by Kathy-Jo Wargin. Illustrated by Anne Yvonne Gilbert. Mitten Press, 2007. (Grades 1–3)

This Brothers Grimm tale of a spoiled princess finding her handsome prince by breaking a witch's spell has enchanted readers since it was written in the early 1800s. Children will delight in the princess's distaste as she shares her meal and bed with the slimy, green frog, who is really a prince enchanted by a wicked witch, whose spell can be released by the princess if she is willing enough.

Iron John, by Eric Kimmel. Holiday House, 1999. (Grades 2–4)

Hans, a young prince, has heard many eerie tales about the man-beast who rules the enchanted woods. Yet when Iron John is brought to the castle in chains, Hans is more fascinated than frightened. The boy not only frees the gentle savage but accepts him as a second father, and he runs away with Iron John to start a new life of growth and discovery beyond his imagination.

Sleeping Beauty, by Mahlon Craft. Seastar Books, 2002. (Grades 2–4)

From the Brothers Grimm comes the tale of a princess cursed at birth by a witch who is unhappy at not being invited to the christening. The princess leads a happy life until the day of her sixteenth birthday, when the witch's curse comes true. She pricks her finger on a spinning wheel and falls asleep for 100 years, until awakened by a kiss from a prince. This version stays very close to the original Grimm tale and is beautifully illustrated by Kinuko Y. Craft.

Snow White and Rose Red, by Jakob Grimm and Wilhelm Grimm. Illustrated by Gennady Spirin. Philomel Books, 1992. (Grades 2–4)

A BEAR! When they opened the door of their cottage one stormy winter evening, Snow White and Rose Red were astonished, and a bit frightened, to see a huge, shaggy bear standing outside. His fur was covered with snow, and he seemed half frozen, so they took pity on him and invited him to warm himself by the fire. He proved to be a gentle creature and came often to visit during the winter . . . only to disappear mysteriously in the spring. But he was no ordinary bear, as they were soon to discover, and he found a surprising way to repay Snow White and Rose Red for their kindness to him.

The Turnip, by Walter de la Mare. Illustrated by Kevin Hawkes. David R. Godine, 2001. (Grades 2–4)

This retelling of "The Turnip" (originally a tale from the Brothers Grimm) is a real work of art in its own right. There are two brothers: one greedy and duplicitous, the other selfless, compassionate, and poor. Their fates are forever altered when a giant turnip springs from the good brother's field not long after the appearance of a mysterious, squint-eyed old man.

TALES FROM THE BROTHERS GRIMM

Standards: 2, 4, 5, 8, 10

Place the number of each tale beside its description.

1. "Beauty and the Beast"

2. "Princess Furball"

3. "The Frog Prince"

4. "The Goose Girl"

5. "Twelve Dancing Princesses"

6. "The Fisherman and His Wife"

7. "The Bremen Town Musician"

8. "Rumpelstiltskin"

A. _____ The classic tale of the lovely girl and the ugly beast.

B. _____ Four mistreated animal friends set out together and encounter robbers.

C. _____ The fisherman's greedy wife is never satisfied no matter how great the gifts are that they get from a magic fish.

D. _____ A princess makes a promise to an ugly frog who rescues her golden ball from a well.

E. _____ A princess and a maid change identities.

F. _____ Twelve princesses wear out their shoes each night, and no one knows why.

G. _____ A princess with a coat of a thousand furs hides her identity from a king.

H. _____ A miller's daughter makes a foolish promise to a little man who promises to spin straw into gold.

Answer key: A-1; B-7; C-6; D-3; E-4; F-5; G-2; H-8

Greece

Greece covers an area of 51,000 square miles and has a population of 10.5 million people. The language spoken is Greek. The capital is Athens, well known for its beautiful buildings.

Demeter & Persephone: Spring Held Hostage, by Ron Fontes and Justine Fontes. Illustrated by Steve Kurth. Lerner, 2000. (Grades 3–5)

The story of Demeter, the Greek goddess of the harvest, and her daughter, Persephone. Demeter rules over a perpetual summer on earth, where crops, trees, and flowers grow in abundance. Persephone, young and beautiful, unknowingly attracts the attention of the lonely god of the Underworld, Hades. Hades kidnaps Persephone, and a frantic Demeter searches in vain for her daughter. Finally Demeter retreats to her temple in mourning. The goddess's sorrow causes the crops to die and the ground to freeze. The first winter falls over Greece. As people begin to starve, the other Olympian gods and goddesses try to convince Demeter to accept a marriage between Persephone and Hades. But Demeter will not give up her daughter forever to the Underworld. Finally a compromise is struck: Persephone will stay with Hades for half a year (winter). When she comes back from the Underworld to spend half a year with her mother, spring returns to Earth.

The First Olympic Games: A Gruesome Greek Myth with a Happy Ending, by Jean Richards. Illustrated by Kate Thacker. Millbrook Press, 2000. (Grades 3–5)

Tales of the Greek gods were not known for their gentle approach to life. It seems that at the time of the Greek gods, there was a boy named Pelops who was so mean to others that his father, Tantalus, cut him up to make stew out of him. The gods were not happy about this, so they restored Pelops to life. Later on he won both a princess and a kingdom in a horse race, and, so the legend goes, in gratitude for his good fortune he established the Olympic Games.

Greek Myths, by Deborah Locke. Dorling Kindersley, 2005. (Grades 3–4)

This is a collection of myths for third-grade readers and contains "Pandora's Jar," "Labors of Heracles," "Theseus and the Minotaur," "The Fall of Icarus," "The Adventures of Perseus," "The Foolishness of Midas," and "Orpheus and Eurydice."

I Have an Olive Tree, by Eve Bunting. Illustrated by Karen Barbour. HarperCollins, 1999. (Grades 2–4)

If asked what she hoped for as a birthday present, seven year-old Sophia would have answered quickly, "a skateboard." She tries not to show her disappointment when her grandfather's gift is an olive tree. Yet after the death of her grandfather, the tree takes on more importance as a symbol of those who have come before. Sophia and her mother are able to travel to Greece and visit the original family home. There they see a very old olive tree, and following grandfather's wishes, they place grandmother's beads on one of its branches. Sophia begins to fully realize the connectedness of family, past, present, and future.

The Iliad, by Ian Strachan. Kingfisher, 1997. (Grades 4–6)

Retells the events of the war between Greece and the city of Troy, focusing on Achilles's quarrel with Agamemnon.

The McElderry Book of Greek Myths, by Eric A. Kimmel. M.K. McElderry Books, c2008. (Grades 4–6)

Walk among the gods and goddesses, men and monsters, in this enchanting volume of classic Greek myths! Here are 12 of the most beloved legends of Greek mythology, from Pandora and her dreaded box to Icarus with his wings of wax, and, of course, that greedy, gold-fingered King Midas. Vibrant art adds a fresh twist to this collection, giving today's readers their own version of these timeless tales.

Mount Olympus Basketball, by Kevin O'Malley. Walker & Co., 2003. (Grades 2–4)

Imagine a few mortals, even if they are Hercules, Theseus, and others of similar strength and ability, trying to win a basketball game against Greek gods! Blow by blow descriptions of the action are given by sports announcers, who are caricatures of announcers today, complete with sports coats over tunics.

The gods, of course, win the game, but only by using their godly powers. Predictably, the gods trounce the men, thanks to their unfair advantages: Poseidon creates a tidal wave, and Zeus resorts to lightning bolts. Even the trickery of the mortals' Trojan horse is not enough to win the game. But a good time is had by all, especially the reader.

We Goddesses: Athena, Aphrodite, Hera, by Doris Orgel. Illustrated by Marilee Heyer. DK Publishing, 1999. (Grades 4–6)

Three Greek goddesses, Athena, Aphrodite, and Hera, tell their own stories. Includes information about Greek society and religion.

Yanni Rubbish, by Shulamith Levey Oppenheim. Illustrated by Doug Chayka. Boyds Mills Press, 1999. (Grades 2–4)

Yanni must earn enough money to put food on the table for his mother and himself while his father has sought work far away in Germany. The boy and his mother live in a very poor Greek village, but even a small village has trash, and Yanni earns a few coins each day hitching his donkey to a cart and hauling away the town's trash. The other children make fun of Yanni, calling him Yanni Rubbish, until the boy and his mother find a clever way to stop the teasing.

GREEK GODS AND GODDESSES

Standards: 14, 15, 16

Long, long ago the Greeks had three ways of explaining their world: through observation of nature, practical experiences, and imagination. Nature was often explained by giving life to everything and inventing gods with powers far greater than those of humankind. The Greek gods lived on Mount Olympus. Here is one well-known Greek myth in which Bacchus, the god of wine, gives King Midas his wish.

Visit your library to find other Greek myths to read and enjoy.

King Midas

King Midas is granted one wish by Bacchus, the god of wine, for doing him a favor. Midas asks that all he touches turn to gold. Overjoyed at first with this power, he soon realizes his mistake when he touches his little daughter and asks to have his power revoked. He was told to bathe in a certain river where his power is washed away. Some say that that is why gold is found in rivers.

QUESTION: Gold is a very precious and expensive metal. What can you name that is made of gold?

_____ _____ _____ _____

What might happen if YOU had the golden touch?

If I had the golden touch I would be very careful not to touch _____

or _____ or _____. Eating would be a problem

unless I _____.

Clothes made of gold would be very uncomfortable unless _____

_____

If I were offered the golden touch I think I would say _____.

From *Reading the World with Picture Books* by Nancy J. Polette.
Santa Barbara, CA: Libraries Unlimited. Copyright © 2010.

Hungary

Hungary covers 36,000 square miles and has a population of 10 million people. The language spoken is Hungarian. It is a country of many small towns. The people are called Magyars. They are noted for hand embroidery and colorful costumes. The capital is Budapest.

Big Quiet House, by Heather Forest. Illustrated by Susan Greenstein. August House, 2008. (Grades K–3)

"There once was a man whose house was very small," the story opens. "It was cluttered with things from wall to wall." With a tiny, cluttered house, giggling children, and a snoring wife, the poor man can't get a good night's sleep. If only, he thinks, I had a big quiet house! He throws off his covers and goes to visit the wise old woman at the edge of the village. Surely she can help him solve his problem. And she does, but not without giving him some very unusual advice. "Bring a chicken into your house," she suggests. And when that doesn't work, she has him add a goat, a horse, a cow, and a sheep. The ending of the story proves, as so many folktales do, that quite often, nonsense makes the best sense of all.

The Boy Who Stuck out His Tongue, by Edith Tarbescu. Illustrated by Judith C. Mills. Barefoot Books, 2000. (Grades K–3)

When the widow asks her son to light the fire, he just sticks his tongue out at her. "I'm too busy," he laughs, for he would rather make snowballs than help with chores. But when he gets himself into a sticky situation, the kind folk of the little Hungarian village are quick to rally around. The butcher, the baker, the cobbler, the carpenter, and the cook gather up their tools and offer their well-meaning support to the boy, but it is the blacksmith's hot coals that solve the problem.

Feathers, by Heather Forest. Illustrated by Marcia Cutchin. August House, 2001. (Grades 1–3)

Words, like feathers flying in the wind, in the wind. Careless words, tossed about, cannot again be swallowed up. Rumors and gossip can be permanent and damaging. The victim's reputation is harmed, and the trust in the community erodes. In this traditional folktale, a gossip is brought before a wise rabbi, who must concoct a suitable lesson. His clever solution demonstrates vividly the consequence and permanence of words spoken in haste. It is easy to spread gossip, . . . but impossible to take it back

Hanna's Cold Winter, by Trish Marx. Illustrated by Barbara Knutson. Carolrhoda Books, 1993. (Grades 2–4)

This is a true story of how the hippos in the Budapest Zoo were saved from starvation during the German occupation in World War II. Papa was a factory worker who would take his family on Sunday walks throughout the town. A favorite stopping place was the zoo and a visit to the hippos. But the war takes its toll, not only on the people of Hungary, who have less and less food, but on the animals in the zoo. The hippos are suffering from lack of food, and then Papa gets an idea. There are many things made of straw in Hungarian homes: floor mats, shoes, purses, and hats. On their next trip to the zoo, Papa brings the family doormat and starts a campaign in which people bring more than 9,000 items made of straw to the zoo and save the lives of the hippos during one of the coldest winters Hungary has ever known.

BUDAPEST ZOO

Standards: 5, 11, 13, 14

If you traveled to Budapest, the capital of Hungary, you could visit libraries, museums, castles, and the Budapest Zoo. Suppose you visited the Zoo on a cold winter day. List three animals you might see. What would each animal be doing?

1. Hippos are eating straw.

2. _____ are _____ .

3. _____ are _____ .

4. _____ are _____ .

Use the animals and their activities in the following song. Sing to the tune of "Farmer in the Dell."

Example:

The hippos are eating straw,

The hippos are eating straw,

This is true at the Budapest Zoo,

The hippos are eating straw.

The _____ are _____

The _____ are _____

This is true at the Budapest Zoo,

The _____ are _____

The _____ are _____

The _____ are _____

This is true at the Budapest Zoo

The _____ are _____

From *Reading the World with Picture Books* by Nancy J. Polette.
Santa Barbara, CA: Libraries Unlimited. Copyright © 2010.

Iceland and the Far North

Iceland covers an area of about 38,000 square miles and has a population of 302,000 people. The language spoken is Icelandic. Hot geysers provide heat for many of the country's homes and the hothouses where vegetables are grown. The capital is Reykjavik.

Runaway Pony, by Krista Ruepp. Illustrated by Ulrike Heyne. Translated by Marianne Martens. North-South Books, 2005. (Grades K–3)

Prince, a little Icelandic pony, is growing up. He is Anna's pony. She's raised him from a foal and loves him dearly. Whenever Anna calls, Prince comes running right to her and nuzzles her neck. Prince is still too young to be ridden, but it's time to start training him to walk with a halter and lead line. On his very first lesson, Anna accidentally walks him past a noisy tractor. Terrified, Prince rears and runs away. With her wise grandmother's help, Anna manages to find her runaway pony and, with patience and love, win back his trust. Lush paintings of the beautiful Icelandic landscape illustrate this heartwarming story about the special bonds that can exist between horses and young riders.

The Seal Oil Lamp, written and illustrated by Dale DeArmond. Little, Brown, 1988. (Grades 2–4)

A harsh Eskimo law decrees that those who cannot care for themselves are not allowed to live. Seven-year-old Allugua is blind, and when the village people to go to their annual fishing camp, the boy's parents leave him behind to die of cold and hunger. Little does the boy guess that as he sings songs and plays games alone, the mouse people are coming to his rescue!

The Whale Brother, by Barbara Steiner. Illustrated by Gretchen Will Mayo. Walker/Bloomsbury, 1988. (Grades 2–4)

Watching whales with an artist's eye, Omu, an Eskimo boy, tries to carve a seal from bone, but his father and another carver both tell him that he has not been able to put any life into his work. Believing that he is not a carver after all, Omu gives it up; still searching for a talent, he trades his spear for a harmonica. The other boys tease him, for he neither hunts nor carves, but sits around making terrible sounds. So Omu goes out to sea to play his harmonica and becomes friendly with whales, who enjoy his music. When Skana, a great whale, is beached and dies, Omu stays with the once-mighty beast, carving a likeness from ivory. He attains "qarrtsiluni," or the stillness from which real creativity flows.

ICELAND SONG

Standards: 17, 21

Fill in the missing words. Sing the Iceland song to the tune of "Twinkle, Twinkle, Little Star."

Iceland homes have

G_____ heat

Children warm their

Hands and f_____.

Dinner is

A tasty dish

Icelanders eat

Lots of f_____

Off the coast

In Arctic gales

Sailors see both seals

And W_____

Icelanders think

Elves and t_____

Make their homes

In hidey holes.

✂🗝 **Missing words:** feet, fish, geyser, trolls, whales

Ireland

Ireland covers an area of 27,000 square miles and has a population of 4 million people. The languages spoken are English and Irish Gaelic. It is called the Emerald Isle because of its abundant rains and lush grasslands. Another name for Ireland is Eire. The capital is Dublin.

Angela and the Baby Jesus, by Frank McCourt. Illustrated by Raúl Colón. Simon & Schuster Books for Young Readers, 2007. (Grades 2–4)

Based on a childhood story told by the author's mother. At Christmastime, six-year-old Angela takes the baby Jesus from the cold church manger to her warm house in Limerick, Ireland. Angela is six years old and worries about the baby Jesus on the altar of St. Joseph's Church near School House Lane in Limerick, Ireland, where she lives. December nights are damp and cold, and the church is dark. The baby Jesus's mother doesn't even have a blanket to cover him. The baby is sure to need Angela's help, even if she is not allowed to step near the altar, especially by herself.

Children of Ireland, by Michael Elsohn Ross. Lerner, 2002. (Grades 3–5)

Meet the children of Ireland, a nation with a rich and fascinating culture. In Cork, Cormac and Eoghan play the ancient sport of hurling, while Katrina plays rounders. In Donegal, Cait swims in chilly northern waters. John sorts mussels in the seaside village of Cromane. Discover this land of lush hills, busy cities, and ancient stone monuments through the eyes of its children.

A Claddagh Ring for Nuala, by Duncan Crosbie. Illustrated by Peter Rutherford. Pelican, 2008. (Grades 3–5)

The legend of the Claddagh begins in Claddagh, Ireland, with the love of Richard and Nuala, who wish to be married but cannot afford to do so. Richard, in turn, leaves Claddagh in search of his fortune, and along the way his ship is taken over by pirates. Richard is sold as a slave, and many years pass before he is able to return to Claddagh. Much to his surprise, he finds Nuala still waiting for him. As a symbol of their love, friendship, and faithfulness, Richard crafts a ring for Nuala, which is now known as the Claddagh ring, and gives it to her on their wedding day. When the ring is worn on the left hand with the heart facing inward, it means that two loves are forever joined.

Fin M'Coul and the Giant: From Celtic Fairy Tales, by Joseph Jacobs. Scholastic, 1999. (Grades 2–4)

Fin M'Coul and the giant, Cuhullin, were about to meet and have a fight. Fin knew that it was likely he would be beaten yet he could not avoid the fight. Fin was so worried, he asked his wife, Oonagh, for ideas on how to defeat the giant. Oonagh dressed Fin in baby clothes and baked cakes with an iron griddle in the center of each. When Cuhullin arrived, she told him that Fin was out but asked him to sit for some refreshment. She gave the giant a cake with the iron griddle in the center and the "baby" one without. When Cuhullin saw how easily the "baby" devoured the cake, he made a hasty retreat.

Finn MacCool and the Small Men of Deeds, by Pat O'Shea and Stephen Lewis. Holiday House, 1987. (Grades 2–4)

Finn MacCool tries to help a giant rescue his children. One day, as Finn nurses a morning headache, a giant appears and begs for help. The giant wants him to save her newest son. Finn is quite proud to be asked to undertake such a task and agrees to guard the child, but must first locate the eight dwarf men to help him. Thus begins an adventure with many twists and turns, but in the end Finn will have something to brag about.

Fiona's Luck, by Teresa Bateman. Charlesbridge, 2007. (Grades K–3)

The leprechaun king is sure that people are grabbing up and using all of the leprechaun luck. He sends out a decree to all leprechauns that all of the luck is to be gathered up and brought to him. The king then locks the luck up in a large treasure chest, which he hides. Without the luck of the Irish, terrible things happen throughout the land. The potatoes turn black in the ground, and food is scarce. It is then that a young Irish lass, Fiona, comes up with a plan to outsmart the king and get the luck of the Irish back for her people.

Jamie O'Rourke and the Pooka, by Tomie dePaola. Putnam, 2000. (Grades K–3)

From the creator of the much-loved book *Jamie O'Rourke and the Big Potato*, comes another story about the laziest man in all of Ireland, Jamie O'Rourke. This time Jamie's wife has left him alone for a week. All Jamie has to do is clean the dishes and sweep the house. Of course, Jamie's the messiest man in all of Ireland as well as the laziest, but when a magical Pooka comes to do all the housework, he figures he's also the luckiest. But Jamie's luck runs out when he gives the Pooka a warm overcoat as thanks, thus breaking the house-cleaning spell cast on the Pooka. The Pooka runs off, leaving Jamie—and Eileen—with a very messy house indeed!

Leprechauns Never Lie, written and illustrated by Lorn Balian. Abingdon, reissue 2004. (Grades K–3)

Ninny Nanny is so lazy that she and Gram are close to being without home or food. She is so lazy that she won't fill the rain barrel, fix the roof, or dig the potatoes. And there is poor old Gram to take care of as well. So Ninny Nanny decides if she can catch a leprechaun, she can find his pot of gold. What she didn't expect is that it is not wise to try to trick a leprechaun.

Shawn O'hisser: The Last Snake in Ireland, by Peter J. Welling. Pelican Books, 2009. (Grades 2–4)

In this fast-paced new twist on an old tale, whimsical snake Shawn O'Hisser returns to his native Ireland from a visit to England and Wales to find that all of his snake friends have vanished, as has all the leprechauns' gold. Shawn works to solve the mystery, using his wits to avoid being eaten by other inhabitants of the Emerald Isle. Things look pretty hopeless, until Shawn is befriended by Edmund, the natterjack toad, and Kathleen, the orange mouse. Together, they set out to right a wrong, but will they solve the mystery in time? Will they find the leprechauns' gold, or did Dobherchu the Giant Otter take it? What did the monk named Patrick have to do with all those snakes disappearing? Laugh your way along the trail of the disappearing snakes to find the answers to these and other mysteries of the last snake in Ireland.

Small Beauties: The Journey of Darcy Heart, by Elvira Woodruff. Illustrated by Rex Adam. Alfred A. Knopf, 2006. (Grades 2–4)

It is often said that one man's trash is another man's treasure. This is especially true of Darcy Heart O'Hara, a young Irish girl who shares a small cottage with her large family in the 1840s. When circumstances force the family to emigrate to America, Darcy takes with her the small treasures gathered from the Irish countryside. Born with a gift of seeing small beauties, she finds rocks, petals, and feathers and slips them into the hem of her ragged dress. Not surprisingly, during the difficult journey, Darcy's small beauties bring comfort to the family by reminding them of their better times in Ireland.

St. Patrick and the Three Brave Mice, by Joyce A. Stengel. Illustrated by Herb Leonhard. Pelican, 2009. (Grades 1–3)

One sleepless night, with the moon high, the little mouse Tulla scurries from her nest. As she quietly enjoys the evening, the peace is interrupted by Snake slithering from the forest. He is the only snake left in Ireland, the lone creature who has been clever enough to escape St. Patrick and his miraculous bell, and he has a taste for mouse meals. Her whiskers quivering with fright, Tulla watches Snake as he stealthily steals the bell from a sleeping St. Patrick. Despite her fear, Tulla devises a plan just as crafty as Snake's. With the help of two brave mice, she will restore the bell and help St. Patrick rid the Emerald Isle of its last reptile.

Too Many Leprechauns, by Stephen Krensky. Illustrated by Dan Andreasen. Simon & Schuster Books for Young Readers, 2007. (Grades 1–3)

Finn O'Finnegan returns home from Dublin to find his mother complaining that some noisy leprechauns who are making fairy shoes are disturbing her sleep. Finn visits the leprechauns and finds fault with every one of their shoes. When he tells them that their styles are all wrong and their craftsmanship is terrible, they show him their stash of gold to prove that they make fine products. Now that Finn knows where the gold is hidden, it only remains for him to help himself.

Traveling Tom and the Leprechaun, by Teresa Bateman. Holiday House, 2007. (Grades 1–3)

Like many before him, Tom, a traveling minstrel, has fallen in love at first sight with the beautiful princess Kathleen. But Kathleen has vowed only to marry the man who can win a leprechaun's pot of gold. Tom sets out with a clever plan to fool a leprechaun into giving up his fortune. Upon meeting one of the fair folk, Tom charms him with songs and stories. As it turns out, however, Tom's tales hold more truth than trick.

Walking to School, by Eve Bunting. Illustrated by Michael Dooling. Clarion Books, 2008. (Grades 3–5)

Walking to school can be hard if you live in Belfast, Northern Ireland. It's downright dangerous if you're a Catholic, like Allison, and the shortest route to your school goes through a Protestant neighborhood. But sometimes a ray of kindness cuts through the violence. That's what happens when a demonstrator rips a brass button off Allison's new school blazer, and a Protestant girl not only retrieves the button but returns it to Allison. Allison then hands the kind girl a cherished marble, showing that children's friendships would overcome religious differences if adults would stand aside.

The Wee Christmas Cabin, by Margaret Hodges. Illustrated by Kimberly Root. Holiday House, 2009. (Grades 2–4)

All of her life Oona dreams of having a cabin of her own. Left on a doorstep as a baby, she grows to be the prettiest lass in the county, but no lad will marry the daughter of traveling tinkers. So Oona moves from cabin to cabin, helping wherever there is trouble or need. When the Great Famine comes and the last of the potatoes is eaten, Oona knows she must leave. She sets out on a snowy Christmas Eve. To her surprise, the magic of a white Christmas awaits her, as do hundreds of fairies, all wanting to make her dream come true.

The Wishing of Biddy Malone, by Joy Cowley. Illustrated by Denise Christopher. Philomel Books, 2004. (Grades 2–4)

Biddy, a young Irish girl, loves to sing and dance. She is known for her hot temper, which one evening gets the better of her, so she leaves her cottage to cool off and finds herself in a faerie village, where she is given three wishes by a handsome young man. Her wishes, which were "to sing as sweetly as a thrush and dance as lightly as a deer, and for a loving heart" do not come true on her return home, yet years later the faeries' village reappears, and Biddy again meets the young man, who is her true love.

In Ireland they say there is a pot of gold at the end of the rainbow, and you just have to go after it, or try to get it from a leprechaun who hides the gold. It is a way of saying that your own wish can come true, but you must pursue it.

POT OF GOLD

Standards: 5, 8, 21

Draw your own pot of gold. Inside it, draw a picture of what your wish would be. To make a pot of gold:

1. Enlarge a pattern of a pot to desirable size and trace it on heavy yellow tagboard or construction paper.

2. Make a second pot, exactly the same size, out of black construction paper.

3. Glue the top of the black pot across the top of the yellow pot of gold near the pot's rim.

4. You now have a flap. Lift up the black pot, and underneath on the yellow pot, draw what you wish was YOUR pot of gold.

5. If you like, decorate the wish you have put in your pot of gold.

From *Reading the World with Picture Books* by Nancy J. Polette. Santa Barbara, CA: Libraries Unlimited. Copyright © 2010.

Italy

Italy covers an area of 116,000 square miles and has a population of almost 3 million people. The language spoken is Italian. It is the home of the Vatican and St. Peter's Cathedral. The capital of Italy is Rome.

The Bells of Santa Lucia, by Gus Cazzona. Illustrated by Pierr Morgan. Philomel, 1991. (Grades 1–3)

There are many bells in the village of Santa Lucia, and Lucinda loves all them. She even cherishes the small bell her grandmother rings to let her know she is needed. Then Grandmother dies, and the tiny bell is silent. Lucinda, in her grief, would banish all the bells in the town if she could. To make her feel better, a schoolmaster asks her to look after three lambs. Their stall catches fire, which spreads toward the schoolhouse. Only Lucinda can save them. When she rings the largest bell in town, the people come to help, and Lucinda once again values the bells.

Caterina the Clever Farm Girl, by Julienne Peterson. Illustrated by Enzo Giannini. Dial, 1996. (Grades 1–3)

Would you dress in a fishnet and ride a goat to the royal palace? Clever Caterina does. When her poor father offers his gold treasure to the king, Caterina predicts his regal but discourteous response. The strong-willed ruler challenges this unique girl to prove herself, but is so smitten by her wily wit that he asks her to marry him. But he gets much more than he bargained for. Will Caterina be banished from the kingdom? Or will the king realize his true good fortune?

The Flying Bed, by Nancy Willard. Illustrated by John Thompson. Blue Sky Press, 2007. (Grades 1–3)

Guido and his wife were poor. He used poor ingredients in his baked goods, so no one would buy them. He sold all their furniture, but Maria insisted they must have a bed, so Guido found one for free. That night the bed rose into the air and landed in a place full of ovens, where a master baker gave Guido magic yeast. From that day on Guido's baked goods were so good that many customers came, and Maria was worn out. Guido's greed led him to sell the magic yeast to a stranger. When he tried to spend the money, he was arrested because it was counterfeit. Guido and Maria were once again poor. Maria decided to take one last trip on the flying bed, and when it returned her to her room, she found the room filled with delicious apples, enough for all of their customers.

A Gift for the Contessa, by Michael Mele. Illustrated by Ronald G. Paolillo. Pelican Books, 2002. (Grades 1–3)

How do you carry a gift of glass flowers to a contessa? Very carefully—and with a group, if you're Maybellinda. Maybellinda's father has just told her and her family that he may not be able to feed them this winter. Dejected, Maybellinda is nevertheless polite to an old woman who visits her flower stall. When the gray-haired woman requests "a bright yellow flower to match my golden hair," Maybellinda kindly complies. She is rewarded when the old woman gives her a bunch of glistening glass flowers. Maybellinda decides to take them to a count who is giving gold for the world's most beautiful gift for his wife. If she can win the gold, she can take care of her family! Along the way she meets an entertaining mix of people.

The Hinky-Pink, by Megan McDonald. Illustrated by Brian Floca. Simon & Schuster, 2009. (Grades 1–3)

Anabel, a seamstress in Old Italy, dreams of one day sewing a gown for the princess to wear to the Butterfly Ball. The chance comes, but the poor girl has a mere week to make the dress. Nothing goes right, no thanks to a Hinky-Pink in the room. Imagine a buzz saw the size of a flea. Imagine the worst and no sleep for the seamstresses on top of it. This is the tale of how Anabel outwits her challenge and fulfills her dream In Renaissance Italy

The King of Capri, by Jeanette Winters. Illustrated by Jane Ray. Bloomsbury Children's Books, 2003. (Grades 1–3)

The greedy and self-centered king of Capri has a reversal of fortune when the wind blows all of his precious things into the backyard of a kind and generous Naples washerwoman, Mrs. Jewel. Soon the king and the washerwoman meet for the first time, and from that moment both their lives magically change.

Pino and the Signora's Pasta, by Janet Pederson. Candlewick Press, 2005. (Grades K–3)

Every night the signora sets out a bowl of pasta for stray cats. Although the pasta is delicious, Pino, a large stray, starts out to find something better than pasta. As he samples leftovers from various restaurants, he is hit, kicked chased, and thrown out more than once by both waiters and patrons. He returns home to find that the signora has not forgotten him and that pasta served with love is far better than any other food.

Pippo the Fool, by Tracey E. Fern. Illustrated by Pau Estrada. Charlesbridge, 2009. (Grades 1–3)

The Cathedral of Santa Maria del Fiore in Florence was a marvel of art, architecture, and engineering. But it lacked a finishing ornament, a crown, a dome! The city fathers had a solution: to invite the finest masters to compete for the chance to design a dome. The rumors of this contest reached the ears of Filippo Brunelleschi, better known in Florence as Pippo the Fool. As soon as he heard about the contest, Pippo knew it was the chance he had been waiting for. If I can win the contest, I will finally lose that nickname once and for all! This book tells the story of the construction of an architectural masterpiece, Brunelleschi's Dome.

Pizza for the Queen, by Nancy F. Castaldo. Illustrated by Melisande Potter. Holiday House, 2005. (Grades 1–3)

Raffaele the baker and pizza maker buys ingredients for his pizzas that are used by the common folk; tomatoes, mozzarella cheese, and anchovies are foods eaten by peasants. When the queen hears about Raffaels's delicious pizzas, she wants him to bake pizzas for her. Shopkeepers are sure that the pizza maker should purchase only special and exotic ingredients for the queen's pizza, not the peasant food he usually buys. But Raffaele is determined that the queen shall taste the same pizza that her subjects eat. When the anchovies disappear, Raffaele creates a vegetarian pizza with the same colors as the Italian flag. The queen is delighted.

Priceless Gifts, by Martha Hamilton and Mitch Weiss. Illustrated by John Kanzler. August House, 2009. (Grades 1–3)

There is an old saying that "good things come in small packages." In this story from Italy, storytellers Martha Hamilton and Mitch Weiss show us that good things also come in "furry" packages. When a merchant finds himself in a land that is overrun by rats, he realizes that he has the most "priceless gift" in this country, namely his ship's cats. In this classic tale, we learn that one man's cats are another man's treasure and vice versa.

Strega Nona, by Tomie dePaola. Scholastic, 1975. (Grades K–3)

In the town of Calabria there lived an old lady everyone called Strega Nona, which meant "Grandma Witch." The people of the town would go to see her if they had troubles. Since Strega Nona was getting old, she needed help. So she put up a help-wanted sign in the town square. Big Anthony, who didn't pay attention, went to see her and started working for Strega Nona. But there was one condition: he must never touch her cooking pot. However, in her absence he says the magic words that cause the pot to cook. Pasta is everywhere! Unfortunately Big Anthony does not know the words to turn the pot off. Imagine what happens when Strega Nona returns.

Strega Nona's Magic Lessons, by Tomie dePaola. Harcourt, 1992. (Grades K–3)

Strega Nona's two pupils are Bambolona, the town baker's daughter, and "Antonia," who is really Strega Nona's helper, Big Anthony, dressed up like a girl. Bambolona learns quickly and well. Big Anthony is not a very good student. When Strega Nona gives Bambolona a book of magic spells, Big Anthony tries to surprise Strega Nona by learning magic on his own. He turns her into a frog, which does not please her at all. Big Anthony again learns an important lesson: not to do magic until you have learned very well.

There's a Dolphin in the Grand Canal!, by John B. Marciano. Viking, 2005. (Grades K–3)

Luca Buca works in his family's cafe in Venice. One afternoon when he is taking a break from his duties, he sees a dolphin in the Grand Canal. Dolphins, of course, are found at sea. They are not found in the canals of Venice. At least this is what his parents tell him when Luca Buca reports his sighting. At a second sighting, Luca joins the dolphin in the canal and sits astride the soaring creature, waving to everyone, including Mama and Papa, as he goes by.

Tony's Bread: An Italian Folktale, by Tomie DePaola. Putnam, 2005. (Grades K–3)

Serafina wants a husband, but her father Tony, the baker, has found no man he thinks is good enough for her. He gives her everything she wants except the thing she wants most, a husband. Knowing she will end up an old maid, the girl spends her days sitting at her window crying and eating candy. A young suitor, Angelo, wants Serafina for his wife and cleverly asks the help of three aunts to get Tony's approval. Angelo promises Tony a bakery of his own in return for Serafina's hand. The two are married, and Tony becomes rich from inventing and baking a special bread called panettone.

Zoe Sophia's Scrapbook: An Adventure in Venice, by Claudia Mauner. Illustrated by Elisa Smalley. Chronicle Books, 2003. (Grades 1–3)

Visit Italy's palaces and piazzas with nine-year-old Zoe, who travels to Italy from her home in New York to visit her great-aunt in Venice. Traveling with Zoe is her pet dachshund, who accompanies the child and her aunt through shops and museums and even on a ride in a gondola. At one point in the story the dog disappears, but gondolier Ludovico saves the day.

LEARNING ABOUT ITALY

Standards: 10, 11, 13

Cover up the paragraph at the bottom of the page. Working in pairs, guess yes or no as each statement is read aloud. Make any needed corrections after reading the paragraph about Italy.

_____ 1. Italy is shaped like a question mark.

_____ 2. Italy is located in southern Europe.

_____ 3. There are many high mountains in Italy.

_____ 4. Italy is surrounded by land.

_____ 5. The mountain people of Italy raise sheep and goats.

_____ 6. The Alps are found in Italy.

_____ 7. Madrid is a city in Italy.

_____ 8. Many Italians are fond of opera.

Italy is a country in southern Europe. It is shaped like a boot and is noted for its beautiful scenery and very old buildings. Italy has many high mountains, and no place in the "boot" is more than 65 miles from the sea. The people love art and music and good food. In the mountains they raise sheep and goats, olives, and grapes. If you visited Italy you could go to an opera and hear beautiful music or visit one of the many art museums. You could ride in a gondola on the Grand Canal of Venice or climb the Alps, one of the most famous mountain chains in the world.

From *Reading the World with Picture Books* by Nancy J. Polette.
Santa Barbara, CA: Libraries Unlimited. Copyright © 2010.

Lithuania

Lithuania is a tiny northern European country of about 25,000 square miles and has a population of 3.7 million people. Reading is very important to the people, many of whom can read in three languages, Lithuanian, Polish, and Russian. The capital is Vilnius.

Eli Remembers, by Ruth Vander Zee and Marian Sneider. Illustrated by Bill Farnsworth. Eerdmans Books for Young Readers, 2007. (Grades 2–4)

Year after year, Eli watches the solemn lighting of seven candles at his family's celebration of Rosh Hashanah, the Jewish New Year. On such a happy occasion, his parents and grandparents always seem sad, and Eli can't understand why.

Then one year Eli travels to Eastern Europe to learn more about his family history. There, he learns how the candles represent his family's connection to the Holocaust in Lithuania, and how remembering his ancestors can help heal years of grief and shame.

TRADITIONS

Standards: 3, 4, 8

Many families have traditions that are passed down to each new generation. Some traditions might involve an object. Others might call for special gifts or for a special dish that is not served at other times of the year.

Ask students to draw a picture of an object related to a family tradition or to bring in a recipe for a special dish. Give each child an opportunity to talk about his or her object or recipe. Encourage children who don't have objects or recipes to think of a new tradition that would be good for the family and draw a picture of it.

Monaco

This tiny country covers less than one square mile and is home to about 32,000 people. Languages spoken are French, English, and Italian. It is home to many casinos, and the capital is Monaco.

A Brave Little Princess, by Beatrice Main. Illustrated by Octavia Monaco. Barefoot Books, 2000, 1999. (Grades 1–3)

Here are three adventures of a very tiny princess who is tired of being so very tiny. On every walk she takes, people point and whisper how very small Princess Leonora is. Leonora tells her grandmother that the thing she wishes for most is an adventure of her own. She receives not only the adventure she asked, for but two other adventures as well. In one village, she defeats a dragon with bold threats and her tiny arrow. In the next, she uses her tiny hands to undo the magic knots in the flour sacks that prevent the baker from making bread. In her third adventure, she bests a flock of vultures by scaring them with their own reflections in her hand mirror, showing that one doesn't have to be big to do the right thing at the right time.

The Storytelling Princess, by Rafe Martin. Illustrated by Kimberly Bulcken Root. Putnam, 2001. (Grades 1–3)

This princess may be lost, but she's not helpless. She told her parents she'd rather be swept overboard in a storm at sea than marry a prince she didn't choose for herself-and that's exactly what happened! Yet it wasn't a disaster. For with a little luck, a lot of pluck and a special way with words, the princess turns this accident into a wildly entertaining adventure for herself and the prince of her dreams.

MYSTERY WORD GAME

Standards: 4, 5, 9

To play the game:

1. One person is the clue caller. That person asks for a volunteer to give a number between one and five. The clue caller then reads the word for the number given.

2. If the volunteer cannot guess what the word describes, the clue caller asks for another volunteer to give a different number and reads the word for that number. The game continues until a correct guess is made or all numbers are used.

Following are some clues that are important to the story.

ROUND 1	ROUND 2	ROUND 3
1. tiny	1. brown	1. small
2. wood	2. full	2. circular
3. sharp	3. bulging	3. look
4. pointed	4. knots	4. glass
5. stick	5. flour	5. reflection
(arrow)	(sack)	(mirror)

The Netherlands

The Netherlands covers 16,000 square miles, about 40 percent of which was reclaimed from the sea. Large dikes keep the sea water from flowing over the land. It is home to 16.5 million people, which means it is a very crowded country. It has gentle winters and cool summers and was home to two very famous painters, Rembrandt van Rijn and Vincent van Gogh. The language spoken is Dutch, and the capital is Amsterdam.

Blueberries for the Queen, by John Paterson and Katherine Paterson. Illustrated by Susan Jeffers. HarperCollins, 2004. (Grades 1–3)

The time of the story is World War II, and young William longs to do something to help the war effort. Perhaps if he picks a basket of blueberries and gives it to the queen, she might be able to forget her worries about her country for a brief time. This is just what he does. Little does he know that it will be Princess Juliana who accepts the gift and invites him in to meet Queen Wilhelmina.

The Boy Who Held Back the Sea, by Lenny Hort, Thomas Locker, and Mary Mapes Dodge. Puffin, 1993. (Grades K–3)

Grandmother tells Pieter, who has been sent to his room, the story of "The Boy Who Held Back the Sea." Jan is a troublemaker who tells tales about sea serpents to the dike's watchmen, plays hooky from church, and throws a rock through a school window. The troublemaker becomes a hero when on his way home he sees a hole in the dike and plugs it with a finger until help comes.

The Greatest Skating Race: A World War II Story from the Netherlands, by Louise Borden and Niki Daly. Margaret McElderry Books, 2004. (Grades 3–5)

In the winter of 1941, 10-year-old Piet, a strong skater, is asked to help two children escape to safety in Belgium. He must race with Johanna and her little brother, Joop, along the frozen canals, past German guards, and over the border to safety. They outwit and hide from German soldiers and make it to their destination in one long, difficult day. In saving the children Piet has become as much of a champion as if he had won the Elfstedentocht, a 200-kilometer skating race.

Hana in the Time of the Tulips, by Deborah Noyes. Illustrated by Bagram Batoulline. Candlewick Press, 2004. (Grades 1–3)

In seventeenth-century Holland, tulips were among the most prized possessions. Hana's father has bulbs that he fears might be onions and spends his time worrying with others about whether there will be tulips. Hana misses evenings with her father and then discovers that a painting can be as prized as a flower. She paints the rare tulip for her father, and for the first time in a long time, she sees him smile.

Hans Brinker, by Bruce Coville. Illustrated by Laurel Long. Dial, 2007. (Grades 3–5)

The story of Hans Brinker is a true classic, but few still read the novel, which was written in the 1860s. Now Bruce Coville and Laurel Long are reintroducing the charming tale in this glorious picture book version. This is a tale of a family sticking together through hardship, and of wishes granted just in the nick of time. The race to win the silver skates is well known, but the mystery of the watch and the missing riches is equally enticing. This is the best kind of fairy tale, and kids will be riveted by its drama. For the winter holidays or anytime, this is a book to cherish.

Katje, the Windmill Cat, by Gretchen Woelfle and Nicola Bayle. Candlewick, 2006. (Grades K–3)

Like many pets, Katje the cat is well cared for and the center of attention, until her owner, the miller, marries and a new baby, Anneke, arrives. Katje wants to play with the baby, but the baby's mother chases the cat away to live in the mill instead of the house. A terrible storm causes flooding that breaks through the dike and sweeps the cradle away. Katje saves Anneke's life by leaping from side to side to keep the cradle upright.

THE TULIP SONG

Standards: 3, 4

Sing the song to "She'll Be Comin' 'Round the Mountain."

We will plant bulbs in the garden
Yes we will
We will plant bulbs in the garden
Yes we will
We will plant bulbs in the garden
We will plant bulbs in the garden
We will plant bulbs in the garden
Yes we will.

We will water bulbs quite often
Yes we will
We will water bulbs quite often
Yes we will
We will water bulbs quite often
We will water bulbs quite often
We will water bulbs quite often
Yes we will

We will pull weeds in the garden
Yes we will
We will pull weeds in the garden
Yes we will
We will pull weeds in the garden
We will pull weeds in the garden
We will pull weeds in the garden
Yes we will

We will watch the tulips blossom
Yes we will
We will watch the tulips blossom
Yes we will
Purple, yellow white and red
See them in the t ulip bed
We will watch the tulips blossom
Yes we will

Norway

Norway covers 125,000 square miles and has a population of 4.5 million people. Two forms of Norwegian are spoken. For several months of the year the sun shines both night and day in the northern part of the country. Norway is a country of many deep waterways, with tall mountains on either side. The capital is Oslo.

Boots and the Glass Mountain, by Claire Martin. Illustrated by Gennady Spirin. Dial Books, 1992. (Grades 2–4)

It is midnight on St. John's night, and Cinderlad is crouched in the hayloft waiting to see what strange creature comes on this special night each year to eat all of the grass in the meadow. The two previous years his brothers had been sent to watch, but they were so frightened by the clatter and the noise that they ran away. A rumble in the distance grew louder and louder. The hayloft shook, and Cinderlad was thrown to the floor. Picking himself up, he marched outside to see a huge, gleaming horse with the copper armor of a knight on the ground beside it. Cinderlad jumped on the horse and rode it to a hiding place and then went home to his family. For three years in a row, Cinderlad kept watch and each year found a horse larger and grander than the last.

Now in this same country there was a king whose daughter he would give to any man who could ride up a mountain of glass and take three golden apples from her lap. The knights came from far and wide; even Cinderlad's brothers came, but no one could ride up the mountain. Finally one last knight rode up to the base of the mountain. He was on a large, grand horse and wore a suit of copper. Who do you suppose he is? And will he win the hand of the princess?

Christmas Trolls, written and illustrated by Jan Brett. Putnam, 2000. (Grades K–3)

Christmas is Treva's favorite time of the year. But this year, decorations and presents are mysteriously disappearing. When Treva follows a small creature making off with the Christmas pudding, she discovers two irresistible trolls, who want to have Christmas, but don't understand it. Jan Brett's trademark luminous paintings give readers a magical Christmas full of surprises.

The Legend of the Christmas Rose, by William H. Hooks. Illustrated by Richard Williams. HarperCollins, 1999. (Grades 1–3)

When news of the birth of the Christ child is delivered by an angel, three shepherds want to go to Bethlehem to take the child the gift of a lamb. Dorothy, their sister, is not allowed to go, but she follows her brothers at a distance. When they arrive at the stable, she realizes that she has no gift to give. An angel appears to the sad child and hands her a small white flower. Soon she is surrounded by white flowers and takes these as her gift to the Christ Child. A touch of the child's hand turns them pink. The pink rose is known to this day as the Christmas Rose.

Master Maid: A Tale of Norway, by Aaron Shepard. Illustrated by Pauline Ellison. Dial, 1997. (Grades 2–4)

A troll gives young Leif three tasks to perform. At first the tasks seem impossible, but imagine the anger of the troll when his cook, a young girl who is the Master Maid of the tale, helps Leif do each of the tasks. When the furious troll decides to put Leif in a stew, he and the girl run away, and because of the cleverness of the girl, they are able to escape. When the two marry, Leif speaks up when the minister asks the girl if she will "love, honor and obey." Leif recognizes the many gifts his wife has and says that he is the one who should obey, and he does.

Trouble with Trolls, by Jan Brett. Putnam, 1999. (Grades K–3)

Treva's trouble with trolls begins when she climbs Mount Baldy with her dog, Tuffi. The trolls who live there long for a dog, and they try to kidnap him. But Treva is brave and quick-thinking. She outwits one troll after another, until she reaches the very top of the mountain, where five trolls are waiting—and they want her dog! From underground to mountain peak, Jan Brett's story is filled with adventure and eye-catching details.

Who's That Knocking on Christmas Eve?, by Jan Brett. G.P. Putnam's Sons, 2002. (Grades K–3)

Every year, trolls knock down Kyri's door and gobble up her Christmas feast. But this year the trolls are in for a surprise: a boy and his pet ice bear on their way to Oslo have come in from the cold. And once the ice bear is finished with the trolls, you can bet they won't come knocking next Christmas Eve!

CREATE A TROLL

Standards: 2, 14, 16, 21

To reinforce the idea that many creatures in stories are imaginary, ask children to bring to class old magazines from home that can be cut up. Each child may decide what kind of troll he or she wants to create. Have the children look for and cut out a picture of a person, then paste it on a plain piece of paper. The children may then add lines and features to create their trolls.

Other cuttings from the magazines may be used as well to add to the troll/person. The creature should be given a name and a two-line description telling what magical powers the troll has. Some children may want to make the two lines rhyme.

What other stories can children name that have a troll as a character?

Poland

Poland covers an area of 121,000 square miles and has a population of 38.5 million people. Polish music is embodied in the works of Frédéric Chopin. The language spoken is Polish. The Polish name for the country is Polska. The capital is Warsaw.

Butterflies Under Our Hats, by Sandy Eisenberg Sasso. Illustrated by Joani Keller Rothenberg. Paraclete Press, 2006. (Grades 1–3)

There are many tales of the people of Chelm in Jewish folklore. In this tale the people are discouraged because nothing good ever seems to happen. A wise woman tells them that what they need is hope, and the way to get hope is to keep a butterfly under one's hat. As foolish as this seems, the idea begins to work when they spot something on the hat left by the butterfly.

The Cats in Krasinski Square, by Karen Hesse. Illustrated by Wendy Watson. Scholastic Press, 2004. (Grades 2–4)

Based on a true event, this is an account of how a young girl and her friends smuggled food to those imprisoned in the Warsaw ghetto in1942. Abandoned cats show her holes in the ghetto wall that can be used to pass food shipped by train to Warsaw. Somehow the Gestapo has heard of the plan and has its own dogs to sniff out the bundles of food arriving on a train. The children arrive at the train station with covered baskets. When the train with the food supplies pulls in, the cats in the baskets are let loose. The dogs chase the cats, and the children are able to pass the food through the chinks in the wall.

Just Stay Put: A Chelm Story, by Gary Clement. Groundwood Books, 1995. (Grades 1–3)

Mendel spends his whole life dreaming his days away in the little village of Chelm, until one day he decides to set off for Warsaw. Along the way he stops for a nap, pointing his shoes in the direction of Warsaw so he won't lose his way, but a passerby turns the shoes backward, sending him back to Chelm. Once there, Mendel is amazed to find that Warsaw is just like home, and he decides from then on to just stay put.

MY NAME IS . . .

Standards: 2, 4, 6, 14, 16, 21

Visit the library and find an easy-to-read book about Poland.

Follow the pattern from the old rhyme "My Name Is Alice" to include information about Poland.

The children's names must begin with the letter P. Products may begin with any letter. Animals must be found in Poland and, if possible, begin with the letter P.

YOUR TURN:

GIRL'S NAME: P _____ my name is _____

BOY'S NAME: My best friend's name is P _____

COUNTRY: We come from Poland.

PRODUCTS: And we sell _____ and _____ and _____ .

ANIMAL: P _____ is a _____ .

ANIMAL: P _____ is a _____ .

From *Reading the World with Picture Books* by Nancy J. Polette.
Santa Barbara, CA: Libraries Unlimited. Copyright © 2010.

Portugal

More than 10.5 million people live in Portugal, which covers an area of 35,600 square miles. The language is Portuguese. The capital is Lisbon. Because this is a land nearly surrounded by ocean, Portugal is a land of many fishermen. It is also the country from which Vasco da Gama and Magellan set sail on their famous voyages.

My Very Own Lighthouse, by Francisco Cunha. Winged Chariot Press, 2005. (Grades 2–4)

Many stories that have Portugal as their setting center around the sea, and this is no exception. When the fishermen go out the families worry, especially if there are storm warnings. A little girl creates her own lighthouse to ease her worries about her father, who is a fisherman. In this tale children will learn about Portugal and about the ties that hold a caring family together.

SIMILES

Standards: 12, 14, 16, 21

Try to describe Portugal by using similes. List adjectives that describe the country:

_____   _____

_____   _____

Now use these words to write sentences about the country. Each sentence must contain a simile: a comparison using the words like or as.

Example: The lighthouse stood tall like a soldier guarding the sea.

The simile, helps the reader develop better mental images about the country you are describing.

Write your similes below.

1. _____ .

2. _____ .

Russia

Russia covers an area of about 6.6 million square miles and is home to 142 million people; it is sixth in world population. It is the world's largest country and has been independent since 1991. The language spoken is Russian. The capital of Russia is Moscow.

Annushka's Voyage, by Edith Tarbescu. Illustrated by Lydia Dabcovich. Clarion Books, 1998. (Grades 2–4)

How important can the gift of a candlestick be? Anya finds out when her grandmother gives a candlestick each to her and her little sister to take with them on their trip to America. Mother is dead, and father has sent tickets so the two girls can travel alone. At one point they are separated, but they find each other by waving the candlesticks. When they finally arrive at their new home with their father, the precious candlesticks become part of their Sabbath celebration.

Babushka Baba Yaga, by Patricia Polacco. Putnam, 1999. (Grades 2–5)

Year after year Baba Yaga the witch has watched other old women with their grandchildren, and she longs to be like them. She disguises herself as an old peasant woman and is welcomed in the home of a young family, where she becomes very fond of the child, Victor. But old wives' tales will not die, and when she hears the old women talking about how terrible Baba Yaga is, she sheds her human clothes and goes back into the forest to live alone. Victor, who had become fond of this new grandmother, goes into the woods searching for her and is rescued by Baba Yaga from wolves. The old women accept her as one of them, and she has truly become a babushka.

Brother Bartholomew and the Apple Grove, by Jan Cheripko. Illustrated by Kestutis Kasparavicius. Boyds Mill, 2004. (Grades 1–3)

In this tale a wise older monk, Brother Bartholomew's, task is to oversee the apple orchard, which he does by allowing the deer to come into the orchard and eat the apples. Young Brother Stephen comments that this should not be, but the old monk simply replies, "God will provide." When Brother Bartholomew dies, Brother Stephen builds a barbed wire fence around the orchard and is pleased with himself. Then a beautiful buck gets caught in the wire and injures itself. At this, Brother Stephen realizes that his pride has led him to not understand the phrase "God will provide."

A Confused Hanukkah: An Original Story of Chelm, by Jon Koons. Illustrated by S. D. Schindler. Dutton, 2004. (Grades 1–3)

Hanukkah is fast approaching in the village of Chelm, but the Rabbi is away. Unfortunately, not one of the villagers remembers how Hanukkah is supposed to be celebrated. So they send Yossel, a simple young man, to the neighboring village to learn what he can. Yossel makes a wrong turn, but he does find some people celebrating a holiday. The question is: Is it the right holiday?

The Enormous Turnip, by Alexei Tolstoy. Illustrated by Scott Goto. Houghton Mifflin, Sandpiper, 2003. (Grades K–2)

An old man plants a turnip that grows and grows and grows. In fact, it grows so big that he cannot pull it out of the ground by himself. He calls his wife to help, she calls the children, and more and more helpers are called, until finally the turnip comes up from the ground, proving that some tasks are better done when everyone helps.

The Firebird, retold and illustrated by Rachel Isadora. Putnam, 1994. (Grades 2–4)

The author/artist is a former ballerina who tells the tale of this famous ballet. When Prince Ivan first discovers the Firebird in an enchanted forest, he never imagines the extraordinary events that will follow. He meets 10 beautiful princesses and falls into the hands of the evil sorcerer, Katschei, who tries to trap them all. But it is the Firebird alone who possesses the means to free them and end the reign of Katschei forever.

The Fool and the Fish, by Alexander Afanasyev. Illustrated by Gennady Spirin. Dial, 1990. (Grades 1–3)

As in many tales, the foolish brother turns out not to be as foolish as everyone thinks. A magic fish that is willing to grant Ivan's every wish enables the lazy young man to outwit his older brothers, angry villagers, and even the Tsar, ultimately winning him an enchanted palace and the Tsar's daughter in marriage.

Grandma Chickenlegs, by Geraldine McCaughrean. Illustrated by Moira Kemp. Carolrhoda Picture Books, 2000. (Grades 1–3)

Tatia knows she should stay away from Grandma Chickenlegs, but when her new stepmother orders her to visit the old witch, Tatia must obey. Bravely, she sets out through the woods with her dear doll, Drooga, as her only companion. Grandma Chickenlegs clearly has terrible plans for her. To escape, Tatia must be courageous and clever, and she must rely on the kindness of friends.

Grandmother and the Runaway Shadow, by Liz Rosenberg. Illustrated by Beth Peck. Harcourt Brace, 1996. (Grades 2–4)

Imagine having a shadow as a best friend! This is what happened to Grandmother when the soldiers raided her small village and she had to flee. She manages to make the difficult journey to the New World, accompanied by the shadow. When Grandmother finds work in a garment factory, the shadow tells "funny stories that made all the women laugh." Of all the brave young women who fled persecution in Russia and made their way to the United States, only Grandmother can tell the tale of being accompanied by a shadow.

Luba and the Wren, by Patricia Polacco. Philomel, 1999. (Grades K–2)

Luba lives happily in her dacha with her parents until she helps a frightened wren. When the wren returns the favor, telling her to ask for anything she wishes, how her life changes! She wants nothing, but her parents want a rich estate, then to be lords, then czar and czarina, and then rulers of the world! Where will it end?

The Magic Nesting Doll, by Jacqueline K. Ogburn. Illustrated by Laurel Long. Dial, 2000. (Grades 1–3)

Katya's grandmother took a little matryoshka, a nesting doll, out of a small box. "If your need is great, open the doll and help will come. But you may only do so three times. After that the magic will be gone." A wicked spell has changed a handsome young prince into a pale, glassy figure made of "living ice," and his kingdom into a frozen landscape of night without moon, darkness without dawn. Katya knows that it's up to her to rescue the prince and undo the evil spell that has banished the sun. Armed with only the magic nesting doll and her own valiant heart, she is determined to succeed. But will the combined effort of her courage and the mysterious nesting doll be strong enough to prevail?

Martha, by Gennady Spirin. Philomel Books, c2005. (Grades 2–4)

The author relates how he and his Moscow family rescued Martha, a crow with a broken wing, and how she joined their household. This is Gennady Spirin's own dear story about the day his son Ilya found a crow with a broken wing and brought it home. The veterinarian told the boy that it would never fly again. "Put it to sleep!" he urged the parents. But the wild crow—Martha, they called her—was full of surprises. She most certainly made their home, her home, and one day she did fly! Would there be one more surprise? When she flew away that fall, would she return again?

Nikolai, the Only Bear, by Barbara Joosse. Illustrated by Renata Liwska. Philomel Books, 2005. (Grades 2–4)

Nikolai, a bear who lives in the orphanage in Novosibirsk, Russia, does not seem to fit in, until the day some visitors arrive from America. There are 100 orphans at the Russian orphanage, but Nikolai is the only bear. He growls when he speaks and claws the air when he plays. "Play nice, Nikolai," the keepers say. No one wants to take Nikolai home. Then one day a fur-faced man and a smooth-faced woman come to visit from America. They growl with him and play with him, and sing songs that make him feel soft-bearish. And when it's time for them to go home, Nikolai knows that he has found the right family at last.

Peter and the Wolf, retold and illustrated by Chris Raschka. Simon & Schuster, 2009. (Grades 1–3)

Here in the setting of a theater, the tale is told of a boy who outsmarts a wolf with the help of a bird, a duck, a cat, a grandfather, and some huntsmen, plus an additional character not found in the original tale. Sergei Prokofiev composed *Peter and the Wolf* in 1936 to introduce children to the instruments of the orchestra. The dramatic tale is retold here and will prove an excellent follow-up to listening to the orchestral piece.

Petrosinella, retold and illustrated by Diane Stanley. Dial Penguin, 1995. (Grades 1–3)

Once upon a time there was a woman who longed so fiercely for the rich, green parsley in the ogress's locked garden that she climbed over the wall and took some. But she was caught and tricked into promising her future child to the hideous ogress. When the enchantress claimed little Petrosinella, she locked her in a high tower, using the girl's long golden hair as a ladder, until one day a handsome prince came along. Petrosinella used both her wits and magic to outsmart her captor.

Philipok, by Anne Beneduce. Philomel Books, 2000. (Grades K–2)

Philipok wants to go to school like his older brother. But his mother says no, he must stay home with Grandma. Little Philipok is determined to go and slips out of the house to make his way to school through the snow. He is cold and frightened when he arrives, and soon finds that he must earn the privilege to stay.

The Sea King's Daughter, retold by Aaron Shepard. Atheneum, 1997. (Grades 1–3)

With magnificent illustrations by Gennady Spirin, here is the classic tale of the Sea King, who has decided that his daughter should marry a talented musician. The daughter, however, has other ideas. After all, the Sea King has more than one daughter.

Vassilisa the Wise: A Tale of Medieval Russia, by Josepha Sherman. Illustrated by Daniel San Souci. Harcourt, 1988. (Grades 1–3)

Vassilisa's husband boasted once too often, and this time in the presence of Prince Valdimir. The angry prince has the poor fellow imprisoned in the dungeon. Vassilisa is determined to free her husband, so she disguises herself as a Tartar nobleman and challenges the prince to contests of his own choosing. She wins the contests and asks for the release of her husband as a prize. The prince, of course, quickly agrees.

When the Chickens Went on Strike: A Rosh Hashanah Tale, by Erica Silverman. Adapted from a story by Sholom Aleichem. Illustrations by Matthew Trueman. Dutton Children's Books, 2003. (Grades 1–3)

During Rosh Hashanah, a young boy overhears the chickens in his village planning a strike. They are sick of being used for Kapores, a custom practiced in his Russian village, where people wave chickens over their heads to erase bad deeds. But the boy needs Kapores! How else will he make his father proud? He tries to warn his father, but the villagers cannot find a way to bring the chickens back to the village. Finally the boy makes his own plea. Will the chickens listen, or will he find a new way to overcome his bad behavior?

RUSSIA: YES OR NO?

Standards: 2, 8, 17

Locate Russia on a map. Read aloud the following statements. Have the children guess YES or NO. Then read the paragraph about Russia to allow children to verify their guesses.

1. _____ Russia was once ruled by a king called a czar.

2. _____ Another name for St. Petersburg is Vladivostok.

3. _____ There are few private homes in Russia.

4. _____ Russian children go to school for 10 years.

5. _____ Moscow is the largest city in Russia.

6._____ A kopeck is a Russian hat.

Today Russia is an independent nation but was until recently a republic in the Soviet Union. Many years ago all of the land was ruled by a king called a tsar (or czar). Most of the royal families lived in St. Petersburg, which is today called Leningrad. In Moscow, the largest city in Russia, families live in apartments. There are very few private homes. Russian children go to school for 10 years. A kopeck is a Russian coin. Until *glasnost*, or the time of openness, the people of Russia did not have a great deal of freedom, but this is rapidly changing. At the time of the tsars the land they ruled was so vast that when people in Moscow were going to bed, those in Vladivostok were having breakfast.

From *Reading the World with Picture Books* by Nancy J. Polette.
Santa Barbara, CA: Libraries Unlimited. Copyright © 2010.

Scotland

Scotland is part of the United Kingdom, which is made up of England, Scotland, Wales, and Northern Ireland. The total area of the United Kingdom is 94,525 square miles, and the total population is about 61 million people. Languages spoken are English, Welsh, and Scots Gaelic. The capital of Scotland is Edinburgh.

Andrew McGroundhog and His Shady Shadow, by Peter J. Welling. Pelican, 2005. (Grades 1–3)

A story about how Groundhog Day came into existence with the help of a little Scottish groundhog and his shady shadow. One day Andrew McGroundhog climbed up Hadrian's Heights to go fishing. As he was climbing, he repeatedly heard someone cry out and found that it was his shadow. His shadow was upset about being dragged up the mountain, dunked in the water, and stepped on by a pony. Andrew's shadow wanted the groundhogs to hibernate because winter was too cold for shadows. Andrew then wondered when he could stop hibernating. His shadow said he would give a thumbs-up if it was springtime or would bonk him on the nose if it was winter. Even now, if the groundhogs don't see the thumbs-up, they sleep for six more weeks.

The Ghost of Greyfriar's Bobby, written and illustrated by Ruth Brown. E. P. Dutton, 1995. (Grades 2–4)

Two children tour an Edinburgh churchyard and come upon the grave of a dog named Bobby. The church gardener tells the children Bobby's tale. It seems that when the dog's master passed away in 1858, he was buried in Greyfriar's churchyard. Bobby, the faithful dog, remained near the grave site until his own death, when he was buried next to his master, Jock.

The Luck of the Loch Ness Monster, by A. W. Flaherty. Houghton Mifflin, 2007. (Grades 1–3)

Katrina Elizabeth travels by ocean liner with her nanny to visit her grandmother in Scotland. Following the ship is a tiny worm that eats the oatmeal Katrina throws out of the porthole each morning. On arrival in Scotland the worm becomes the Loch Ness Monster and is delighted to find a home in a loch with lots of visitors, who throw him food. He gives Katrina a good-bye kiss when it is time for her to return home. A charming tale!

Pirican Pic and Pirican Mor, retold by Hugh Lupton. Illustrated by Yumi Heo. Barefoot Books, 2003. (Grades 1–3)

Suppose you and your friend went out one day to gather walnuts. You find a walnut tree and many walnuts scattered on the ground. It is a beautiful day, and forest animals are hiding in the shadows, watching. You are so busy gathering the walnuts that you do not notice what is happening to them. Your friend is eating every one!

The Selkie Girl, by Susan Cooper. Illustrated by Warwick Hutton. Atheneum, 1986. (Grades 2–4)

A young fellow, Donallan, falls in love with one of three beautiful selkie-maidens that he sees sitting on the rocks. He steals her sealskin so that she cannot return to the sea, and marries her. As the years pass the girl longs for her home in the sea, even though she and Donallan have five children whom she loves. At last she learns where her skin is hidden, and putting it on, she returns to the sea. But every year Donallan and his children go down to the sea, and when they return, there is "a look on their faces like sunlight."

The Serpent Came to Gloucester, by M. T. Anderson. Illustrated by Bagram Ibatoulline. Candlewick Press, 2005. (Grades 3–5)

Over hundreds of years, sailors have reported sighting sea monsters, yet none has ever been captured. This tale tells of the sighting of such a monster in Gloucester harbor in 1817. A year later sailors were sure they had spotted the monster once again, far out to sea. This time, after much effort in attempting to capture the monster, they found that it was a huge mackerel. The fish that got away!

Tam Lin, by Jane Yolen. Illustrated by Charles Mikolaycak. Harcourt Brace, 1990. (Grades 3–5)

When the worlds of humankind and the Faery Folk sit side by side, with moonlight and mist the only door between, young Jennet MacKenzie defies her parents' warning and embarks on a quest to win back the forbidden Carterhaugh, her ancestral home. One evening at the dilapidated mansion Jennet comes upon a blood red rose amid the twining thorns. When she plucks it, it summons forth Tam Lin, a handsome captive of the Faery Queen. With courage and spirit, Jennet challenges the power of the Queen to save the life of Tam Lin and win back the home that is rightfully hers.

The Wee Scott Book: Scottish Poems and Stories, by Aileen Campbell. Pelican, 2002.
   (Grades 2–4)

   Gather around children, for there are stories told of a world of Highlands and stone castles. Here the blow of the bagpipes ushers in the sheep from the hills and sailors on the coast. And in the dreamy night, fairies scurry about and the sandman Angus sells dreams to the little ones. This is a real place called Scotland, and here in this book are the poems and stories of its children. Filled with lullabies, folktales, and playful rhymes, *The Wee Scot Book* is an open invitation to youngsters from all over to join the Scots at playtime. These are authentic songs and tales from the Scottish childhood of author and illustrator Aileen Campbell. She combines fascinating English text with verses from the old Scots language.

Whuppity Stoorie, by Carolyn White. Illustrated by S. D. Schindler. Putnam, 1997.
   (Grades 2–4)

   Another Rumpelstiltskin variant in which an evil fairy cures a poor woman's prize pig and demands as payment the woman's daughter, Kate, unless the woman can guess her name. The pig leads Kate deep into the forest, where she hears the evil fairy chant her name, Whuppity Stoorie.

A NESSIE POEM

Standards: 2, 12, 13, 14, 15

Use the pattern that follows to tell what you think Scotland's famous Loch Ness Monster, Nessie, looks like.

Line 1: One word _____

Line 2: Two words _____

Line 3: Three words _____

Line 4: Four words _____

Line 5: Five words _____

Spain

Spain covers an area of about 195,000 square miles and has a population of 41.5 million people. Languages spoken are Castilian Spanish, Catalan, Galician, and Basque. Spain is the closest European country to Africa and is known worldwide for its annual "running of the bulls." The capital is Madrid.

Conejito, by Margaret Read MacDonald. Illustrated by Geraldo Valério. August House, 2007. (Grades K–2)

When Conejito (Little Rabbit) begins his school holiday, he goes to visit his Tía Mónica, across the mountain. He loves his Tía Mónica—or is it the cakes and cookies he knows she will feed him when he arrives? But Conejito runs into a few obstacles on the way to his auntie's, including Señor Zorro, Señor Tigre, and Señor Leon. Conejito may want to eat Auntie Mónica's treats, but Mr. Fox, Mr. Tiger, and Mr. Lion want to eat him! With his own quick thinking and a little assist from Tía Mónica, Conejito outwits his predators and makes his way safely home.

Ferdinandus Taurus, by Munro Leaf. Illustrated by Robert Lawson, David R. Godine, 2000. (Grades 1–3)

Once upon a time, there lived in Spain a bull named Ferdinand. While his brothers liked to charge around the field, butt their heads together, and generally act ferocious, Ferdinand liked nothing better than to sit under the cork tree and smell the flowers. He was, you see, a placid and gentle bull whose only desire in life was to be let alone. And his life would have proceeded very nicely had he not one day placed his considerable rump on a bumblebee.

The Goat-Faced Girl: A Classic Italian Folktale, by Leah Marinsky Sharpe and Jane Marinsky. David R. Godine, 2009. (Grades 2–4)

A large lizard, ever conscious of tripping hazards, picks up the infant and takes her home, where she soon grows into a pretty, pampered, and generally useless young woman named Isabella. Despite her adoptive mother's efforts (for the lizard is really a witch in disguise) to shape her up, the girl prefers the alluring life offered her by the charming Prince Rupert, a world of cooks and servants, palaces and jewels, luxury and indolence. Luckily, the lizard woman is a canny, concerned parent. She does not suffer fools lightly and is not about to let her daughter's too-easy transition to palace life go unchallenged. And so she arranges a surprise transformation for her daughter, one that puts the prince's marital plans on hold and gives the witch just enough time to hammer home a few lessons about the downside of idleness, the inanity of vanity, and the satisfactions of self-reliance.

Isabel Saves the Prince: Based on a True Story of Isabel I of Spain, by Joan Holub. Illustrated by Nonna Aleshina. Aladdin, 2007. (Grades 2–4)

Young Isabel loves her peaceful life. But when the king summons her and her brother, Alfonso, to live with him, Isabel knows they have no choice but to go. She is worried because the king's way of life is very different—what if she and her brother don't fit in? Then the king's men accuse Alfonso of treason, and Isabel knows she must step up and do what's right—for her brother and for Spain.

The Little Matador, by Julian Hector. Hyperion Books for Children, 2008. (Grades K–2)

The Little Matador comes from a long line of proud bullfighters, but he would rather draw a bull than fight one! Despite his father's best efforts to get him to follow tradition, the Little Matador spends most days daydreaming and sketching animals in the meadow.

One day when the Little Matador is caught "making a scene" in the town square—drawing a scene, that is—his father decides he's had enough! The Little Matador gets dragged to the arena to face his first bull. He may have decided he's not going to fight, but the bull has other plans. That is, of course, until the Little Matador pulls out his sketch pad. Our talented hero may have won over the bull, but can he overcome his father's disapproval?

Saint Francis & the Wolf, by Jane Langton. Illustrated by Ilse Plume. David R. Godine, 2007. (Grades 2–4)

This lovely retelling of one of the less known Saint Francis lessons centers on the legend of the great wolf of Gubbio, a ferocious canine who terrorized the town and was slowly reducing it to penury and starvation. In nearby Assisi, Brother Francis heard of their plight and came to their rescue. Unbelievingly, the villagers watched from the ramparts as Brother Francis called to the wolf, tamed it with his tenderness, and made it pledge that if the people of Gubbio would care for it, he would do them no harm. He took the pledge and lived in harmony with the citizens of the city until his death.

Señor Felipe's Alphabet Adventure, by Sharon Hawkins Vargo. Illustrated by Sharon Hawkins Vargo. Millbrook Press, 2001. (Grades K–2)

Señor Felipe, a photographer, finally has an assignment. He imust make a set of photographs of objects, beginning with each letter of the Spanish alphabet. Yes, amigo, Señor Felipe can speak Spanish! Join him and his trusty parrot on their remote island for an action-packed alphabet adventure.

SINGING ABOUT SPAIN

Standards: 2, 4, 9, 11, 14, 15, 16

1. With your teacher's help, find the country of Spain on a world map or on a globe. What direction is Spain from where you live?

2. Find the article on Spain in the encyclopedia. Look in the article for a box that gives facts about Spain. Answer these questions:

   a. What is the capital city of Spain? _____

   b. Name two animals found in Spain. _____ _____

   c. Name an activity one can do in Spain. _____

   d. Name two foods served in Spain. _____ _____

Use your information from the blank spaces in the song below. Sing it to the tune of "Here We Go 'Round the Mulberry Bush."

Come with us to visit Spain, to visit Spain, to visit Spain,

Here we are in old M_____, the capital of Spain.

We can see _____ and _____ (2 animals),

_____ and _____, _____ and _____.

We can see _____ and _____,

Animals of Spain.

We will eat _____ and _____ (2 foods)

_____ and _____, _____ and _____.

We will eat _____ and _____

When we dine in Spain.

Then we'll go to _____ (one activity or sight)

Then we'll go to _____

While we visit Spain.

From *Reading the World with Picture Books* by Nancy J. Polette. Santa Barbara, CA: Libraries Unlimited. Copyright © 2010.

143

Sweden

Sweden covers an area of 173,700 square miles and is home to 9 million people. The language spoken is Swedish. It is the home of the Nobel prizes, given for outstanding achievement in many fields by Alfred Nobel, the inventor of dynamite. The capital is Stockholm.

Henrietta and the Golden Eggs, by Hanna Johansen. Illustrated by Kathi Bhend. David O. Godine, 2002. (Grades 1–3)

Henrietta has big dreams for a little chicken: learning to sing, to swim, to fly, and, most important of all, to lay golden eggs. Even when her 3,333 fellow inmates in the old henhouse laugh at her ambitions, Henrietta holds fast, practicing day and night. And while she's honing her talents, she's also getting ready to move on to the bigger, brighter world she can see through the tiny hole in the henhouse wall. Whether Henrietta achieves her dreams is debatable, but through her persistence and her resolute belief in herself, she does manage to change the lives of everyone in the hen house for the better.

Mirabelle, by Astrid Lindgren. Illustrated by Elisabeth Kallick Dyssegaard. R. & S. Books, 2003. (Grades 1–3)

Imagine having a doll that comes to life and talks only when others are not around! Britta is from a very poor family who cannot squander money on such things as a doll when food is needed for the table. A stranger, however, gives Britta a seed and tells her to plant it and care for it. She does, and the seed grows to be a magical doll, who tells Britta her name is Mirabelle. Join Britta and Mirabelle as their adventures unfold in the pages of this book.

Pippi Goes to the Circus, by Astrid Lindgren and Michael Chesworth. Puffin, 2000. (Grades 2–4)

Step aside, ringmaster. Pippi's in charge! Pippi Longstocking has her own special way of doing everything. When she goes to the circus, she doesn't just watch—she takes over! She stands on the back of a trotting horse, does spectacular tricks on the tightrope, and lifts the strongest man in the world over her head. You've never seen a circus like this before! Books about Pippi have been enjoyed by children all over the world for 50 years.

The Red Bird, by Astrid Lindgren. Illustrated by Marit Trnqvist. Arthur A. Levine Books, 2005. (Grades 2–4)

With *The Red Bird,* Lindgren turns her attention to two very different orphans, Matthew and Anna, who are sent to live with the stern farmer in Myra. The work is hard; the food is scarce; the days are cold. But then Anna and Matthew follow the red bird to Sunnymead, where they find hope, sunshine, and in the end, freedom. This extraordinary story of hope and redemption is certain to become a modern classic.

The Tomten and the Fox, by Astrid Lindgren. Putnam, 1997. (Grades 1–3)

Here is a peaceful solution to an ongoing problem. Moonlit scenes of the farmyard under snow show Reynard the fox prowling near the henhouse. He's hungry, but Tomten, the kindly old troll who guards the henhouse at night, shares his porridge with the fox, and the hens are safe—for another night.

SING A SWEDISH ANIMAL SONG

Standards: 4, 12, 14, 21

Follow the pattern and add one more animal found in Sweden. Sing the song to the tune of "Skip to My Lou."

Describe	Name	Action	Where?
Gray	wolf	hiding	in the trees
Red	fox	prowling	near the henhouse

Animals found in Sweden!

Switzerland

Switzerland covers an area of 16,000 square miles and is home to 7.5 million people. Languages spoken are German, French, and Italian. It is one of Europe's oldest democracies and has never fought in a war. The literacy rate is 99 percent, and the capital is Bern.

The Chocolate Cow, by Lillian Obligado. Simon & Schuster, 1993. (Grades 1–3)

For the first time, Pierre and Valerie will be part of the annual spring procession. Pierre's joy at the coming event is mixed with apprehension because his cow, Melody, who is old and gives little milk, is to be sold. On a day when Pierre and Valerie have made a long walk to the meadow, a sudden violent storm comes up and the cattle scatter for shelter among the rocks. Pierre cannot find Melody or hear her distinctive bell. Little can he guess that the cow will become famous throughout the village.

Dreamflight, by Brigitta Garcia López. North-South, 2005. (Grades 1–3)

When can you fly? In your dreams, of course, especially if you have a guardian angel named Wilbur as your teacher. Young Max is happy to meet Wilbur, who says he has always been around. The two do dream flying together. However, when your guardian angel eats too much chocolate and is too heavy to fly, a crash is likely to happen. Wilbur must once again become invisible, and while Max will miss him, he can still fly in his dreams.

Little Donkey's Wish, by Udo Weigelt. Illustrated by Pirkko Vainio. North-South, 2005. (Grades K–2)

Being the smallest of a group often means being ignored. This is just what happens to Josie when the other donkeys in the barn start making their Christmas wishes for a new hat or blanket or more carrots. Josie knows she will be laughed at if she shares her wish to become big and strong. She has a very secret wish as well that does come true on Christmas Eve, when Santa chooses her from all the other donkeys to join his reindeer team.

William Tell: One Against an Empire, by Paul D. Storrie. Illustrated by Thomas Yeates. Lerner, 2009. (Grades 2–4)

He wanted nothing more than to live in peace, until a petty tyrant forced him into a cruel choice: Swiss hunter William Tell is famous for his great skill with a crossbow. A mild-mannered husband and father, he just wants a quiet life for his family. Yet his homeland's brutal foreign rulers are making such an existence impossible. Then one day a ruthless official forces Tell into a terrible choice: shoot an apple off his son's head—or be killed along with his son. Will he accept this awful challenge?

A PROBLEM TO SOLVE

Standards: 1, 7, 8

Switzerland is a land of mountains, trees, and streams. In one tiny Swiss village the people heard a beautiful melody when the wind sang through an old fir tree, which grew partway up the mountain. The people loved the music from the tree. Then one day a woodcutter decided to cut down the tree and use its wood to make a beautiful clock for the village square. Each hour the people would hear the lovely chimes from the clock.

Should Pierre cut down the tree to make a clock? Give reasons for and against.

YES	NO
_____	_____
_____	_____
_____	_____
_____	_____
_____	_____
_____	_____
_____	_____
_____	_____
_____	_____

From *Reading the World with Picture Books* by Nancy J. Polette. Santa Barbara, CA: Libraries Unlimited. Copyright © 2010.

Ukraine

Ukraine covers an area of 233,000 square miles and has a population of 46 million people. Ukraine is the top steel producer in the world and grows more sugar beets than any other country. The capital is Kiev.

The Bird's Gift, by Eric Kimmel. Illustrated by Katya Krenina. Holiday House, 1999. (Grades K–2)

When winter comes too early one year, hundreds of little birds are caught in the snow and ice. Katrusya can't bear to see the delicate creatures suffer, so she begs her family and neighbors to help her save them. Soon everyone in the village is out gathering up the birds and bringing them back to town, where the birds fill their cottages, their church, but most of all, their hearts. Toward the end of winter the birds begin behaving strangely, chirping wildly and flinging themselves against the glass window panes. The villagers release the birds, and within minutes they are gone. But that Easter Katrusya finds in the grass beautifully decorated eggs.

Easter Eggs for Anya, by Virginia Kroll. Illustrated by Sally Wern Comport. Zonderkidz, 2007. (Grades K–2)

Anya's family is too poor to buy eggs to decorate for Easter. Father is away, and mother is struggling to make ends meet and put food on the table. But then Anya discovers an abandoned nest of goose eggs and plans an Easter surprise. Yet there's more than one surprise when the eggs begin to hatch and spring shows once again that it is a time of new beginnings.

The Mitten, by Jan Brett. Putnam, 1989. (Grades K–3)

Nicki's grandmother knits mittens for him and warns him not to lose them in the snow because they are snow white. The boy loses one of the mittens and along come a whole series of animals, thinking it is a fine shelter from the cold. A mole, a rabbit, a hedgehog, an owl, a badger, and a fox all climb in the mitten. Then along comes a bear who climbs in as well. The animals are packed in tight, When a tiny mouse squeezes in, her whiskers tickle the bear's nose. He sneezes, and "Aaaaa-aaaaa-ca-chew!" all the animals fly out of the mitten. As the mitten sails through the air, Nicki spots it, reclaims it, and takes it home to show his smiling grandmother.

Rechenka's Eggs, by Patricia Polacco. Putnam, 1995. (Grades 1–3)

Babushka spends the cold winters painting Easter eggs, and her unique designs and intricate artwork win her the first prize in the Easter festival. This year she has 12 beautiful hand-painted eggs to enter in the contest.

Then one morning she finds a goose that has been hurt and brings it into her cottage and nurses it back to health. She names the geese Rechenka. Then the disaster strikes. The lively goose, now well, flies around the cottage knocking over Babushka's paints and breaking the eggs. But all is not lost.

Rechenka lays 12 beautifully decorated new ones to replace them. While Babushka is in Moscow winning a prize, the goose flies away, but she leaves one last egg in her basket. From it a gosling hatches that becomes Babushka's companion.

COLOR THE EASTER EGGS

Standards: 19, 21

Look in the card catalog or on the shelves of the library for these books. Find the missing color in the title. Draw an egg. Add the complete title and decorate the egg with the missing color(s). Hang your decorated egg on a tree branch . When all the decorated eggs are added, you will have a class Easter tree.

1. _____ *Leaf,* _____ *Leaf* by Lois Ehlert.

2. *Old* _____ *Fly* by Jim Aylesworth.

3. _____ *Snow, Bright Snow* by Alvin Tresselt.

4. *Is It* _____, *Is It* _____ *Is It* _____? by Tana Hoban.

5. _____ *and Say* by Patricia Polacco.

6. _____ *Bear,* _____ *Bear* by Bill Martin Jr.

7. *Lilly's* _____ *Plastic Purse* by Kevin Henkes.

Answer key: 1-*Red, Yellow*; 2-*Black*; 3-*White*; 4-*Red, Yellow, Blue*; 5-*Pink*; 6-*Brown, Brown*; 7-*Purple*

From *Reading the World with Picture Books* by Nancy J. Polette.
Santa Barbara, CA: Libraries Unlimited. Copyright © 2010.

Wales

Wales is a small country that is part of the United Kingdom and forms the westward extension of the island of Great Britain. At one time coal mining was an important industry, but the mines are nearly depleted today. Many citizens of Wales would their country to be independent of the United Kingdom. The languages spoken are English and Welsh. The capital of Wales is Cardiff.

A Child's Christmas in Wales, by Dylan Thomas. Illustrated by Edward Ardizzone. David O. Godine, 1984. (Grades 2–4)

This is one of the illustrator Ardizzone's last books, and in our mind one of his best. It is a gentle and beguiling memoir of a Christmas spent in Cardiff when Dylan Thomas was a child. Ardizzone's quick, sure brushwork is not only the perfect complement to a timeless classic but also a wonderful evocation of a gentle and seemingly endless Christmas in a faraway land made charming and endearing through language.

The Seal Children, by Jackie Morris. Frances Lincoln Children's Books, 2004. (Grades 2–4)

When a fisherman called Huw falls in love with a selkie (half-woman, half-seal), she gives him her sealskin as a sign of her love. She bears him two children, Ffion and Morlo, before returning to her own people. A few years later a stranger comes to the village, telling of a land far away, and Ffion and Morlo remember their mother's stories of the glittering cities underwater. Will they be able to find those places, and their mother? This lovely, lyrical story of love and freedom was inspired by Welsh myth and a real deserted village in west Wales.

The Silver Cow: A Welsh Tale, by Susan Cooper. Illustrated by Warwick Hutton. McElderry, 1991. (Grades 2–4)

From Wales comes this tale of young Huw, whose lilting harp music enchants Tylwyth Teg, the magic people of Bearded Lake. From the depths of the black lake comes the gift of a beautiful silver cow, and the cow is magic, for her milk is three times as rich as the milk of an ordinary cow, and she gives three times as much. Huw's father is a selfish and greedy man, and his wealth makes him greedier than ever. Huw tries to make his father see the magic, but he scoffs at the Tylwyth Teg . . . until they seek their revenge.

WELSH TALES

Any of these tales might be read twice to the class. The first reading will tell the story and capture the beauty of the language. The second reading will give students a chance to note all the sighs and sounds of the ocean.

Let each student choose one living thing found in or around a lake or an ocean and find out more about it. Use the information in this pattern:

Choose a sea or lake animal _____

How does it move?_____

What sound does it make?_____

Use your answers on the lines in the poem.

Example:

In the ocean an octopus was floating along
In the ocean an octopus was squirting all day long
Octopus goes sSquish, squish, squish

In the ocean(lake) a/an_____
                                                    (sea/lake animal)

Was _____along
                                    (how does it move?)

In the ocean/lake a/an _____
                                                    (sea/lake animal)

Was _____ all day long

_____ goes
                    (sea/lake animal)

_____
                    (What sound does it make?)

From *Reading the World with Picture Books* by Nancy J. Polette.
Santa Barbara, CA: Libraries Unlimited. Copyright © 2010.

Part Four

North and Central America

Facts about North and Central America

North America is 9,357,293 square miles. There are more than 435 million people living in North America. Mt. McKinley, in Alaska, is the highest point, at 20,320 feet above sea level. The lowest point is Death Valley, in California, at 282 feet below sea level. The longest river in North America, the Mississippi, is 2, 320 miles long. Lake Superior, the largest lake in North America, is 31,699 square miles, and is located between the United States and Canada.

COUNTRIES OF NORTH AND CENTRAL AMERICA

Booktalks have been provided for the countries in boldface.

Anguilla	Honduras
Antigua and Barbuda	Isla Aves
Aruba	**Jamaica**
Bahamas	Martinique
Barbados	**Mexico**
Belize	Montserrat
Bermuda	Navassa Island
British Virgin Islands	Netherlands Antilles
Canada	**Nicaragua**
Cayman Islands	**Panama**
Clipperton Island	**Puerto Rico**
Costa Rica	Saint Barthelemy
Cuba	Saint Kitts and Nevis
Dominica	**Saint Lucia**
Dominican Republic	Saint-Martin
El Salvador	Saint Pierre and Miquelon
Greenland	Saint Vincent and the Grenadines
Grenada	**Trinidad and Tobago**
Guadeloupe	Turks and Caicos Islands
Guatemala	**United States**
Haiti	**Virgin Islands (U.S.)**

1. Play the X Game (see page 5) using the countries of North America.

2. Create a word search with the 10 largest countries of North America.

Belize

Belize covers an area of 8,865 square miles and is home to almost 295,000 people. It is the only English-speaking country in Central America. The capital is Belmopan.

Children of Belize, by Frank Staub. Lerner, 1999. (Grades 2–5)

Meet the children of Belize, a small Central American nation of lush rain forests, sandy shores, and rugged mountains. Belize's rich cultural life has been shaped by the many groups that have called Belize home. Through words and pictures, these portraits of real children will help readers understand what it's like to grow up in Belize.

The Village Basket Weaver, by Jonathan London. Illustrated by George Crespo. Penguin Group, 1996. (Grades 1–3)

Tavio and Policarpio are Caribs, a coastal people native to Belize. Carpio is a very important man, for he alone remembers the art of basket weaving and the secrets of the patterns, and can make the new cassava squeezer that is necessary for the survival of the village. Tavio, realizing that his grandfather's health is failing, his eyes growing weaker and his hands more feeble, decides to apprentice with Carpio so that someday he, too, can become the village basket weaver. He knows how important it is that these skills not be lost.

RHYMING RIDDLES

Standards: 2, 4, 6

Belize is about 50 percent forest, with more than 50 different kinds of trees.

Complete these rhyming riddles. Name five trees found in Belize.

1. Its name rhymes with leader. This tree is a _____.

2. It often makes the holiday scene. This tree is an _____.

3. This tree is not a joke. It is strong and sturdy. It's an _____.

4. I'd make furniture if I could,

    From this beautiful _____ wood.

5. On a Christmas tree a star will shine,

    It's not a cedar, it's a _____.

Answer key: 1-cedar; 2-evergreen; 3-oak; 4-mahogany; 5-pine

From *Reading the World with Picture Books* by Nancy J. Polette.
Santa Barbara, CA: Libraries Unlimited. Copyright © 2010.

Bermuda

Bermuda is a self governing British colony of seven islands. The largest is 14 miles long and 1 mile wide. It depends on tourism for its economy, and the capital is Hamilton.

Caribbean Journey from A to Y, by Mario Picayo. Illustrated by Earleen Griswold. Companita Books, 2000. (Grades 2–4)

Although this is not a story book it is a picture book about the Caribbean islands, from A to Z, one letter at a time. You will learn the names of cities, towns, and islands and where they are located as well as many of the things that grow there and the wildlife found on the islands. Take a mini-vacation to this part of the world in this beautifully illustrated book.

Terrific, by Jon Agee. Hyperion Books for Children, 2005. (Grades 1–3)

Eugene Mudge lives in Dismal, North Dakota, and has a little problem with negativity. "Terrific," says Eugene when he wins an all-expenses-paid cruise to Bermuda. "I'll probably get a really nasty sunburn." But Eugene's luck is much worse than that. His ship sinks, and he ends up stranded on a tiny island. But no matter how many bad things happen, his response is always a sarcastic "Terrific," until a talking parrot changes Eugene's grumpy attitude.

SEA CREATURES

Standards: 13, 14, 15

The ocean around the Bermuda Islands will reveal many sea creatures: jellyfish, swordfish, dolphins, starfish, octopus, and sharks. Choose one and complete this pattern. Illustrate your sea creature page for a class book.

I saw a _____

(name a sea creature)

and the _____ saw me

It was _____ along in the deep blue sea

(tell how it moves)

_____ goes _____ _____ _____

(Name the creature)   (tell what it does)

Canada

Canada covers an area of nearly 4 million square miles and has a population of 33,390,000. The official languages are English and French. Canada is the world's second largest country physically, with ten provinces and three territories. It is a leading mineral producer and manufactures iron and steel used in the automobile industry. The capital is Ottawa.

Amtrak, by Jim Jessell. Creative Company, 1994. (Grades 2–4)

A young boy hears the eerie howl of a wolf as he is climbing into bed. His grandfather comforts the frightened boy by telling him a story. At the beginning of time the Great Sky God created the man and woman and their sons to live on Earth. He also populated the land with wild animals, but it seems that the caribou, who were last to be created, were prone to sickness and the herds were disappearing due to disease. It was then that the Great Spirit God created the wolves, who would take the sick caribou from the herds, leaving only the healthy to grow and increase. Thus the caribou became strong once more.

Anne of Green Gables, by Lucy Maud Montgomery. Groundwood Books, 1990. (Grades 4–6)

Imagine the reaction of a brother and sister, set in their ways, who decided to adopt a boy to help on their farm. Instead of a boy, a young girl called Anne shows up. She is not afraid of anything, is a nonstop talker, and is somewhat stubborn. Although it takes a bit of time and many adventures, which include being accused of stealing a brooch, attending a picnic and tasting ice cream for the first time, being in a school play, and dying her bright red hair green, Anne soon becomes a beloved part of the family.

Arctic Adventures: Tales from the Lives of Innuit Artists, by Raquel Rivera. Groundwood Books, 2008. (Grades 4–6)

Here are four exciting tales from the Innuits, illustrated by four different artists, including the precarious position of a boy and his dog adrift on shifting ice; the meeting of a hunter and a polar bear; the frightful adventure of a shaman to appease a sea goddess; and a child and mother being rescued by the Royal Canadian Air Force. Beautiful illustrations in colored pencil and mixed media show the individual people and creatures in the Arctic landscape close up, sometimes with an edge of magical realism. After each story there is a brief, straightforward biography of the artist, a photo, and a reproduction of his or her work.

All Along the River, by Blair Drawson. Groundwood Books, 2006. (Grades 2–4)

Grandpa Joe sits by the river having tea with his granddaughter. Then out comes a most wonderful tale of his boyhood feats of derring-do. He paddled down the river in search of a great river giant, and along the way he came upon huge fish, fierce pirates, beautiful mermaids, wild animals, and friendly Chipewyans, and before he knew it he was having an amazing adventure, culminating in the pirate's ship sailing over a waterfall the size of Niagara Falls. Finally, the river giant appeared, and somehow they all end up back having tea with Grandpa Joe and his granddaughter, sitting by the river.

As Long as the Rivers Flow, by Larry Loyie. Illustrated by Heather D. Holmlund. Groundwood Books, 2006. (Grades 4–6)

In the 1800s the education of First Nations children was taken on by various churches, in government-sponsored residential schools. Children were forcibly taken from their families in order to erase their traditional languages and cultures. *As Long as the Rivers Flow* is the story of Larry Loyie's last summer before entering residential school. It is a time of learning and adventure. He cares for an abandoned baby owl and watches his grandmother make winter moccasins. He helps the family prepare for a hunting and gathering trip

Aunt Olga's Christmas Postcards, by Kevin Major. Illustrated by Bruce Roberts. Groundwood Books, 2007. (Grades 1–3)

Great-great Aunt Olga has been a collector of Christmas postcards all her life. She's 95, and many of the cards come from very long ago. The Yuletide season is the occasion to share her postcards and her Christmas memories with her favorite niece, Anna. Decked out in red, Aunt Olga is not averse to a little fun over tea, teaching Anna how to write her very own Christmas rhymes.

Bashful Bob and Doleful Dorinda, by Margaret Atwood. Bloomsbury Children's Books, 2006. (Grades 1–3)

Imagine a baby abandoned and raised by dogs! This is what happened to Bashful Bob, whose mother left him behind in a beauty parlor. Not until he meets Dorinda does he learn to talk. Dorinda has also lost her parents and is treated like a servant by the relatives who took her in. Using lots of alliteration, together they prove themselves brave and daring. Finally their parents find them, and they all live together in "blinding bliss, delirious with delicious delight."

Bella's Tree, by Janet Russell. Illustrated by Jirina Marton. Groundwood Books, 2009. (Grades 1–3)

Bella's grandmother, Nan, has become "crooked." All those berries that she used to love picking are lying under the snow. Even worse, she's too old to go out and find the perfect Christmas tree. But spunky Bella and Bruno, the dog, are certain that they can find a tree and smooth out Nan's misery. It takes them a few trees, some songs, and the help of some birds, but the end result is perfect, leaving grandmother, girl, and dog with "their eyes blinking from the beauty, the beautier, the beautiest."

A Brave Soldier, by Nicolas Debon. Goundwood Books, 2008. (Grades 4–6)

When World War I broke out in August 1914, Canadians rushed to join the army, thinking they could fight for king and country and be back home for Christmas. This is the story of Frank, whose experience of the war brings him from this initial enthusiasm to bitter disillusionment. The especially brutal conditions that faced soldiers in the First World War is portrayed in a spare, straightforward style, which neither glorifies fighting nor dwells on the horror. However, no one reading this book can come away with anything other than a sense of the tragic waste and futility of war, and especially of "the war to end all wars."

Dancing Through the Snow, by Jean Little. Kane-Miller, 2008. (Grades 3–5)

Ten-year-old Min, abandoned at age three, has spent years in foster care. When she's dumped by her latest foster mother just before Christmas, Jess Hart, a former Children's Aid doctor who knows Min and sees past her hardened shell, decides to take her home for the holidays. On their way to find a Christmas tree, Min discovers a young dog near death and brings it home. As the dog's timidity and distrust of people begin to lessen, Min realizes how much she herself has been "walling" people out. Min starts to open up, makes some new friends, and even stands up to her old nemesis, the bullying and taunting Laird.

Dawn Watch, by Jean E. Pendziwol. Illustrated by Nicolas Debon. Groundwood Books, 2001. (Grades 1–3)

This is the story of a child and her father making a night crossing of Lake Superior on their sailboat. As first mate, the child's job is to watch for ships, lights, land, and logs while the autopilot steers the craft. Above, the Big Dipper, North Star, Milky Way, and Northern Lights illuminate an inky night sky. And as dawn breaks, the horizon begins to glow and land appears, a black line between sky and sea.

Evangeline for Children, by Alice Couvillon and Elizabeth Moore. Illustrated by Alison Davis Lyne. Pelican, 2005. (Grades 4–6)

In the shadow of enemy British ships, Evangeline and Gabriel invite all the Acadian villagers to come dance and celebrate young love at the couple's engagement party. Instead of wedding toasts, the British shout out a proclamation saying, "Because you refused to honor your new ruler, the King of England, His Majesty commands that all of your possessions be taken from you and that you be sent far away to distant lands." Shouting soldiers rip children from their mothers' arms, and Gabriel and Evangeline are pushed onto separate ships. Evangeline spends years searching and praying for a safe reunion with her one true love, Gabriel. She follows Indian guides and smoke trails, only to find she has again missed Gabriel by a few days. "And while her youth and beauty gradually faded, her love for Gabriel never died."

The Fiddler of the Northern Lights, by Natalie Kinsey-Warnock. Illustrated by Leslie W. Bowmann. Penguin Group, 1996. (Grades 2–4)

The Pepin family lived in the north woods along the wild St. Maurice River, and Henry learned all of Grandpa Pepin's stories by heart. Everyone says they are just stories, until the night Grandpa and Henry go upriver in search of the fiddler and something strange and wondrous does happen. At first Henry is disappointed to return home without seeing the fiddler's lights. Then the fiddler's music summons the dancing colors of the aurora borealis and turns the black river into a "ribbon of sparkling, dancing light."

The Ghost Horse of the Mounties, by Sean O'Huigin. Illustrated by Barry Moser. David R. Godine Publishers, 1996. (Grades 4–6)

This legend told in verse begins on a black summer's night on a lonely Canadian plain. Six Mounties are watching over 250 wild horses when a terrible storm bears down upon the camp. The horses stampede, and in the rush to capture them, one young man is tossed aside and trampled. His own horse sees his master fall, then takes off in fright with the others. The young Mountie dies of his injuries, and the only horse that is not recaptured is his. The horse roams the plains and after many years feels a strange force pulling him toward a weathered mound of earth with a broken wooden cross. The horse has at last found its master.

The Ghost on the Hearth, by Susan Milord. Illustrated by Lydia Dadcovich. August House, 2004. (Grades 2–4)

In the summer of her twelfth year, a poor girl named Emily leaves home to work on a farm in rural Quebec. The farmer and his wife love Emily, but when she falls ill and dies, another girl is hired to take her place. Soon a strange event keeps recurring in the farmhouse. What is going on? On the first night, the farmer fails to solve the mystery. But on the second night, the farmer's wife snaps awake to find herself staring at a ghost!

The Huron Carol, by Ian Wallace. Groundwood Books, 2007. (Grades 4–6)

The Huron Carol is a beautiful and unusual Christmas song with a rich history. In the early 1600s, Father Jean de Brébeuf came to Canada from his native France as a Jesuit missionary. He settled among the Huron, or Ouendat, people in what is now Midland, Ontario. Despite his missionary zeal, Brébeuf was sensitive to the people with whom he lived. He learned their language and he wrote, in Huron, the original version of this famous Christmas carol. Brébeuf's carol continued to be sung by successive generations of Hurons. Then in 1926, Toronto writer Jesse Edgar Middleton, inspired by Brébeuf, wrote his own version of the carol in English. His are the familiar words we sing today, describing the Huron landscape, flora, and fauna in telling the Christmas story.

Kiviok's Magic Journey, by James Houston. A Margaret K. McElderry Book. Atheneum, 1973. (Grades 3–5)

Shortly after the sun and the moon came to light the world, Kiviok appeared and took as a wife a beautiful girl, whose white feather coat was snatched up by a wicked raven one day while she bathed in the lake with her sisters. The sisters, quickly pulling on downy coats, turned back into snow geese and soared into the sky, but Kungo was left behind. For seven years, she and Kiviok and their two children lived joyfully together, until the wicked raven came again and spirited Kungo and the children away.

Kiviok began a long and dangerous journey to search for his lost family . . . a journey that took him far to the South and across a mighty ocean, there to confront the raven in a life or death situation.

The Loup Garou, by Berthe Amoss. Pelican, 2009. (Grades 4–6)

Based on the actual expulsion of French Acadians from Nova Scotia in the eighteenth century, *The Loup Garou* recounts the adventures of Robert and his two friends, Louis and Little Otter, as the English try to force them from their homes. Having been tricked with other boys and their fathers into being taken prisoner in a church, Robert crawls through a small window to find his way back to his mother and home. With Robert's bravery, and the help of the Micmac Indians and the mysterious Loup Garou, a legendary creature who turns from man to wolf at twilight, Robert's family struggles to stay together in their homeland. This tale, set in 1755, encompasses both history and imagination.

Malian's Song, by Marge Bruchac. Illustrated by William Maughan. August House, 2008. (Grades 4–6)

In the words of a young Abenaki girl, *Malian's Song* tells the true story of the deliberate English attack by British Major Robert Rogers on the St. Francis Abenaki community near Montréal in 1759. Jeanne Brink, a descendant of Malian living in Vermont, told the little-known

Abenaki version of the brutal attack—which stands in direct contrast to Rogers's surviving journal records—to the Vermont Folklife Center

Marja's Skis, by Jean E. Pendziwol. Groundwood Books, 2008. (Grades 1–3)

Marja admires her big, brave older sister and is waiting until she too can ski and go to school. When Marja turns seven she is finally ready. Her father tells her, "When you are strong inside, you can do anything." And despite her mother's objections, she skis off to school on her own. It's hard to stay true to her father, though, when he dies in a logging accident and the family must struggle to survive. But Marja persists, skiing to school each day, learning her sums and letters and how to speak English, just as her father had always wanted. Then one sunny spring afternoon as she is skiing home alone, Marja's newfound strength is put to the test.

The Mummer's Song, by Bud Davidge. Illustrated by Ian Wallace. Groundwood Books, 2009. (Grades 1–3)

On a cold, clear Newfoundland night shortly after Christmas, several outlandishly costumed mummers appear, and Granny's house suddenly erupts in a burst of joking and tomfoolery, raucous singing, and exuberant dancing. Granny and her two young charges are instantly caught up in the merriment. When the evening's festivities come to a close, the mummers bid a fond farewell until next year.

Music from the Sky, by Denise Gillard. Illustrated by Stephen Taylor. Douglas & McIntyre, 2001. (Grades 1–3)

The setting of this tale is Novia Scotia, where one of Canada's oldest black communities is found. A little African American girl longs to make music with a flute and is fascinated by the idea that her grandfather can make her a flute. It takes a while, but they find a branch, and Grandpa whittles it carefully until the girl can use it to create her own sky music.

Old Mother Bear, by Victoria Miles. Illustrated by Molly Bang. Chronicle Books, 2007. (Grades K–2)

A 24-year-old grizzly bear gives birth to her last litter of cubs, then spends three years teaching them what they need to know to survive in their southern British Columbia home before they go off on their own. Includes facts about grizzlies and the Khutzeymateen Grizzly Bear Sanctuary

One Hundred Shining Candles, by Janet Lunn. Illustrated by Lindsay Grater. Scribner's, 1991. (Grades 2–4)

The year is 1800. In the dark woods of upper Canada there are few luxuries. Christmas will bring little cheer to the Jamieson family. When 10-year-old Lucy hears the visiting schoolmaster describe the wonderful Christmas he has seen, with roast goose, toys, and bright ribbons, her imagination is fired. What if she and her small brother, Dan, were to make their parents the most splendid gift of all, 100 shining candles? But the best plans can sometimes go awry.

Paddle to the Sea, written and illustrated by Holling C. Holling. Houghton Mifflin, 1984. (Grades 2–4)

Imagine a small carved Indian figure in a 12-inch canoe that makes a trip from the Canadian wilderness to the Atlantic ocean! A young boy carves the figure and sets it on its journey, beginning on a snow bank near a river that eventually leads to the Great Lakes, the St. Lawrence River, and finally the Atlantic Ocean. The small figure meets many dangers, including wild animals, sawmills, fishing nets, and a shipwreck, before finally reaching its destination.

The Patchwork Path: A Quilt Map to Freedom, by Bettye Stroud. Illustrated by Erin Susanne Bennett. Candlewick Press, 2007. (Grades 3–5)

The images stitched into Hannah's patchwork quilt lead to secret signposts on the Underground Railroad as she and her father take flight from slavery on a perilous path to freedom. The wagon wheel, the bear's paw and flying geese are some of the squares in the quilt Hannah's mama helped her to sew before Hannah's sister was sold to another plantation and Mama died of a broken heart. Now that Hannah's papa has decided to make the run for freedom, this patchwork quilt is not just a precious memento of Mama; it's a series of hidden clues that will guide them along the Underground Railroad to Canada, where they'll finally be free. This is the story of a brave father and his young daughter, two of thousands who escaped a life of slavery and made the dangerous journey to freedom—a story of courage, determination, and hope.

Rabbit and the Moon, by Douglas Wood. Illustrated by Leslie Baker. Simon & Schuster Books for Young Readers, 1998. (Grades K–2)

Rabbit wants to view the earth from the vantage point of the moon. He asks all the birds to take him to the moon, but only Crane is able to oblige. The flight leaves Rabbit thrilled with his new perspective and provides Crane with his long legs and red headdress. Rabbit had a strong desire to go to the moon. He could not jump far enough, and none of the birds would agree to fly him there. Finally, Crane saw Rabbit's disappointment and decided to take him. During the flight, Rabbit held on to Brother Crane's legs, stretching them into the long legs that cranes have today. Rabbit's bloody paw touched the Crane's head, which gave him his characteristic red headdress as Rabbit achieved his dream.

The Red Sash, by Jean E. Pendziwol. Illustrated by Nicolas Debon. Groundwood Books, 2006. (Grades 2–4)

This is the story of a young Métis boy who lived near the fur trading post of Fort William, on Lake Superior, nearly 200 years ago. His father spends the long winter months as a guide leading voyageurs into the northwest to trade with native people for furs. But now it is Rendezvous, when the voyageurs paddle back to Fort William with their packs of furs, and North West Company canoes come from Montreal bringing supplies for the next season. It is a time of feasting and dancing and of voyageurs trading stories around the campfire.

With preparations underway for a feast in the Great Hall, the boy canoes to a nearby island to hunt hare. But once there, a storm begins to brew. As the waves churn to foam, a canoe carrying a gentleman from the North West Company appears, heading toward the island for shelter. The boy helps land the canoe, which has been torn by rocks and waves. Then he saves the day as he paddles the gentleman across to Fort William.

A Salmon for Simon, by Betty Waterton. Illustrated by Ann Blades. Atheneum, 1978. (Grades K–2)

Young Simon, a Canadian Indian, sets out to catch a salmon. He has no luck on his fishing trip until an eagle, who has caught a salmon, drops the fish into a water-filled hole. As Simon looks at the beautiful fish, he wants to return it to the sea, but the fish is too big and too slippery for Simon to hold. So Simon begins to dig and eventually creates a water-filled channel that allows the salmon to make its way to the sea.

Shin-chi's Canoe, by Nicola I. Campbell. Illustrated by Kim LaFave. Groundwood Books, 2009. (Grades 3–5)

The story of two children's experience at residential school. Shi-shi-etko is about to return for her second year, but this time her six-year-old brother, Shin-chi, is going, too. As they begin their journey in the back of a cattle truck, Shi-shi-etko takes it upon herself to tell her little brother all the things he must remember: the trees, the mountains, the rivers, and the tug of the salmon when he and his dad pull in the fishing nets. Shin-chi knows he won't see his family again until the sockeye salmon return in the summertime. When they arrive at school, Shi-shi-etko gives him a tiny cedar canoe, a gift from their father. The children's time is filled with going to mass, school for half the day, and work the other half. The girls cook, clean, and sew, while the boys work in the fields, in the woodshop, and at the forge.

Shin-chi is forever hungry and lonely, but finally the salmon swim up the river, and the children return home for a joyful family reunion

The White Stone in the Castle Wall, by Sheldon Oberman. Illustrated by Les Tait. Boyds Mill, 2005. (Grades 4–6)

It may not be true but it could be: this story of how a single white stone came to be in the wall surrounding Casa Loma, the magnificent medieval castle that stands in the middle of Toronto. John Tommy Fiddich lives in Yorkville, tends the family vegetable patch, and considers himself the "luckiest boy in town." When a hailstorm wipes out the vegetables, he goes from being the luckiest to the unluckiest. Then word gets out that Henry Pellatt, the eccentric millionaire who brought light to the city and built Casa Loma, is offering one dollar for brown stones to place in the wall going up around the castle. After trudging through the city all day with his stone, John reaches the castle, only to find that rain has washed it white. But Henry Pellatt accepts the stone for his wall, rewarding John for his hard work, making him again "the luckiest boy in town." The trip through the streets of Toronto, from Yorkville to Casa Loma, makes for a book as enchanting to young and old as the fabulous castle that inspired it.

WHAT DOES CANADA PRODUCE?

Standards: 2, 4, 6, 21

List three things mined or manufactured in Canada.

_____

_____

_____

List five facts about a product the country is best known for without naming the product.

1._____

2._____

3._____

4._____

5._____

Ask a classmate to say a number between one and five. Read the clue for that number. The student may guess or pass. The game continues until the product is guessed or all clues have been read.

⚷ **Answer key:** The product is _____

From *Reading the World with Picture Books* by Nancy J. Polette.
Santa Barbara, CA: Libraries Unlimited. Copyright © 2010.

ACROSTIC POEM

Describe one of the provinces of Canada as an acrostic poem.

Example:

O   ccupies Eastern Canada

N   ickel extensively mined

T   oronto a major city

A   jumping off place for westward
       migration

R   ichest province

I   ndustrial economy

O   ne third Canada's population

_____

_____

_____

_____

_____

_____

_____

_____

S _____

A _____

S _____

K _____

A _____

T _____

C _____

H _____

E _____

W _____

A _____

N _____

_____

_____

_____

_____

_____

Costa Rica

More than 4 million people call the island of Costa Rica home. The name means "rich coast," and the island covers 19,730 square miles. One-third of Costa Rica is rain forest, abundant with wildlife. Spanish is the language spoken. The capital is San Jose.

The Far-flung Adventures of Homer the Hummer, by Cynthia Furlong Reynolds. Illustrated by Catherine McClung. Mitten Press, 2005. (Grades 1–3)

This is a beautifully illustrated tale of the migration of the ruby-throated hummingbird from the rain forests of Costa Rica to northern Michigan. As one would expect on such a long trip for such a tiny creature, many things happen to the ruby-throated traveler. A frog spies the bird and plans on a delicious dinner. Weather is a great danger, as is getting trapped in a farmer's barn, but the bird does eventually make the journey successfully, just in time to start a new family.

When the Monkeys Came Back, by Kristine L. Franklin. Illustrated by Robert Roth. Atheneum, 1994. (Grades 1–3)

As an old woman listens to the chatter of the howler monkeys in the trees on the hillside. She remembers when the monkeys disappeared. When she was a child, her father sold the hillside to men who cut down all the trees. The monkeys, having no place to live, left. Marta the child grew to be Marta the woman. She married and asked her husband to let her plant seedlings on the hillside. Many, many years later, when the seedlings have become full-grown trees, the monkeys return, finding their home once again.

RAIN FOREST ANIMALS

Standards: 13, 14, 15

Costa Rica's rain forest is home to monkeys, anteaters, deer, wildcats, weasels, otters, coyotes, and foxes. Choose one.

_____

(Animal)

Complete the missing information.

Animal Report

Choose an animal _____

Tell two things it has. _____ _____

Tell four things it does. _____ _____ _____ _____

Tell where you would find the animal _____

Use the information in a song. Sing it to the tune of "Mary Had a Little Lamb"

Example:

Howler monkeys have a tail
Big brown eyes, soft brown fur
They shriek and bark
And hoot and howl
And live in Costa Rica

_____ have a _____

_____ and _____

They _____ and _____

And _____ and _____

And live in Costa Rica.

Cuba

Cuba is 42,803 square miles and is home to 11.5 million people. The main crops are coffee, rice, and sugar cane. Animal life is abundant and includes 7,000 different kinds of insects. The language spoken is Spanish, and the capital is Havana.

Amelia's Show-and-Tell Fiesta, by Mimi Chapra. Illustrated by Martha Avilés. HarperCollins, 2004. (Grades 1–3)

Amelia is a little girl who has come to the United States from Cuba. When she hears about sharing at show and tell, she wears her fanciest fiesta dress. Then she sees a basket on the teacher's desk with small show and tell items and realizes she has made a mistake. However, an understanding teacher and curious classmates help to make things right.

The Dog Who Loved the Moon, by Cristina Garcia. Illustrated by Sebastia Serra. Simon & Schuster, 2008. (Grades 1–3)

Pilar's whole family loves music and dancing, so Pilar is overjoyed when she receives new dancing slippers and a puppy as birthday gifts. She expects the puppy, who plays with her by day, to be her new dancing partner in the evening, but unfortunately this is not to be. Paco, the puppy, has fallen in love with the moon, and only Pilar's musical uncle and a dose of magic can cure his ailment

Mama Does the Mambo, by Katherine Leiner. Illustrated by Edel Rodriguez. Hyperion, 2001. (Grades 1–3)

At Carnival time in Havana, Mama and Papa were a sensation as they danced together. "Papa held the beat, and Mama, the rhythm." But following the death of her Papa, Sophia fears that her Mama will never find another dancing partner for Carnival. Now men line up in the courtyard in hopes of becoming Mama's dance partner, but "her heart is not in it. Her skirts stay in the closet, her feet, bare." Mama's favorite suitor is Eduardo, a kind fellow who displays his cooking talents in the kitchen but demonstrates little skill on the dance floor. Finally, at Carnival, as their favorite Mambo begins, Sofia and mama dance it together, to the delight of all.

Papa Tells Chita a Story, by Elizabeth Fitzgerald Howard. Illustrated by Floyd Cooper. Simon & Schuster, 1995. (Grades 1–3)

The stories parents tell have even more magic when they are true. Chita is fascinated by her Papa's stories about when he was a soldier in Cuba during the Spanish–American War. He tells about delivering a secret message to the troops across the island of Cuba, through the dangers of snakes, alligators, predatory birds, thorns, and brambles. As he recounts the events, each peril grows to monstrous proportions in Chita's imagination, but the message is delivered and Papa earned a medal to prove it.

The Road to Santiago, by D. H. Figueredo. Illustrated by Pablo Torrecilla. Lee & Low Books, 2003. (Grades 2–4)

This is a true tale of a family determined to let nothing interfere with their celebration of Christmas with family members who live some distance away. When they arrive at the train station to begin their journey, they find that civil war has broken out and rebels have destroyed the train tracks. Papa does not turn back. He finds a farmer, who gives the family a ride to the next bus station. With the help of other kind people, the family does make it to grandmother's house, where they celebrate Midnight Mass together followed by their holiday celebration.

SPIDER STORY

Standards: 4, 14, 16

Among the 7,000 kinds of creepy crawly creatures in Cuba are scorpions, tarantulas, and many other kinds of spiders. Fill in the blank spaces to write a spider story.

Some spiders spin their own _____

where they _____

_____

_____

_____.

Sometimes they go around _____

_____

_____

_____ , or sometimes they just

_____

_____

_____

_____. But to this very day some spiders spin their own

_____

_____

_____

_____.

El Salvador

El Salvador is a tiny country of only 8,124 square miles, yet it is home to almost 7 million people. It is bounded on the south by the Pacific Ocean but has no Caribbean coast. It has an abundant bird population but is less rich in mammal. The capital is San Salvador.

Alfredito Flies Home, by Jorge Argueta. Illustrated by by Luis Garay. Groundwood Books, 2007. (Grades 1–3)

Alfredito and his family are getting ready to return to El Salvador for Christmas. It will be their first visit back since they left as refugees and made their way to California on foot. But this time they're flying! Excitement mounts as Alfredito and his family soar over the earth and finally arrive at their beloved home to reunite with family and friends.

Magic Dogs of the Volcanoes, by Manlio Argueta. Illustrated by Elly Simmons. Children's Book Press, 1990. (Grades 2–4)

It might be dangerous living at the foot of a volcano, but not if you are protected by magic dogs. For generations, the cadejos, wolflike, magical animals, have cared for the people who live at the foot of the volcanoes. But then the landowner decides to do away with them in the hopes of making the campesinos harder working, and he sends soldiers made out of lead to kill them. In desperation the cadejos call upon their great-great grandparents, the volcanoes, who defeat the soldiers and, by extension, the landowner.

Waiting for Papa, by René Colato Laínez. Illustrated by Anthony Accardo. PiZata Books, 2004. (Grades 2–4)

When revolution causes an upheaval in a country, innocent people suffer. When a factory is bombed, their home is burned, and a family loses all their possessions, the mother is able to escape with the children to the United States, where she finds a job in a sewing factory. Three years pass, and efforts to get Papa to the United States are not going well. Beto misses his papa and longs for the time when the family can be together again. Then at school he is able to write his papa a letter, and after he reads his letter on the radio, wonderful things begin to happen.

DUCK SONG PATTERN

Standards: 13, 14, 15

Read about El Salvador's wild duck or royal heron. Use the information in the song pattern below.

Example: A BIRD SONG

Name the bird.

Tell one thing the bird does.

Use the information in the song and sing it to the tune of "Did You Ever See a Lassie?"

Did you ever see a robin (name the bird),

A robin, a robin

Did you ever see a robin (name the bird)

Make a nest in a tree (name one thing it does)

Did you ever see a _____

(name of bird)

A _____, a _____

(name of bird)   (name of bird)

Did you ever see a _____

(name of bird)

_____

(one thing it does)

Greenland

Greenland covers 840,000 square miles. It is the world's largest island, being three times the size of Texas, and is a dependency of Denmark. The population is about 56,000 and the capital is Nuuk.

Call Me Ahnighito, by Pam Conrad. Illustrated by Richard Egielski. HarperCollins, 1995. (Grades 3–5)

Told in the first person, a huge meteorite describes how it lies half-buried in Greenland for centuries until it is finally excavated by members of a Peary expedition and begins a new journey to New York City in 1897. "They call me Ahnighito [Ah-na-HEET-o]. And they tell me I am made of star stuff, but I don't remember my birth." Named for Peary's four-year-old daughter, it now resides in the American Museum of Natural History.

Grandmother's Pigeon, by Louis Erdrich. Illustrated by Jim Lamarche. Hyperion, 1996. (Grades 2–4)

The eccentric, well-traveled grandmother of two young kids decamps in mid-vacation, riding a porpoise to Greenland and leaving behind a trove of strange treasures and artifacts, including a collection of bird's nests and three old eggs, which hatch, marvelously, into passenger pigeons. Erdrich wields her Native American ancestry and her worldiness—Grandmother owns an original Klee—to give young readers a sense of the world's wonders and the wisdom of the elders, the old wisdom of the natural cycles that we are losing. A letter from Grandmother, promising to return, winds up this fetching tale.

WHAT MIGHT HATCH?

Standards: 2, 19, 21

Ask children to bring to class old magazines that can be cut up.

Decide what rare bird might hatch from one of the eggs the grandmother leaves. Look for and cut out a picture of a common object. Paste the picture on a plain piece of paper, then add lines and features to create a rare bird. Give the creature a name.

Older children may want to compose a couplet to describe what their bird does.

Grenada

Twenty-one miles long and twelve miles wide, with an area of 120 square miles, Grenada is known as the "Isle of Spice." The population is about 90,000. Bananas and many spices are exported, along with a large variety of tropical fruits. The capital is St. Georges.

The Nutmeg Princess, by Richardo Keens-Douglas. Illustrated by Annouchka Galouchko. Annick Press, 1992. (Grades 2–4)

In this joyous, modern fable, only those with goodness of heart can see the elusive vision. On the Caribbean island called the "Isle of Spice," there was a lake with a nutmeg grove nearby. On the lake, some said, lived the Nutmeg Princess, but she would only appear when the nutmeg was ready for picking and the sweet smell of the spice filled the air. If you were lucky, you might see her, but to do so you had to rise at 4 a.m. and sit just so by the edge of the lake. Two children are determined to do just that, and the townspeople follow along. Only the two children are gifted with a vision of her and her wisdom. "Go now, follow your dreams, and if you believe in yourselves, all things are possible." And then she was gone, never to reappear.

SPICE OR FRUIT RESEARCH

Standards: 2, 4, 6

Read about one of these spices (nutmeg or cinnamon) or one of these fruits (mangos, passion fruit, guavas, bananas, or tamarind). Complete the questions below with information about the spice or fruit.

1. What are you? _____

2. Where do you live? _____

3. Favorite colors _____

4. Favorite clothes _____

5. What is your job? _____

6. Who are your family/friends? _____

7. Where do you vacation? _____

8. Favorite holiday _____

9. How do you move? _____

Guatemala

Guatemala borders Mexico on the west and north and covers 42,000 square miles. It has a population of 12,778,000. Chief crops are bananas and coffee beans. More recently, oil is being shipped to countries around the world. The capital is Guatemala City.

Abuela's Weave, by Omar S. Castaneda. Illustrated by Enrique O. Sanchez. Lee & Low, 1995. (Grades 1–3)

A young Guatemalan girl and her grandmother grow closer as they weave some special creations and then make a trip to the market in hopes of selling them. A story about intergenerational trust, love, and independence, this book introduces children to the culture of Guatemala through the story of a little girl selling her grandmother's beautiful weaving at the public market.

Mama and Papa Have a Store, by Amelia Lou Carling. Dial, 1998. (Grades 1–3)

The youngest child in a Chinese family that has emigrated to Guatemala City describes a typical day, from early morning to night, in her parents' dry goods store. Her parents, whose Chinese names mean Lady Who Lives in the Moon and Fragrant Pond, are Dona Graciela and Don Rodolfo to the customers who frequent their general store. Going past the paper lanterns and firecrackers on display, a weaver pores over "rows and rows of colored strands [of thread] arranged like schools of fish in glassy water," and chooses "volcano purple, maize yellow, hot pepper red." Lunch in their home behind the store is cooked in a wok and served with tortillas.

My Pig Amarillo, by Ichikawa, Satomi. Philomel Books, c2002. (Grades K–2)

Amarillo is Pablito's best friend. They do everything together—run, hide from each other, jump in the mud. They are inseparable, just like many best friends. But Amarillo is a bit different—he is a little yellow pig. When Pablito comes home from school one day and Amarillo isn't there, Pablito is devastated. Where could he be? Pablito can't eat; he can't sleep. His heart feels as if it will break wide open. But Grandfather has an idea, a way for Pablito to send a message to Amarillo, and help him say good-bye to his best friend.

Race of Toad and Deer, by Pat Mora. Illustrated by Domi. Groundwood, 2001. (Grades K–2)

An arrogant deer who is always boasting about his speed and strength is finally challenged to a race by a wily toad. All the jungle's inhabitants—the jaguar, the toucan, the tapir, and the armadillo—gather to watch this unlikely competition. But with the help of his friends, the toad manages to defeat his adversary, proving the value of brains over brawn.

The Sleeping Bread, by Timothy Rhodes. Illustrated by Stefan Czernecki. Hyperion, 1992. (Grades 1–3)

All beggars must be banned from the town at festival time when visitors come. Zafiro, the beggar, bids a tearful good-bye to his friend, Beto, the baker. A tear falls in the bread dough, and the next morning the dough refuses to rise. The people try to wake the sleeping bread, but to no avail. Beto brings Zafiro back and the two solve the problem.

Song of Chirimia: A Guatemalan Folktale, by Jane Anne Volkmer. Lerner, 1990. (Grades 2–4)

A bilingual retelling of a Guatemalan folktale about a young man who tries to win the hand of Moonlight, a Mayan princess, by making his song as sweet as that of the birds. It seems that the once happy princess has become silent, and Clear Sky, her father, decides it is time for her to wed. He sends for all the young men of the kingdom, and Black Feather is the one who brings a smile to her face with his singing. But before she agrees to marry him, she asks him to complete a nearly impossible task. He carries out the task, which results in the invention of the chirimia, a recorder-like instrument.

GUATEMALAN GAMES AND CRAFTS

Standards: 2

Visit the library to find books about games children around the world play. Teach the class a game that Guatemalan children play. Here are some books you might look for:

- *Play with Us: 100 Games from Around the World,* by Oriol Ripoll. Chicago Review Press, 2005. Paperback.

- *Sidewalk Games Around the World,* by Arlene Erlbach. Millbrook Press, 1998.

- *Games Around the World,* by Teacher Created Materials, 2008.

- *Kids Around the World Play!: The Best Fun and Games from Many Lands,* by Arlette N. Braman. Wiley, 2002.

Visit the Internet to find crafts you can do from Guatemala:

Guatemala for Kids! (www.rainbowkids.com/HTMLFiles.aspx?page= GuatemalaAct–Cached). Free crafts, coloring pages, puzzles, and maps. Kids have fun exploring the culture of Guatemala through puzzles, coloring pages, games, and crafts. This area keeps growing every month, so check back.

Arts and Crafts from Guatemala (www.dltk-kids.com/Crafts/friendship/ mbracelets.htm). In Guatemala, tiny worry dolls are made out of scrap materials.

Haiti

More than 8.5 million people live in Haiti's 10,714 square miles. It is a very poor country, and the average life expectancy is only 52 years. Less than half of the people can read. Coffee is Haiti's main cash crop. The capital is Port-au-Prince.

Circles of Hope, by Karen Lynn Williams. Illustrated by Linda Saport. Eerdmans, 2005. (Grades 2–4)

In Haiti it is the custom to plant a tree upon the birth of a child. When his sister is born, Facile decides to do just that, but at first the fruit tree he plants won't grow. Then his sister becomes ill, and mother must take her to a city far away for treatment. Facile plants his tree in a circle of stones, and this time the tree takes root and grows. When mother and sister return, Facile is proud to show his tree.

Josias, Hold the Book, by Jennifer Riesmeyer Elvgren. Illustrated by Nicole Tadgell. Boyds Mills Press, 2006. (Grades 1–3)

"Holding the book" means attending school, but Josias is too busy trying to make the beans in his garden grow to attend school. He tries everything from watering to fertilizing the plants, but nothing seems to work. It looks as if his family will go hungry. He asks a friend who does attend school if the answer might be found in a book. What Josias learns convinces him to ask his parents if, in addition to tending the garden, he can go to school. A schoolteacher helps him with a book that explains that because the soil is tired, Josias must change crops. Now Josias's father sees school as a good idea, though the boy's attendance will be a hardship.

Open the Door to Liberty! A Biography of Toussaint L'Ouverture, by Anne Rockwell. Illustrated by R. Gregory Christie. Houghton Mifflin, 2009. (Grades 3–5)

Toussaint L'Ouverture led a revolution to free the enslaved people of Haiti. At one time Haiti was a French colony, and white plantation owners owned thousands of black slaves brought from Africa. Toussaint was born a slave on this island in 1743. He was a small and sickly baby but battled to survive. He strengthened his body by swimming and riding horseback. He sharpened his intelligence with books about history and philosophy. Toussaint dreamed that he was destined to be a great leader who would lead his people to freedom. He was right.

Painted Dreams, by Karen Lynn Williams. Illustrated by Catherine Stock. HarperCollins, 1998. (Grades 1–3)

Using whatever she can find—a scrap of wastepaper, a bit of charcoal—Ti Marie makes beautiful art. If only she had real paint and clean white canvas, what wonderful pictures she could paint then! Mama says there is no money for such things, but Ti Marie finds a surprising way to make her dreams come true and to create pictures that make the heart sing .

Running the Road to ABC, by Denize Lauture. Aladdin, 2000. (Grades 1–3)

Six island children are running at daybreak—over the hills, through the fields, across the city square—to school! Never before has the love of learning (and learning together) been such a joyous time. Denise Lauture's buoyant, poetic text captures the happiness and youth of the children. Illustrations show the rich beauty of Haiti with the bright-colored vibrancy of Haitian folk art.

PUZZLE STORY

Standards: 2, 3, 17

Ask students to make up an island story using only three sentences. Make a second copy of the story to check later. Cut the story into 10 pieces, cutting only around the words, not through them. Exchange story puzzles and give the students three minutes to complete them. The winner is the one who finishes first.

Jamaica

Jamaica is the third largest island in the Caribbean Sea, covering 4,244 square miles, and is home to 2.5 million people. The island has varied terrain, with both desert and rain forests as well as the coastal areas. Tourism is the major industry. The capital is Kingston.

The Crab Man, by Patricia E. Van West. Illustrated by Cedric Lucas. Turtle Books, 2001. (Grades 2–4)

Neville's family has no money for such luxuries as a new dress for his mother. Workers in the fields receive barely enough money to feed their families, yet the young boy, who earns a few pennies catching and selling crabs, wants more than anything to buy his mother a new dress. Then trouble comes, when Neville realizes he must make a choice between giving up his savings to save the crabs and not protecting the wildlife that is in danger,

A Season for Mangoes, by Regina Hanson. Illustrated by Eric Velasquez. Clarion Books, 2005. (Grades 2–4)

In Jamaica, when a person passes on, a sit-up is held to celebrate the life of that person. The sit-up lasts all night. A little girl, Sareen, is to take part in her first sit-up for her grandmother, who has died. As various family members recall incidents from grandmother's life, Sareen discovers that sharing her stories of Nana's passion for mangoes helps lift the sadness. Her brother and parents listen raptly as she tells Nana's love of mangoes and of her own efforts to find the sweetest mango for her sick grandmother. Sareen is happy she could contribute to the celebration and takes part in a final activity, the sunrise dance.

The Tangerine Tree, by Regina Hanson, Jane Feder, and Harvey Stevenson. Clarion Books, 1995. (Grades 1–3)

Ida's papa must leave the family to start a new job in New York. There are few jobs to be had in Jamaica, so papa has no choice but to leave his family. Ida is so upset that she hides in a tangerine tree. Papa finds her and gives her a book, telling her that when she can read it by herself, he will be home. She gives papa juice from the tree, liquid sunshine to keep him warm.

Tiger Soup: An Anansi Story from Jamaica, by Frances Temple. Scholastic, 1994.
  (Grades 1–3)

  Anansi tricks Tiger into leaving the sweet coconut-mango soup he has been cooking by
tempting Tiger to take a cool dip in "Blue Hole." Thinking he'll soon be rid of the menace,
Tiger dives into the water, leaving his meal unattended. Anansi eats the soup himself and
manages to put the blame on the monkeys.

TREASURE HUNT

Standards: 1, 3, 4

Draw a path on the chalkboard with letters along the way and a "treasure" at the end. Ask for a volunteer to seek the treasure. To get to the treasure the student must say a word beginning with each letter along the way. If possible, the word must have something to do with the story or with an island. If the child has difficulty, allow classmates to help him or her. When the treasure is reached, print the child's initials on it.

Mexico

Mexico covers an area of 761,600 square miles. The population is nearly 200 million people. It shares a border with the United States and is rich in mineral resources. Two-thirds of the people live in the larger cities. Much of northern Mexico is desert. Tropical hurricanes occur in the coastal lowlands. Few live in the northern or southern parts of the country. The national sport is bullfighting. The capital is Mexico City, the second most heavily populated city in the world.

Abuelos, by Pat Mora. Illustrated by Amelia Lau Carling. Groundwood Books, 2008. (Grades K–2)

This is the story of a small girl whose family moves to a New Mexican village, where she meets the traditional "los abuelos," old mountain monster men who come down from their dark, smoky caves in winter to make sure that children are behaving. The girl is teased by her older brother. ("Oooooo . . . Da-a-a-ark . . . They're com-m-m-ing.") Then at a community bonfire, village men disguised as the hairy, sooty abuelos come stomping down through the snowy night, asking the children if they have been good. Amid all the chaos, the girl recognizes her uncle behind a mask and joins in the uproarious laughter. The abuelos encourage the little ones to dance and sing around huge bonfires. Afterward everyone enjoys cookies and empanadas.

Adios Oscar!: A Butterfly Fable, by Peter Elwell. Blue Sky Press, 2009. (Grades 1–3)

When Oscar the caterpillar discovers that he will one day become a butterfly, he's overjoyed. And his friend Edna the bookworm encourages his hopes of flying to Mexico with the other monarch butterflies. To prepare, Oscar learns Spanish and dreams of flying through the purple Sierra Madre Mountains. But when Oscar emerges from his cocoon with stubby little wings, a craving for the taste of designer sweaters, and the urge to take a spin around the bathroom lightbulb, his dreams are dashed. There will be no trip to Mexico for Oscar—or will there?

Armando and the Blue Tarp School, by Edith Hope Fine. Illustrated by Hernán Sosa. Lee & Low Books, 2007. (Grades 2–4)

Armando and his father are trash pickers in Tijuana, Mexico. They spend their days at the trash dump picking out items they can use or sell. Then one day a man arrives and spreads out a blue tarp on the ground. He invites all who are willing to come to his school, where they can learn English and many other things. Armando's father thinks that going to school is a very good thing, and Armando becomes one of Señor David's pupils. Based on a real event, this tells of the work of a New York teacher, David Lynch, who in his small way brought education to poor children in Mexico.

Bravo, Tavo!, by Brian Meunier. Illustrated by Perky Edgerton. Dutton Children's Books, 2007. (Grades 2–4)

Tavo dreams of nothing but being a famous basketball star and getting new shoes so that he can practice better, for he plays so much that he wears out his sneakers. The village is facing a serious drought, and Tavo's father, Gustavo, is too busy worrying about the drought to pay attention to new sneakers for Tavo. Gustavo thinks he can solve the water shortage by using some of the old ways, but the other villagers think his ideas are foolish. Tavo puts aside basketball to help prove his father right. In return, something miraculous happens to his sneakers, and he's the hero of the next game.

Butterflies on Carmen Street by Monica Brown. Illustrated by April Ward. Piñata Books, 2007. (Grades 2–4)

Today is the day Julianita and her friends have been waiting for: they're going to learn about monarch butterflies. But what's even more thrilling is they're each going to receive their very own caterpillar to raise! When Julianita gets hers, she names him Tiger because of his striking yellow and black stripes. Ms. Rodríguez teaches her students all about the monarch. But Julianita already knows that they fly south thousands of miles every winter, because her grandfather remembers seeing the beautiful monarchs in his village in the highlands of Mexico. As the children feed and care for their caterpillars, they anxiously anticipate the transformation from caterpillar to chrysalis to butterfly. When Tiger finally emerges from his chrysalis, Julianita doesn't want to let him go. "Tiger knows the way to Mexico because it's in his heart," her Abuelito reassures her. She feels sad to see Tiger fly away, but Julianita knows that someday, she will follow him to her grandmother's magical Mexico.

Charro Claus and the Tejas Kid, by Xavier Garza. Cinco Puntos Press, 2008. (Grades 1–3)

Suppose that Santa Claus did not speak Spanish and had no idea what children along the U.S./Mexico border wanted for Christmas. This problem is quickly solved when Santa recruits a farmer named Pancho, who calls the land around the border home. Pancho and his cousin, Vincente, take over Santa's gift giving to the children who live near the border. Instead of reindeer, Pancho uses flying burros and now has a new name, Charro Claus.

Chato and the Party Animals, by Gary Soto. Illustrated by Susan Guevara. Putnam, 2000. (Grades K–2)

Chato, the coolest cat in el barrio, loves to party—but not his best buddy, Novio Boy. Birthday parties always make him blue. "I'm from the pound," he tells Chato. "I don't know when I was born. I never knew my mami. I never even had a birthday party, or nothing." So Chato plans the coolest surprise party for Novio Boy, inviting all of el barrio and cooking up a storm. But he forgets the most important thing—inviting Novio Boy! Luckily, just as everyone starts remembering all the things they used to love about their long-lost friend, the birthday boy arrives with his own surprise—himself!

Domitila: A Cinderella Tale from the Mexican Tradition, by Jewell Reinhart Coburn. Illustrated by Connie McLennan. Shen's Books, 2006. (Grades 1–3)

Domitila is not only "sweeter than a cactus bloom in early spring," she is also a talented cook and an amazing leather artist. Most of the classical elements of a Cinderella story can be found in Domitila. A gentle weaving of her mother's nurturing with strong family traditions is the secret ingredient for Domitila to rise above hardship to eventually become the governor's bride. Moreover, with a firm belief in simplicity and realism, Domitila makes a lasting impression as a triumphant Cinderella in her humility, service, and unassuming modesty.

Unlike most ivory tower Cinderellas, the only transformation in this story is Timoteo's—Domitila's suitor—as we watch him mature from an arrogant politician's son into a compassionate family man. There is no glass slipper to fight over, and no fairy godmother to save the day. All Domitila has are her innate qualities and her family legacy.

Dream Carver, by Diana Cohn. Illustrated by Amy Cordova. Chronicle Books, 2002. (Grades 2–4)

Here is a tale based on the work of the renowned Oaxacan woodcarver Manuel Jimenez, who bravely broke with a generations-old artistic tradition. With small knives, the men of the village carve juguetes, tiny wooden animals so small they could fit in the palm of a hand, which are painted in fiesta-bright colors by women and girls. But Mateo dreams of carving life-sized animals, with surfaces that tingle with vibrant, improbable colors and surreal patterns. When Mateo ultimately produces a glorious wooden menagerie, including a quetzal with majestic feathers, he wins over not only Papa, but the entire village, and a new way of carving is born.

Elena's Serenade, by Campbell Geeslin. Atheneum Books for Young Readers, 2004. (Grades 2–4)

Who ever heard of a girl glassblower? In Mexico, where the sun is called el sol and the moon is called la luna, a little girl called Elena wants to blow into a long pipe and make bottles appear, like magic. But girls can't be glassblowers. Or can they? Join Elena on her fantastic journey to Monterrey—home of the great glassblowers!—in an enchanting story filled with magic realism.

Erandi's Braids, by Antonio Hernandez Madrigal. Illustrated by Tomie dePaola. Putnam, 1999. (Grades K–2)

Erandi is excited. Tomorrow is her birthday, and Mama has promised her a present. But tomorrow brings unexpected worries. Their fishing net is full of holes and beyond repair. Suddenly Mama needs money to buy a new one. Erandi knows that the hair buyers have come up from the city to buy the beautiful thick black braids of the village women. Is Mama going to sell Erandi's braids? Antonio Hernandez Madrigal draws upon a past custom of buying the hair of the Tarascan women of Mexico in this tender story of a little girl's selflessness.

F Is for Fiesta, by Susan Middleton Elya. Illustrated by Brian Karas. Putnam, 2006. (Grades 1–3)

From adornos (decorations) going up all over the house, biscochitos (cupcakes) baking in the oven, and a special treat of churros (doughnut sticks) for breakfast, this can only be the beginning of a fabulous cumpleaños (birthday)! As the alphabet continues, the story highlights fun elements of a boy's never-ending birthday celebration.

Ghost Wings, by Barbara M. Joosse. Illustrated by Giselle Potter. Chronicle Books, 2001. (Grades 2–4)

A child looks forward to the days when grandmother takes her to the Magic Circle, where monarch butterflies adorn the trees. When it is time for the butterflies to migrate north, one lands on the child's arm, and she feels the tickle of its wings long after it has gone. "That's because they carry the souls of the old ones," Grandmother says. After Grandmother dies, all the sad little girl can think about is that her arm doesn't feel the tickle anymore, and her grandmother's scent of cornmeal and roses is fading as well. It's not until the season for the Day of the Dead, the time to remember the old ones, that the girl discovers the truth of her beloved grandmother's words. A butterfly alights on the girl's arm, melting her sadness: "In my head, I heard Grandmother's songs. I remember how she smelled, like cornmeal and roses."

A Gift for Abuelita, by Nancy Luenn. Illustrated by Robert Chapman. Northland, 1998. (Grades 2–4)

When Rosita's grandmother passes away, the little girl is inconsolable. She and her grandmother had been very close, doing many things together like working in the garden and in the kitchen. To help the little girl cope with her grief, her grandfather tells her that grandmother's spirit will visit the family on the Day of the Dead, and on that day the child must have a gift for her beloved grandmother. The little girl thinks long and hard. What would make a perfect gift?

The Gold Coin, by Alma Flor Ada. Illustrated by Neil Waldman. Aladdin Books, 1994. (Grades 1–3)

Juan has been a thief for many, many years. So many, in fact, that he can't even remember what it's like to be anything else. When he tries to steal Dona Josefa's gold, something strange begins to happen to Juan. His skin becomes tan instead of pale, his body straight instead of bent, and his face has smiles instead of scowls. Juan also begins to remember things. He remembers good home-cooked food, being among friends, and laughing. When the opportunity arrives for him to take Dona Josefa's gold, a strange thing happens. Juan realizes he can't. Maybe he isn't a thief anymore.

Gonyo and the Princess: A Mexican Tale, by Verna Aardema. Dutton, 1991. (Grades 2–4)

Gonyo Gonzales lives in the palace of the king. When the king hears about a princess with golden hair, he sends Gonyo to find her. With the help of a fly, a dove, and a small fish, Gonyo finds the princess and takes her to the king. The princess is dismayed to find that the king is very old and insists that she will not marry him until he sends someone to fetch water from the Spring of Life. Again Gonyo sets out, and once again he is successful. Before trying the water himself, the king orders Gonyo to be put to death, then sprinkled with the water to see if it will bring him back to life. Gonyo dies, and the princess steps forth to sprinkle the water from a small pearl bottle. Will the water bring him back to life? If it does, will the princess have to keep her promise and marry the king?

The Miracle of the First Poinsettia: A Mexican Christmas Story, by Joanne Oppenheim. Barefoot Books, 2003. (Grades 1–3)

Originally native to Mexico, beautiful poinsettia plants decorate homes around the world every holiday season. But few people who love the plant s deep red tones know the traditional Mexican tale about how the poinsettia first came to be. Glowing scenes transport readers to Old-World Mexico and into the arms of a young girl as her trust leads her straight into a miracle.

Nana's Big Surprise, by Amada Perez. Children's Book Press, 2007. (Grades K–2)

Nana's visit from Mexico should be a joyous occasion. But this summer she's coming to California because Tata has died. Amada and her five brothers hope to cheer her up with a surprise gift of a coop full of fluffy yellow chicks, just like the ones Nana raised with Tata in Mexico. But no matter how hard everyone tries to make Nana feel better, it seems like nothing can bring a smile to her face. That is, until one day the chicks reveal a little surprise of their own.

***Pancho's Piñata*, Vol. 1,** by Timothy Rhodes. Illustrated by Stefan Czernecki. Hyperion, 1994. (Grades 1–3)

Years ago, at Christmastime in the village of San Miguel, young Pancho had rescued a talking falling star lodged atop the cactus in the town square. This deed has brought Pancho happiness for many years, and one Christmas he decides to share his joy—and some gifts—with the town's children. Thus the piZata, a decorated clay pot filled with toys and sweets, was born.

Pedro and the Padre: A Tale from Jalisco, Mexico, by Verna Aardema. Illustrated by Frisco Henstra. Dial, 1991. (Grades 1–3)

Indolent Pedro never hesitates to lie to avoid pain or punishment. His disgusted father has had enough of the boy when he again falls asleep during chores. The father sends Pedro out into the world to make his own way. A kindly padre takes the boy in, but not only does Pedro not repay the kindness by doing chores, he steals the padre's burro and sombrero and continues to swindle travelers with schemes involving a money tree and a magic bird. Eventually he does mend his ways and discovers it doesn't pay to be a thief.

The Rowdy, Rowdy Ranch, by Ethriam Brammer. Piñata Books, 2003. (Grades 1–3)

On El Rancho Grande, the grandchildren are not so interested in how Grandpa bought the ranch, but in what can be done on the ranch. The children play hide and seek in cornfields, under "the canopy of green leaves, golden threads and giant ears of corn." They feed the family horses, ride the rambunctious pigs, and take frolicking dips in the duck pond. But through all of the outdoor escapades, their family stories are circling in the air, like the "sunflower wind" blooming around them. While drinking ice-cold lemonade in the sunshine, they hear about how Grandpa's song of sorrow won him El Rancho. They hear about chickens that have abandoned their coops to live in Abuela's chicken tree, and they even discover a story about a boy who cried chocolate tears. In those days of running and jumping, the narrator, Tito, did not realize that he was hearing the stories that would wrap him up "like an enchanted sarape to keep me warm for the rest of [his] life."

The Twelve Days of Christmas: A Piñata for the Piñon Tree, by Philemon Sturges. Little, Brown, 2007. (Grades 1–3)

"On the first day of Christmas mis amigos brought to me: a piñata for the piñon tree." Spice up Christmas with a Southwestern spin! Celebrate the holidays with Philemon Sturges's lively adaptation of the classic Christmas carol, "The Twelve Days of Christmas." Instead of leaping lords and drummers drumming, our favorite friends from Readerville bring us cowgirls yodelin', poinsettias bloomin', and much more!

NAME GAME

Standards: 4, 9

After establishing a listening mood, say: "I know a child whose name is Pedro/Lupita (use names from stories recently shared). Will all the children whose names start with the same sound as the name Pedro please stand?" Have the children prove the similarity by saying Pedro/Paul or Lucy/Lupita.

Without saying the name, describe a character in a story recently shared. Give a physical description rather than telling what the character did. Have teams take turns guessing the character and give them five points for each correct guess.

MEXICAN ANIMAL RIDDLE

Following is a poem about an animal found in Mexico that contains three facts. Use this poem as a model. Find interesting information about another animal and include the facts you find in a riddle poem.

WHAT IS IT? A MEXICAN ANIMAL	WHAT IS IT? A _____ ANIMAL
This riddle poem, if you're a whiz, Will tell you what this creature is.	This riddle poem, if you're a whiz, Will tell you what this creature is.
How big is it do you suppose? 48inches from its tail to its nose.	How big is it do you suppose? _____ inches from its _____ to its nose.
Gray and black its color(s) will be These are the colors you can see.	_____ and _____ its color(s) will be These are the colors you can see.
When looking for a tasty treat small game are what it likes to eat	When looking for a tasty treat _____ are what it likes to eat
Now you've played a guessing game Can you guess this creature's name?	Now you've played a guessing game Can you guess this creature's name?
Coyote	

Nicaragua

Nicaragua covers almost 50,000 square miles and has a population of more than 5.5 million people. It is a land of valleys, mountains, and volcanoes. It was the home of Dario, a man known as the "prince of Spanish-American poetry." The capital is Managua.

Invisible Hunters, by Octavio Chow. Illustrated by Joe Sam. Children's Book Press, 1993. (Grades 3–5)

Late one Saturday afternoon, three brothers leave their village to hunt wari, the wild pig their people depend on for food. While hunting they discover a magical vine that can make them invisible—but they will only enjoy this power if they promise never to sell the meat they hunt, and never to hunt with guns, only with sticks. All is well until European traders arrive to buy the precious wari meat—and the brothers forget the promises of caring for the environment they made so long ago. They find that the very thing that gives you power can turn against you if not respected and used properly.

Mother Scorpion Country, by Dorminster Wilson. Illustrated by Virginia Stearn. Children's Book Press, 1987. (Grades 2–4)

From the folklore of the Miskito tribe in Central America comes the tale of a brave young Miskito Indian who follows his wife from the land of the living to the spirit world. Naklili cannot truly be a part of the spirit world known as Mother Scorpion country because he still belongs to the living. He finally accepts the fact that he must return to the living world, but promises to tell no one what he has experienced in Mother Scorpion Country. Because of his refusal to tell what he has seen, he loses all of his friends and has a lonely existence, until at last he dies and can rejoin his wife.

NICARAGUAN POEMS

Use the patterns to write a poem about Nicaragua. Find information about volcanoes. Report the information as an acrostic poem.

V _____

O _____

L _____

C _____

A _____

N _____

O _____

Adverb Poem

1	Adverb	Abruptly
2	Adverb	Majestically
3	Adverb	Proudly
4	Noun	Rugged mountains
5	Verb	Dissect
6	Noun with	the East from the West
7	Any words	in Nicaragua.

Phone Number Poem

Choose a phone number and put each number on a separate line. Then for each line, choose words that have the number of syllables in that line's number.

3	deep valleys
4	rugged mountains
5	awakened from sleep
5	by rumblings within
8	volcanoes catch the morning light
5	rivers of lava
5	set fire to the land

From *Reading the World with Picture Books* by Nancy J. Polette.
Santa Barbara, CA: Libraries Unlimited. Copyright © 2010.

Panama

Panama covers an area of 30,193 square miles and has a population of more than 3 million people. It is home to the Panama Canal, which links the Atlantic and Pacific Oceans. It is also home to mountain ranges and the rain forest, with abundant wildlife including the giant sea turtle, which lays its eggs on the beaches. The capital is Panama City.

A Christmas Surprise for Chabelita, by Argentina Palacios. Illustrated by Lori Lohstoeter. BridgeWater Books, 1996. (Grades K–2)

Chabelita is a little girl who lives with her grandparents in Panama. She misses her mother, who must earn money for the family by working in the city, so she memorizes her mother's favorite poem to recite at a Christmas program at her school. But she is also in for a wonderful Christmas surprise from her grandparents.

The Panama Canal, by Lesley A. DuTemple. Great Building Feats. Lerner Books, 2003. (Grades 3–5)

It took 40 years and cost nearly 25,000 lives, but on August 15, 1914, the Panama Canal was completed. For hundreds of years, adventurers, politicians, sailors, and soldiers had dreamed of shortening the long, harrowing journey from the Atlantic to the Pacific Ocean. Yet Panama's geography made that task nearly impossible. Understand the tireless spirit of those who succeeded in building this remarkable canal and those who died along the way.

Panama in Pictures, by Tom Streissguth. Lerner Books, 2003. (Grades 3–5)

Panama is the wealthiest nation in Central America. This is due mainly to the Panama Canal, which connects the Atlantic and Pacific Oceans and is a major trade and transportation route. A wide economic disparity between the rural and urban areas of the nation, political instability, and harsh dictators have made further economic advancement difficult.

PANAMA DATA BANK

Standards: 2, 4, 5, 15

THE PANAMA SEA TURTLE:

EATS	LIVES	HAS	DOES
sea grass	warm climate	bone armor	born on dry land
crabs	in the sea	hard shell	breathe air
shrimps	Pacific Ocean	flippers	lay eggs on sandy beaches
			glide with ease through the water
			live fifty years

Use information from the data bank in this pattern. Illustrate your pattern page.

Big sea turtles eat _____ and _____

_____ and _____

_____ and _____

Big sea turtles eat _____ and _____

And (name something they do) _____

Puerto Rico

The Island of Puerto Rico covers an area of 3,515 square miles and has a population of nearly 8 million people. It is one of the more prosperous of the Caribbean Islands because of its ties to the United States. It lies in a region hit by hurricanes from June through November. It is a self-governing island. The capital is San Juan.

A Doll for Navidades, by Esmeralda Sántiago. Illustrated by Enrique O. Sanchez. Scholastic, 2005. (Grades K–3)

Las Navidades are coming. In preparing for Christmas in Puerto Rico, the house smells of cinnamon and coconut, crepe paper festoons the yard, and best of all, the Three Magi will soon bring presents to all the children. Esmeralda hopes they will bring her a baby doll. But instead, she receives something far more precious: she experiences firsthand the magic of giving and the power of her family's love for her.

How the Sea Began: A Taino Myth, by George Crespo. Houghton Mifflin, 1993. (Grades 2–4)

The gourd containing the bow and arrow of the great departed hunter Yayael produces a torrent of water that becomes the world's ocean. When Yayael disappears during a hurricane, his parents place his powerful bow and arrow in a gourd hanging from the ceiling. One day the gourd fills with fish, enough for all the hungry villagers; but when some curious boys are asked to protect this magical food source, catastrophe occurs. They inadvertently break the gourd, and "in an instant everything in the hut was afloat." Torrents "flowed and rose to cover the land" and eventually "all kinds of sea creatures came out of the gourd to fill the water with life"—the villagers will never hunger again.

Mimi's Parranda, by Lydia M.Gill. Piñata Books, 2006. (Grades 2–4)

Like most young children, Mimi loves Christmastime, so much so that she doesn't even mind the bitter cold. But while her friends plan to ask for skates, sleds, coats, and boots for Christmas, Mimi wants a straw hat, new sandals, a polka-dot bathing suit, and maybe even a beach ball. She'll need toys and clothing for warm weather because she goes to Puerto Rico every Christmas, and she can't wait to go again this year! Mimi especially looks forward to her annual parranda, the Puerto Rican version of Christmas caroling. She loves it when everyone arrives late at night and wakes her up by playing their instruments—guiros, palitos, maracas, guitars, tambourines. And the food—she dreams about a table brimming with all her favorites: roasted pork, pasteles, and arroz con leche. But when she learns that her family won't be able to go to Puerto Rico this year, Mimi is crushed. She is so sad that she loses interest in her class's holiday party, and on the day of the party, she decides to stay home in bed. Just as Mimi is falling asleep, though, she hears the unmistakable sounds of musical instruments. Could it be that she'll get her parranda after all?

Paco and the Witch, by Felix Pitre. Illustrated by Christy Hale. Penguin/Dutton, 1995. (Grades 1–3)

At Paco's house, everyone is busy preparing for a fiesta. So when his mother realizes that she has one last thing to fetch from the store, Paco volunteers to make the long trip down through the woods to the village below. The woods are beautiful, but Paco is wary, for his grandmother has warned him of the evil witch who lives there. Paco knows he shouldn't stop, but he is so tired. Surely if he sat down just for a moment . . . ?

Vejigante-Masquerader, by Carmen Lomas Garza. Scholastic, 1993. (Grades 1–3)

In the town of Ponce on the island of Puerto Rico, a young boy dreams of taking part in the carnival festivities by becoming a vejigante, one who dresses up like a clown with a devil mask. He saves his money to buy material and manages to make his own costume. How excited and proud he is as he joins the other vejigantes becoming part of El Gallo's pranksterish vejigante band—and finally bravely tangling with a goat that tears his costume.

ISLAND ANALOGIES

Standards: 2, 4, 6

How many can you write?

Example: Coral is to island as claws are to bear. (Both protect themselves by ripping and tearing.)

What can you do with:

Sharks are to _____ as _____ are to _____ .

Palm trees are to _____ as _____ are to _____ .

Coconuts are to _____ as _____ are to _____ .

Wild birds are to _____ as _____ are to _____ .

Hurricanes are to _____ as _____ are to _____ .

Tide pools are to _____ as _____ are to _____ .

Saint Lucia

The Island of Saint Lucia covers 617 square miles and has a population of 14,300. It is a member of the British Commonwealth and is noted for its sulphur springs and beautiful tropical birds and orchids. The capital is Castries.

My Grandpa and the Sea, by Katherine Shelley Orr. Carolrhoda, 1990. (Grades 1–3)

A little girl, Lisa, tells about her Grandpa, who had never had a formal education but who was very wise. He understood messages from both the sea and sky as he sailed in his small boat, catching the fish that he would sell. Then larger and more efficient boats entered the waters off the shores of Saint Lucia. The large boats hauled in many ore fish, and soon there were no fish in the waters. Grandpa had to find another way to make a living. Using his knowledge of the sea, Grandpa solves his problem by starting a sea moss farm.

OCEAN RESEARCH QUESTIONS

Here are questions Lisa might have asked Grandpa. Choose one question to research. Share the answer with your class.

What makes waves curl as they reach the shore?

Why can't you see the wind?

Why are water and the sky blue?

Do flying fish really fly?

Do sharks really eat people?

Trinidad and Tobago

The Republic of Trinidad and Tobago covers an area of 1,980 square miles and has a population of slightly more than 1 million people. It is home to the Caroni Swamp, a wild bird sanctuary where white flamingoes and the scarlet ibis are found. The capital is Port-of-Spain.

Coconut Kind of Day, by Lynn Joseph. Illustrated by Sandra Speidel. HarperCollins, 1990. (Grades 1–3)

Experience the sights and sounds of Trinidad by going with a young girl as she hears the beat of the steel drums, goes to the colorful market with her mother, buys treats from the coconut man, helps the fishermen "pullin' seine," and sees the "rows of scarlet ibis/race across the sky/chasing the red ball sun/into the sea." The child's experiences are told in 13 verses, offering a fascinating look at another culture.

Fish for the Grand Lady, by Colin Bootman. Holiday House, 2006. (Grades 1–3)

In Trinidad, two brothers, Colly and Derrick, try fishing in a new place, hoping to bring home a big catch for their grandmother. They are determined to catch more than she can cook in one day. They buy new hooks, dig lots of worms, and head out before dawn for a new angling spot. After a morning spent losing bait to fish that slip away, Derrick throws the bucket of worms into the river. Suddenly their luck changes in a surprising way. Perhaps they can keep their promise to grandmother after all.

Jump Up Time: A Trinidad Carnival Story, by Lynn Joseph. Illustrated by Linda Saport. Clarion Books, 1998. (Grades 1–3)

Carnival time is coming, and for six months the family has been putting together the beautiful hummingbird costume to be worn by Lily's sister Christine. Christine is to join other children on stage "jump up," or parade across the stage, during the Children's Carnival. Lily is green with envy at all the attention her sister is getting. All goes well until the actual moment when Christine is to go on stage. She freezes, and it is only with Lily's help that she is able to do her part. As a way of saying thank-you, Christine lets Lily wear her hummingbird headdress.

A WALK AROUND TRINIDAD

Standards: 4, 14, 16

Suppose you took a walk around Trinidad and Tobago. Use this pattern to tell what you would see. Add more verses.

On the first day of spring,

What did I see but a _____

Looking at me.

On the second day of spring,

What did I see but a _____

Nodding at me.

United States

The United States covers an area of 3,317,972 square miles and has a population of more than 301 million people. It is the third largest country, and Alaska is the largest of its 50 states. The capital is Washington, D.C.

It has a wide variety of landforms, from deserts to mountains to prairies, and an abundance of wildlife. It is still considered a new country compared to the ancient civilizations that existed in Europe and Asia.

The books that best represent the culture of the United States are the tall tales. These are tales of heroes and heroines that demonstrate super powers at birth and the ability to move ahead alone and accomplish whatever goals they have set for themselves. This contrasts with the European philosophy reflected in European folktales, which show the young hero needing help and guidance from an older, wiser person until able to tackle the problems of the world.

American Tall Tales, by Mary Pope Osborne and Michael McCurdy. Scholastic, 2005. (Grades 2–4)

Meet America's first folk heroes in these nine wildly exaggerated and downright funny stories. Here are Paul Bunyan, John Henry, Sally Ann Thunder Whirlwind, and many other uniquely American characters, together in one superb collection.

The Bunyans, by Audrey Wood. Illustrated by David Shannon. Scholastic, 1996. (Grades 2–4)

You may know that Paul Bunyan was taller than a redwood tree and stronger than 50 grizzly bears—but you may NOT know that he also had a wife and two kids, a "jumbo boy" named Little Jean and a "gigantic girl" named Teeny, who helped him create some of the most striking natural wonders of North America! Here are the tall-tale beginnings of Niagara Falls, the Rocky Mountains, Old Faithful (Ma Bunyan creates Old Faithful by poking holes in Wyoming with her pickax to release hot water for the laundry and dishes), Bryce Canyon, and more. The Bunyans are a family you will never forget!

Clever Beatrice and the Best Little Pony, by Margaret Willey. Atheneum Books for Young Readers, 2004. (Grades 1–3)

Everyone knows that Beatrice of the north woods is clever. But did you know that she's also mighty brave? In this tale our heroine proves that she's a pint-sized force to be reckoned with when she discovers that someone has been sneaking into the barn at night to ride her beloved pony. But who? The village bread maker, who specializes in solving "things not easily explained," claims he can help Beatrice, given enough time. But Beatrice doesn't have time, so she starts thinking herself.

Davy Crockett Gets Hitched, by Bobbi Miller. Illustrated by Megan Lloyd. Holiday House, 2009. (Grades 1–3)

Davy Crockett shouldn't have any problem wooing a gal. But a shortcut through the woods puts a bodacious burr in his britches and leaves him acting more like a clown than the king of the wild frontier. At stake is the favor of Miss Sally Ann Thunder Whirlwind, a gal so special she can outdance any fool on two feet.. Davy must gather all his gumption to whirl his way into Miss Sally Ann's heart.

The Dinosaur Tamer, by Carol Greathouse. Dutton, 2008. (Grades 2–4)

Back when the old, old West was still as green as a bristlecone pine and cowboys were as common as warts on a stegosaurus, one cowboy stood out among all cowboys. With the strength of an iguanodon and the speed of a Utah raptor, lasso-tossing, pleiosaurus-riding Rocky is legendary. There isn't a dinosaur in the land that would think of giving Rocky a lick of trouble. That is, until he meets T. rex, the most rip-roarin', snip-snortin', flame-breathin' reptilian ever to stomp the earth. But Rocky is up to the challenge, and his efforts to tame T. rex take the disagreeing duo on a Western adventure of epic proportion.

The Ghosts of Luckless Gulch, by Anne Isaacs. Illustrated by Dan Santat. Atheneum Books for Young Readers, 2008. (Grades 2–4)

Meet Estrella. She can run so fast that she burns up the air, leaving trails of flames wherever she goes. Her pets, a Kickle Snifter, a Sidehill Wowser, and a Rubberado puppy, are as untamed as California, and the pride and love of Estrella's heart. When the greedy ghosts of old gold miners steal her pets, Estrella will need every bit of her pluck and nimble-footedness to rescue them. Here is a tale as unpredictable as the California Gold Rush, as tall as a redwood tree, and as surprising as a skunk selling perfume. Pull a chair up to the wood stove and get ready to laugh!

The Great Texas Hamster Drive, by Eric A. Kimmel. Illustrated by Bruce Whatley. Marshall Cavendish, 2007. (Grades 2–4)

When Pecos Bill's daughter gets two pet hamsters, they soon multiply into 18,376 hamsters, swarming over the prairie, nibbling down the grass, and spooking the longhorns, so Bill decides to take them all to Chicago, where lots of boys and girls want pet hamsters. Unfortunately, they'll first have to be rounded up and herded to the railyard in Abilene.

Jess and the Stinky Cowboys, by Janice Lee Smith. Dial Books for Young Readers, 2004. (Grades 1–3)

Dry Gulch becomes the smelliest town in the West when a posse of stinky cowboys arrive and refuse to take baths. Things get so bad, even the stinkbugs leave. No baths today! No baths tomorrow! No baths ever! roar the funky cowpokes. And pretty soon all of Dry Gulch is up in arms—while holding their noses! Luckily Deputy Jess and her aunt Gussie are determined to make the No Stink Law stick. With a clever plan, and a little soap, can they solve the P.U. problem?

John Henry, by Julius Lester. Illustrated by Jerry Pinkney. Puffin, 1999. (Grades 2–4)

The tale is told that John Henry was born with a hammer in his hand, when all the animals came to see him and the sun wouldn't go to bed. As a child he helped his father build a house in record time. But this tall tale hero is best known for his battle against the steam drill, as he raced the machine to cut through "a mountain as big as hurt feelings." He won the race but hammered so hard that his heart burst, and he died as he was born, with a hammer in his hand.

Kissimmee Pete, Cracker Cow Hunter, by Jan Day. Pelican Publishing, 2005. (Grades 1–3)

Just like cowboys out west, "cracker cow hunters"—so called because they used the crack of their whips to scare cows out of the brush—rounded up their cattle and drove them to market, encountering unpredictable situations along the way. Here, the tender-hearted, courageous, clever cracker cow hunter Kissimmee Pete, his horse Blaze, his dog Mud, and his green cow String Bean, sing, swim, push, and wrestle their way across grasses, prairies, and swamps, finally arriving safely at port with their herd.

Mike Fink, by Jeni Reeves. Illustrated by Stephen Krensky. Lerner, 2007. (Grades 2–4)

Mike Fink was the best keelboater on the river, and he was the first to admit it. He knew the river's tricks. He could ride a waterfall like a bucking bronco, and he even wrestled alligators. What would happen when he made a bet with Davy Crockett? Could he win the race with Powder Keg Pete? Hop on board this rollicking story of an American tall-tale hero.

Mississippi Jack: Being an Account of the Further Waterborne Adventures of Jacky Faber, Midshipman, Fine Lady, and Lily of the West, by Louis A. Meyer. Houghton Mifflin, 2007. (Grades 2–4)

The intrepid Jacky Faber, having once again eluded British authorities, heads west, hoping that no one will recognize her in the wilds of America. There she tricks the tall-tale hero Mike Fink out of his flatboat, equips it as a floating casino showboat, and heads south to New Orleans, battling murderous bandits, British soldiers, and other scoundrels along the way. Will Jacky's carelessness and impulsive actions ultimately cause her beloved Jaimy to be left in her wake?

Paul Bunyan and Other Tall Tales, by Jane Mason. Scholastic, 2002. (Grades 2–4)

Here is the tale of the giant of the great North Woods. No lumberjack had ever been bigger, taller, or stronger. As a lumberjck he felled trees for cities and towns and fed his co-workers using the biggest pancake griddle ever. Here is the tale of an American tall-tale hero that should be part of every child's reading.

Paul Bunyan's Sweetheart, by Marybeth Lorbiecki. Sleeping Bear Press, 2007. (Grades 2–4)

Paul Bunyan has a BIG problem. He's in love, but the lady who has caught his eye will have nothing to do with him. What's a giant lumberjack to do? When Paul Bunyan meets pretty Lucette, he knows she's the gal for him. After all, she's so tall she can't fit into an ordinary cabin. She can churn butter into a thick creamy river, and when she cleans house she can twirl up a tornado! Why, it's a match made in heaven! But to win Lucette's heart, Paul must prove his worth in a love test.

Pecos Bill: The Greatest Cowboy of All Time, by James Cloyd Bowman. Illustrated by Laura Bannon. New York Review of Books, 2007. (Grades 2–4)

Imagine a family traveling west in a covered wagon. In the back of the wagon are 18 children, making the space way too crowded. So what do 17 of the children do? They toss their four-year-old brother out the back of the wagon. Having so many children, ma and pa don't miss four-year-old Bill who, left alone in the desert, is raised by a pack of coyotes. For a long time Bill thinks he is a coyote, although it is strange he doesn't look like one. Finally he realizes he is a human being, but one with very unusual habits!

Railroad John and the Red Rock Run, by Tony Crunk. Peachtree, 2006. (Grades 2–4)

TODAY IS THE DAY Lonesome Bob is set to marry Wildcat Annie. The wedding ceremony begins at two o'clock in Red Rock, and Wildcat Annie waits for no one. "I've driven this train for 40 years, and we've never been late once yet!" Railroad John says proudly, as Lonesome Bob and Granny Apple Fritter board the train for Red Rock. But Bad Bill and his outlaw gang are waiting up around the bend, and a fierce thunderstorm kicks up. Now the

Sagebrush Flyer train and Lonesome Bob are 22 minutes behind schedule! Can Granny Apple Fritter's Hard-Shell Chili-Pepper-Corn-Pone Muffins help save the day?

Steamboat Annie and the Thousand-pound Catfish, by Katherine Wright. Philomel Books, 2001. (Grades 2–4)

A thousand-pound catfish? There's no such thing! Well, of course there is: His name's Ernie, and he's an ornery, stubborn, hot-tempered thousand-pound catfish at that. What's a town called Pleasant to do when this worthless whiskered rascal and his wormy sidekick are making it downright unpleasant? Call Steamboat Annie, that's what!

Swamp Angel, by Anne Isaacs. Illustrated by Paul O. Zelinsky. Dutton, 1994. (Grades 2–4)

When Angelica Longrider was born, she was scarcely taller than her mother and couldn't climb a tree without help. She was a full two years old before she built her first log cabin. But by the time she is fully grown, Swamp Angel, as she is known, can lasso a tornado and drink an entire lake dry. She single-handedly saves the settlers from the fearsome bear known as Thundering Tarnation, wrestling him from the top of the Great Smoky Mountains to the bottom of a deep lake. The fight lasts five days. When both Swamp Angel and the bear are too tired to fight, they go to sleep, and Swamp Angel's snores are so loud that she snores down a huge tree, which lands on the bear and kills it. Swamp angel pays tribute to her foe and then has enough bear meat to feed everyone in Tennessee.

TALL-TALE SONGS

Standards: 9, 10, 12

Many popular songs and tales were a part of the wilderness years. One song that the settlers especially liked was about Old Dan Tucker, who "combed his hair with a wagon wheel."

How could Dan Tucker have a toothache in his heel?

Answer: If a bear bit him on his heel he would have a toothache in his heel.

Read the words to the following "tall-tale" song. Choose one or more lines from the song and explain how it could be true.

Traveling Around the World by Nancy Polette

Once I had a little cat , its color it was taffy
That little cat could sing and dance
and tell jokes that were daffy
She flew to London, Greece and Spain
Despite the snow and wind and rain.
Once I had a little fish, its was bright silver and gold
It swam the world in a single day
Ignored the fishermen bold
One day it flew up in the sky
Waved at me and said goodbye.

Example: A fish might swim the world in a day in a fairy tale.

Write the statement you choose here. Tell how it could be true.

_____

_____

_____

_____

_____

_____

From *Reading the World with Picture Books* by Nancy J. Polette.
Santa Barbara, CA: Libraries Unlimited. Copyright © 2010.

CREATIVE THINKING WITH TALL TALES

Try some of your own exaggerations!

Old Stormalong was so tall that _____

The thunder was so loud that _____

The shark was so angry that _____

The whale was so big that _____

Paul Bunyan

Paul Bunyan is said to have cleared all the cottonwoods out of Kansas and oaks out of Iowa. To get water for his logging camp, he dug ponds, which are today called The Great Lakes. He is probably credited with more inventions than any other tall-tale hero.

Be an inventor! Use five of the items below, with each item acting on the next to create a burglar-proof safe.

sack of potatoes	cat
pigeon	long rope
matches	umbrella
balloon	wooden box
cuckoo clock	tea kettle
50 lb. weight	horn
cannon	candle

Share your tall-tale invention with the class.

Pecos Bill

Pecos Bill was quite a problem solver. When the prairie was parched, he lassoed a cyclone and brought rain to the land; when the cowboys were bored, he composed a number of cowboy songs. Help him to solve this problem!

A varmint got into the mess wagon and stole all the food. Bill and 100 cowboys are one month away from civilization. What will he do? List and rank order three possible solutions.

1. _____

2. _____

3. _____

Virgin Islands (U.S.)

The U.S. Virgin Islands cover 133 square miles and have a population of about 120,000. The islands attract many tourists because of their beautiful beaches, but fresh water is scarce. Sailfish, marlin, tarpon, kingfish, and wahoo are plentiful in the offshore waters. The capital of the U.S. Virgin Islands is Charlotte-Amalie on the Island of St. Thomas.

Rata-pata-scata-fata: A Caribbean Story, by Phillis Gershator. Star Bright Books, 2005. (Grades K–2)

Suppose you could say magic words, and all of your work would be done without you lifting a finger. When Junjun says the words, "rata-pata-scata-fata," he finds that wonderful things begin to happen. He doesn't have to go to market or do any of his chores. Even the rain barrel is filled during a storm. Is this magic or coincidence?

ISLAND FISH

Standards: 2, 4, 6, 9, 11

Choose an island fish to write about.

    sailfish   marlin   tarpon   kingfish   wahoo

Find out:

        Color _____

        Covered with _____

        Lives _____

        Eats _____

        How it moves _____

        Enemies _____

        Sounds it makes _____

Writing pattern:

In offshore waters the _____ hover
                                       (name a fish)

Showing their beautiful_____ cover
                                   (color or colors)

Keeping little ones by its side.

When it sees (a/an) _____ it goes to hide
                        (name of an enemy)

Searching for a tasty treat

_____ and _____ they catch and eat.
           (food)   (food)

As it swims around and around

The _____ makes a _____ sound
       (name of the fish)   (type of sound)

From *Reading the World with Picture Books* by Nancy J. Polette.
Santa Barbara, CA: Libraries Unlimited. Copyright © 2010.

Part Five

South America

Facts about South America

- South America is 6,880,636 square miles.

- There are more than 229 million people living in South America.

- The lowest point in South America is 131 feet below sea level, on the Valdez Peninsula in Argentina.

- The largest country in South America is Brazil. Brazil is almost half the size of South America.

- The longest river in South America is the Amazon River, 4,000 feet long. The Amazon is the second longest river in the world.

- The largest lake in South America is the Maracaibo Lake in Venezuela. It is 5,217 square miles.

- The highest waterfall is Angel Falls in Venezuela. It's 3,212 feet high.

COUNTRIES OF SOUTH AMERICA

Booktalks have been provided for the countries in boldface.

Argentina	Guyana
Bolivia	**Paraguay**
Brazil	**Peru**
Chile	Suriname
Colombia	**Uruguay**
Ecuador	**Venezuela**
French	Guiana

1. Play the X Game (see page 5) using the countries of South America.

2. Create a word search that includes all of the countries of South America.

Argentina

In Argentina, 40 million people live on slightly more than 1 million square miles, more area than Mexico and Texas combined. The official language is Spanish, although English, Italian, German, and French are also spoken there. It is a land of the pampas (wide open plains), with gauchos (cowboys) who herd cattle, Argentina's most valuable export. The capital is Buenos Aires.

Diego's Wolf Pup Rescue, by Christine Ricci. Simon & Schuster, 2006. (Grades K–2)

Introducing Diego! He loves nature, especially animals! When a wolf pup gets into danger, Diego swings into action. With help from his friends and his cousin Dora, Diego finds the lost pup. But can Diego rescue him? Go, Diego, go! This book contains a page of fascinating facts about maned-wolf pups.

The Magic Bean Tree, by Nancy Van Laan. Illustrated by Beatriz Vidal. Houghton Mifflin, 1998. (Grades 1–3)

There came a time on the pampas when water was so scarce that all wildlife was threatened. In the middle of the wide Argentine pampas, there once grew a magic tree. Above this tree slept a bird so evil it could stop the rain from falling. And not far from this tree lived a brave boy, who one day set out to save his village, the llamas, and all the creatures of the pampas from dying of thirst. He felt the hot wind and saw armadillos hiding from the sun and rheas with wing-covered heads. He walked a long way to discover the secret that would rid the pampas of the great bird of the underworld, and with the help of all of the animals, he succeeded.

FREE VERSE PATTERN

Standards: 2, 6, 11, 12

The free verse pattern can be framed in the shape of Argentina. The following example shows how the traditional "book report" can be made into poetry. Fill in the blanks with your own story about Diego.

This is Diego.

This is where

_____

_____

This is where

_____

_____

And you can hear

_____

_____

And you can see

_____

_____

And you can feel

_____

_____

And this is why _____ smile(s).

Bolivia

Bolivia covers an area of 424,000 square miles and is home to about 9 million people. The language spoken is Spanish. It is about five times the size of the United States. People in the highlands raise llamas for their meat, wool, leather, and fuel. The capital of Bolivia is La Paz.

The Children of Bolivia, by Jules Hermes. Carolrhoda, 1995. (Grades 3–5)

This book illustrates children living in various regions of Bolivia. The information is easy to understand, and maps are helpful in locating the children's homes. Information is given about the children's lives and how their parents earn a living as well as the homes in which they live and their daily activities,

Miro in the Kingdom of the Sun, by Jane Kurtz. Illustrated by David Frampton. Houghton Mifflin, 1996. (Grades 2–4)

This is an Inca version of a tale that is told in many different cultures, often called "The Water of Life." A young Inca girl succeeds where her brothers and others have failed, when her bird friends help her find the special water that will cure the king's son. Miro can talk with the birds and run as swiftly as her brothers. To heal an ailing prince, Miro's brothers, like so many men in the kingdom, attempt to fetch water from a lake but fail, and they are cast into a dungeon. With the help of her bird friends, Miro finds the lake, and when she is tested there by huge monsters that rush at her, she stands her ground each time.

Waira's First Journey, by Eusebio Topooco. Lothrop, 1987. (Grades 1–3)

How exciting it is to go to market, especially when market visits are rare, for the market is so far away. A little Indian girl and her parents make the very long journey from their home in the mountains of Bolivia to the market in Topojo; along the way the girl sees many new sights and learns more about her country.

ATTRIBUTE REPORT

Standards: 13, 14, 15, 16

Fill in the blanks in the pattern to describe another Bolivian animal.

Example:

> I am rattlesnake, hear me
>
> Swish through the sand
>
> Lift my tail
>
> Shake my rattles
>
> I am rattlesnake, see my
>
> Yellow cover, diamond blotches, seven foot length, horny rattles
>
> I am rattlesnake, watch me
>
> Sun myself, uncoil my body, shake my rattles, strike a rodent with my sharp fangs
>
> I am rattlesnake, hear me, see me, watch me, but watch out! I may be watching you!

I am _____, hear me

_____

_____

_____

I am _____, see my

_____

I am _____, watch me

_____

I am _____, hear me, see me, watch me, but watch out! I may be watching you!

From *Reading the World with Picture Books* by Nancy J. Polette.
Santa Barbara, CA: Libraries Unlimited. Copyright © 2010.

Brazil

In Brazil 190 million people make their homes on 3,287,000 square miles of land. It is the largest country in South America and the fifth largest country in the world. It is the home of the Amazon rain forest. The language spoken is Portuguese. The Amazon River is home to 1,500 different kinds of fish. The capital of Brazil is Brasília.

The Brave Little Parrot, by Rafe Martin. Putnam, 1998. (Grades K–2)

In this retelling of a traditional Jataka tale from India, when a raging fire threatens to burn down the forest, all of the animals run away in fear. All except for one brave little parrot, who has an idea. "Help me," she cries to the elephants, beseeching them to fill their trunks with water to spray on the flames. "Help me," she begs the cheetahs, even as they urge her to flee and save herself. But the brave little parrot will not be daunted. Can the determination and courage of one small bird be enough to save a forest?

The Dancing Turtle, by Pleasant DeSpain. Illustrated by David Boston. August House, 2001. (Grades K–2)

Turtle loves to dance and play the flute. But her exuberance puts her at risk when her music attracts the attention of a hunter, who brings her home for turtle stew. After she is caught, her only hope for escape is the hunter's children . . . and her own wit. This folktale, first told by the indigenous people of Brazil, is now told throughout Latin America. The versions are as different as the cultures that contain them, but all celebrate Turtle, who carries the world and its wisdom on her back. Like the people of Latin America, Turtle always seems to survive through courage and wit. In watercolors radiant with foliage and wildlife, David Boston guides the reader through the dense and fertile Amazon rain forest.

The Great Kapok Tree, by Lynne Cherry. Harcourt, Brace, Jovanovich, 1990. (Grades 2–4)

In the Amazon rain forest there are many kapok trees. Farmers want to cut the trees down to make room for fields. Other men want the trees for many other uses. In this story a young man falls asleep under a kapok tree after a hard day's work. As he sleeps he dreams that the animals of the rain forest speak to him of the dangers of destroying the rain forest. All of their homes and food supplies will disappear as well as a great source of oxygen for the world. When the young man wakes up, one can only wish that he will heed the warning.

How Night Came from the Sea: A Story from Brazil, by Mary-Joan Gerson. Joy Street Books, 2005. (Grades 1–3)

This tale could be compared with many of the selkie tales of Scotland, in which a creature from the sea assumes human form but longs for the sea. Here a young woman whose mother is the African goddess of the night falls in love with a human, marries, and for the first time lives in the daylight. She misses the night and knows she can only retrieve things from the night from her mother. Servants are sent out to find the goddess of the night, who gives them a gift to take back to her daughter, warning them not to open it. Imagine what happens when the servants do open the gift!

Lost in the Amazon: A Miss Mallard Mystery, by Robert Quackenbush. Pippen Books, 1999. (Grades 2–4)

Here is another delightful Miss Mallard story in which, as always, she solves the mystery and wins the day. The mystery this time centers around the theft of a wonderful liquid developed by her good friend, Dr. Eiderstein. The purpose of the liquid is to preserve the rain forest in its pristine form. The thieves come in disguise, and Miss Mallard must track them down and retrieve the liquid, thus helping to save the rain forests.

Rosa Raposa, by Isabel F. Campoy. Harcourt, 2002. (Grades 2–4)

Here are three tales that have as their setting the rain forest of Brazil. The main character in each tale is a fox named Rosa Raposa. Foxes are small and can make a tasty meal for the fierce jaguar that roams the rain forest in search of food. Each of these tales is based on the old adage, " sly as a fox." for Rosa Raposa is indeed sly, as she outwits the jaguar in three different ways, causing the jaguar to find its dinner elsewhere.

So Say the Little Monkeys, by Nancy Van Laan. Illustrated by Yumi Heo. Atheneum Books for Young Readers, 1998. (Grades 1–3)

A troop of monkeys called Blackmouths live in trees with thorny branches near the Rio Negro in Brazil. Not only are the branches uncomfortable resting places at night, the trees offer little protection from the rains. The monkeys decide to build more comfortable homes when daylight comes but are distracted by singing, jumping, sliding, and eating bananas, and the new homes are forgotten.

Welcome Brown Bird, by Mary Lyn Ray. Harcourt, 2004. (Grades 2–4)

While a boy in North America urges his father not to cut down the trees where the wood thrush lives, a boy in South America awaits the return of the bird that he calls "la flauta" for its flutelike song.

RAIN FOREST CREATURES

Standards: 2, 4, 9, 10, 11

Write about the creatures of the Brazilian rain forest using the following pattern.

One minute after midnight jaguar _____

_____

_____

_____

One minute after midnight crocodile _____

_____

_____

_____

One minute after midnight macaw _____

_____

_____

_____

One minute after midnight anaconda _____

_____

_____

_____

One minute after midnight I sleep while night things are awake.

Chile

Chile covers an area of 292,258 square miles and has a population of about 16 million people. The language spoken is Spanish. Most of Chile is mountains, but the Atacama desert is known as the driest place on Earth. Chile has a small variety of animal life. Llamas are raised in the mountains, and chinchillas and other rodents are found in less mountainous areas. The capital of Chile is Santiago.

A Hen, a Chick, and a String Guitar, retold by Margaret Read MacDonald. Illustrated by Sophie Fatus. Barefoot Books, 2005. (Grades K–2)

A cumulative tale from Chile that begins with a hen and ends with 16 different animals and a guitar. A young boy is given animals by different members of his family: Grandpa gives him a clucking red hen. As each animal has offspring, the child's collection of pets grows: the dog gives him a puppy, the cat a kitten, the duck a duckling, etc.

Mariana and the Merchild, by Caroline Pitcher. Illustrated by Jackie Morris. Eerdman's, 2007. (Grades 1–3)

Old Mariana longs for friendship, but she is feared by the village children and fearful of the hungry sea wolves that hide in the sea caves near her hut. When one day Mariana finds a Merchild inside a crab shell, her whole life changes, but she knows that one day, when the sea is calm again, the Merchild's mother will come to take her daughter back. Yet she cherishes the time she will have raising the child until it is time to return her to the sea.

My Name Is Gabriela: The Life of Gabriela Mistral, by Monica Brown. Illustrated by John Parra. Luna Rising, 2005. (Grades 4–6)

This is a picture book biography of the famous South American poet Gabriela Mistral, who was born in 1889. From the time she was a very little girl in Chile, she had a talent for putting words together. She became a teacher at the age of 15 and later became a college professor, She had a marvelous way of making up words and creating beautiful word images, and she won many prizes in Chile for her poetry. In 1945 she won the Nobel Prize for Literature, the first South American woman to do so.

CHILEAN GAMES

Standards: 3, 17

Visit the library to find books about games children around the world play. Teach the class a game that children of Chile play.

Here are some books you might look for:

- *Play with Us: 100 Games from Around the World,* by Oriol Ripoll. Chicago Review Press, 2005. Paperback.

- *Sidewalk Games Around the World,* by Arlene Erlbach. Millbrook Press, 1998.

- *Games Around the World.* Teacher Created Materials, 2008.

- *Kids Around the World Play!: The Best Fun and Games from Many Lands,* by Arlette N. Braman. Wiley, 2002.

Colombia

Colombia covers almost 500,000 square miles and has a population of 44 million people. The language spoken is Spanish. Coffee is its major crop, and the capital is Bogotá.

The Legend of El Dorado: A Latin American Tale from Colombia, by Nancy VanLaan. Knopf, 1997. (Grades 2–4)

There once was a king whose wife and daughter were lured beneath a lake by a wicked serpent. The serpent had promised that the family would be reunited some day, but year after year passed, and each year the king covered himself with gold dust and was taken to the middle of the lake. He threw in treasures and then jumped in himself, hoping the gold dust from his body would be enough to free his wife and daughter.

One year he doesn't reappear—the serpent has kept its promise; the family is reunited under the waters of the lake. The conquistadors, as American schoolchildren have long been taught, sought vainly for El Dorado; here is the legend that inspired their dreams, based on the 1541 account of an Indian in Colombia.

Mia's Story: A Sketchbook of Hopes and Dreams, by Michael Foreman. Candlewick Press, 2006. (Grades 1–3)

Mia lives with her family in a small South American village below the snowy mountains. Their house is put together from the dumped rubbish of the city; it is not much of a place. One day Mia's father brings her a puppy, which she calls Poco because he's so small. When Poco runs away, Mia travels far up into the mountains to search for him. There she finds some white mountain flowers growing under the stars, as well as something much more powerful: hope.

WHAT YOU CAN DO WITH A PUPPY

Standards: 12, 15

Think of some things you could do with a puppy.

You could _____

And you could _____

It would be fun to _____

And _____

THE RAIN FOREST

Standards: 1, 6

Pre-Reading Activity: Give a Good Guess!

Put a check mark beside any animal that you believe lives in the tropical rain forest. Listen to the booktalk to support or deny your guesses.

_____ sloth	_____ lizard	_____ heron
_____ jaguar	_____ coral snake	_____ bat
_____ monkey	_____ butterfly	_____ hummingbird1
_____ wild pig	_____ panther	_____ ocelot

Welcome to the Greenhouse, by Jane Yolen. Illustrated by Laura Regan. Putnam's, 1993. (Grades 1–3)

    Here is the mysterious world of the tropical rain forest, a house where giant forest trees form the walls, vines frame the views, and there is no roof overhead, only a canopy of leaves. Everywhere color threads through the hot greenhouse. By day you can hear exotic noises, the rustling of the green-coated sloth, or the chatter of monkeys as they make their way from room to room. A flash of the hummingbird or the silver streak of a lizard catch the eye, and the ear picks up the crunch of the wild pig as it bites into tropical fruit. Listen carefully for the wings of the heron flapping to take off in flight, the swoop of the bat as it glides by the sleeping ocelot, and the prowling panther searching for its dinner. Welcome to the greenhouse.

A Writing Activity

Pretend you have stepped into the rain forest. Complete the following lines about your experience.

Into the tropical rain forest

Over _____

Under _____

Above _____

Between _____

Lives a _____

Ecuador

Ecuador covers 109,483 square miles and is home to 13,755 million people. The language spoken is Spanish. The equator runs through it, which is how it got its name. The capital is Quito.

The Shepherd Boy, by Darick Allan. Portal Press, 2003. (Grades 2–4)

In Quito, Ecuador, Tommy, a boy from the United States, strikes out at a shepherd boy for hobbling his sheep. Tommy believes this practice is cruel to the animals. Both boys are affected by the act and have much to learn. Not a picture book, but an excellent read-aloud!

FIVE Ws POEM

Standards: 2, 6, 15

A good reporter always asks Who? What? When? Where? and Why? This poetry form can be instrumental in developing an understanding of the details of a story. Children may read other tales and write a Five Ws Poem about a character in the story.

The pattern:

        Line 1 Who is the poem about?

        Line 2 What are they doing?

        Line 3 When does it take place?

        Line 4 Where does it take place?

        Line 5 Why does it happen?

Who _____

What _____

When _____

Where _____

Why _____

WALKING THAT WAY

Standards: 2, 6, 9, 12

As you "walked" through the pages of the stories set in Ecuador, you saw many new things through the eyes of the author and illustrator. Sing this song to the tune of "Skip to My Lou."

I saw
Spotted jaguars prowling down below
Golden butterflies flying up above
Monkeys and Macaws chattering in the trees
All on a Monday morning.

Write a verse for each day of the week. What would you see? Use the library to research the wildlife of Ecuador's tropical rain forest. Include different animals in each verse. Use this pattern to write more verses.

I see

| (adjective) | (noun) | ("ing word") | (prepositional phrase) |

| (adjective) | (noun) | ("ing word") | (prepositional phrase) |

| (adjective) | (noun) | ("ing word") | (prepositional phrase) |

All on a _____ morning/evening.

From *Reading the World with Picture Books* by Nancy J. Polette.
Santa Barbara, CA: Libraries Unlimited. Copyright © 2010.

Paraguay

Paraguay covers an area of 157,000 square miles and has a population of 6.5 million people. The official language is Spanish. Most workers are found in either agriculture or forestry. The capital is Asunción.

Paraguay: South America Today, by Roger E. Hernandez. Mason Crest, 2005. (Grades 4–6)

A landlocked nation surrounded by its South American neighbors, the Republic of Paraguay has been isolated throughout much of its history. After achieving independence from Spain in 1811, the country suffered under decades of dictatorships and political strife before achieving democracy toward the end of the 20th century. Most of its approximately 7 million citizens are part Guarani Indian and part Spanish and speak both languages. The southward-flowing Paraguay River divides the land in half, with most Paraguayans living in the rolling hills and fertile lands to the east. One of the least industrialized South American nations, Paraguay exports soybeans and cotton, as well as hydroelectric power. Each lavishly illustrated book in the <u>South America Today</u> series teaches about the geography, history, economy, and culture of each nation. Each volume is indexed and contains a bibliography featuring books and Web sources for further information

ACROSTIC SECRET MESSAGE

Standards: 2, 6, 9, 12

A secret message can be found in an acrostic poem. The first letter of each line spells out a word or message going down. The poem can be written like a telegram, with you as the secret sender. Create a secret message that tells about the changes of the forest.

Y   esterday,

O   ld tree branches

U   nfolded the plan.

T   earing up the earth as they fell.

R   ough ends pierced the ground below.

Y   et,

O   ver and over,

N   ew branches appear.

E   ven they, too, know spring is near

Peru

Peru has mountains, deserts, and forests spread over 496,223 square miles. The population is about 28.5 million people. The first immigrants came to Peru more than 13,000 years ago. The Spanish conquered the Inca population in the 1500s, and Spanish is the language spoken today. Major crops are sugar cane and cotton, and Peru has a very large fishing industry. The capital is Lima.

Chancay and the Secret of Fire: A Peruvian Folktale, by Donald Charles. G. P. Putnam's Sons, 2005. (Grades 1–3)

By sparing the life of the water spirit Tambo, Chancay has proved himself kind and worthy. But to win the secret of fire for his people, he must also prove himself strong and brave—braver than anyone has been before.

Over the course of three days, Chancay faces lightning bolts, poisonous spiders, angry panthers, a molten volcano, a terrible condor, and finally the wrath of the moon and the sun. As Chancay reaches the golden temple where the sun and moon live, he knows he must have a clever plan to take the secret of fire home with him, because if he fails, the sun will turn him into a shower of sparks and he will be a star forever. What do you suppose Chancay decides to do?

Isabella's Bed, by Alison Lester. Houghton Mifflin, 1993. (Grades 1–3)

When they visit Grandmother, the children sleep in "Isabella's" handsome bed and explore the trunk of South American treasures at its foot. Grandmother never joins in—"Too many memories," she says—and when her granddaughter asks about the sad song she sings, she tells how Isabella left the Andes after her beloved husband drowned. That night, the children dream of a voyage to the mountain scenes in the pictures on their wall. In the morning, their realization that Isabella and Grandmother are one helps the old woman finally come to terms with her grief and tell them more about her past.

Llama and the Great Flood: A Folktale from Peru, by Ellen Alexander. Crowell, 1989. (Grades 1–3)

A farmer's llama dreams that after a huge flood the world will no longer exist, and he warns his master. The family goes to the top of Mt. Willka Qutu and joins all the animals of the world. After five days of flooding they all descend again to begin building a new life.

Moon Rope: A Peruvian Folktale, by Lois Ehlert. Harcourt Brace Jovanovich, 1992. (Grades 1–3)

Fox persuades Mole to climb with him on a grass rope he has braided and—with the birds' help—hitched to the moon. Fox trains his sight upward and is not seen again except by the birds, who claim they can spy him in the moon still. Mole, nervously looking downward, falls; the birds carry him back to Earth amid the jeers of the other animals, and to this day he prefers his solitary tunnel.

The Stolen Smell, by Mitch Weiss and Martha Hamilton. Illustrated by Tom Wrenn. August House, 2001. (Grades 1–3)

In this story from Peru, we meet a baker who is so stingy that he wants to charge people just for smelling his baked goods. When the baker takes his case to court, the wise judge decides to teach the greedy man a well-deserved lesson

Tonight Is Carnival, by Arthur Dorros. Illustrated by Virgen del Carmen. Dutton, 1991. (Grades 1–3)

A young boy is excited as, for the first time, he gets to join the Carnival band. The boy describes the everyday work that must be finished as he anticipates the festivities and practices the music he will play with his band. The book packs in a lot of detail and would be a useful introduction to the culture.

QUESTION STARTERS

Standards: 1, 4, 8, 16, 20

Choose one story from Peru and write five questions to discuss with friends using these beginnings:

How many ways _____?

What if _____?

If you were _____?

Suppose that _____?

How is _____ like _____?

Uruguay

This is one of the smaller South American countries, covering 8,000 square miles. It has a population of 3.5 million people. It has more farm land than Japan, with far fewer people. Sheep and cattle raising are the chief sources of income. The capital is Montevideo.

Uruguay, by Charles Shields. Mason Crest, 2009. (Grades 2–4)

With its mild climate and vast pasture lands, Uruguay has sustained a strong agricultural economy based mostly on raising sheep and cattle. Family farms and large plantations occupy much of the green rolling plains of this small country, sandwiched between Brazil and Argentina along South America's southeastern coast. Leading manufacturing industries process and export beef, hides, and wool. Most of Uruguay's approximately 3.5 million citizens live in urban areas that have risen on the country's narrow coastal plains, to the west along the Uruguay River, in the south bordering the Rio de la Plata, and in the east along the Atlantic seaboard. Despite social and political unrest toward the end of the twentieth century, Uruguay maintains a high standard of living for its large middle class

CINDERELLA FROM URUGUAY

Standards: 1, 4, 7, 12, 15

Create a Cinderella tale from Uruguay, using these questions.

1. What would be a typical girl's name?

2. In what kind of building would she live? Made of what?

3. What jobs would she have to do?

4. What is an annual celebration the people of Uruguay might attend?

5. Who will help the girl?

6. What will her clothing look like?

7. What male person will she meet?

8. What will she lose?

9. How will she be found?

Venezuela

Venezuela is one of the more prosperous countries of South America, as it exports oil to many countries in the world. It covers 352,143 square miles and has a population of about 26 million. The official language is Spanish, and the literacy rate is 93 percent. The capital is Caracas.

Amazon Diary: Property of Alex Winters, by Hudson Talbot and Mark Greenberg. Photographs by Mark Greenberg. Illustrations by Hudson Talbot. Putnam, 1996. (Grades 4–6)

Told in the pages of a journal, following a plane crash, a young boy describes his adventures on a trip through the Amazon. He lives with a wild tribe, learns to hunt alligator and eat roasted grubs, and battle fire ants and lice. The diary reveals the daily life of those who dwell in the rain forest.

Angel Falls: A South American Journey, by Martin Jordan and Tanis Jordan. Kingfisher, 1995. (Grades 4–6)

The authors travel down the Cacao on their way to view the highest waterfall in the worlds, Angel Falls, 3,200 feet high. On the way they describe the plants and animals of the jungle. Oil paintings show many of the creatures being described, among them morpho butterflies, pygmy kingfishers, azteca ants, and cock-of-the-rock birds,

Great Big Guinea Pigs, by Susan Roth. Bloomsbury Children's Books, 2006. (Grades 1–3)

Did you know that once upon a time, about 8 million years ago, guinea pigs weren't sweet, cute, or little? We all know about the enormous dinosaurs that used to roam the earth, but millions of years ago, there were GREAT BIG GUINEA PIGS, too! During a bedtime story, one little guinea pig learns all about his very big ancestors and how guinea pigs evolved into the lovable pets we have today.

How Iwariwa the Cayman Learned to Share, retold and illustrated by George Crespo. Clarion Books, 1995. (Grades 2–4)

When Kanaporiwa the bird discovers that Iwariwa the cayman secretly possesses fire, the other rain forest animals develop a plan to steal the fire, so that all the creatures can benefit from it.

Jaguar, by Helen Cowcher. Scholastic, 1997. (Grades 1–3)

The story begins with a jaguar looking out over a lagoon, then shifts to a herder hunting the jaguar to protect his cattle. The scene moves back and forth several times, from hunter to hunted, with observations of other animals along the way, until finally the man sees the cat and raises his rifle. Suddenly engulfed by a vision of the jaguar as "an ancestral guardian protecting his own," the man drops his rifle, sinks to his knees, and vows to find another way of safeguarding his herd.

JAGUAR CHANT

Create a jaguar chant. Add an adjective.	Tell where a jaguar might be found:
_____ jaguars	in a _____
_____ jaguars	under a _____
_____ jaguars	between _____
_____ jaguars	over _____
_____ jaguars	beside _____
_____ jaguars	at a _____ , too
Big cats through and through	Here they are,
	From near and far,
	Facts about jaguars!

Part Six

Antarctica

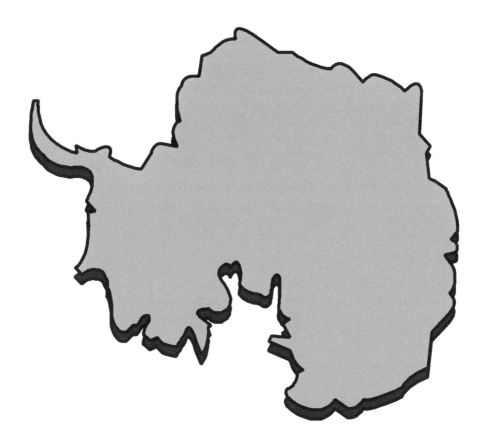

Facts about Antarctica

1. The continent was discovered in 1820 by hunters looking for fur seals.

2. It is fifth in size of the seven continents.

3. It is wholly covered by a vast ice sheet.

4. The average thickness of the ice sheet is 6,500 feet.

5. The name means "opposite of the Arctic."

6. It covers 5.5 million square miles.

7. It is located 600 miles south of the tip of South America.

8. The east and west portions are separated by 1,900-mile-long mountains.

9. There are 800 different species of plants that have adapted to survive on this continent.

10. The Emperor penguins make the Antarctic their home.

11. Forty-five other species of birds are found on islands near the continent.

12. Twelve nations have established bases to study Antarctica.

Penguin and Little Blue, by Megan McDonald. Illustrated by Katherine Tillotson. Atheneum Books for Young Readers, 2003. (Grades K–2)

Penguin and his pint-sized partner Little Blue want to escape their promotional tour for Water World and return to Antarctica to huddle with their penguin buddies. This is easier said than done. They try to re-create their Antarctic world wherever they are, with little success. They enjoy one another's company, but Penguin misses his many friends, with whom he longs to dive, huddle, and chatter. Finally they book passage on a cruise ship heading for home and have a joyful reunion with the friends they had left behind.

Something to Tell the Grandcows, by Eileen Spinelli. Illustrated by Bill Slavin. Eerdmans Books for Young Readers, 2004. (Grades 1–3)

Emmadine Cow wants a wonderful tale of adventure in which she is the star, to tell her grandcows. It is then she hears that Admiral Richard E. Byrd is looking for a few good cows for an expedition. Emmadine volunteers, and away she goes with other cows, dogs, and explorers on a trip to the South Pole in October 1933. The ocean voyage is unpleasant, to say the least, as Emmadine is prone to seasickness. When they reach the South Pole shores, the weather is the coldest man or beast has ever known. She bravely faces the cold, sees seals and penguins, teaches the other cows and the herdsman to dance, and stores away her fantastic experiences to share with her offspring when she returns home.

Some Folk Think the South Pole's Hot: The Three Tenors Play the Antarctic, by Elbe Heinrich. Translated by Audrey M. Woman. Illustrated by Quint Buchholz. David R Godiva, 2001. (Grades 1–3)

What's a penguin to do living at the South Pole, all dressed up and with no place to go? What good is that natty tuxedo if there's no occasion to wear it? Well, these are no dumb penguins. They invite, for their amusement, the Opera Ship from Old Vienna, and who are its illustrious passengers? Well (you guessed it), none other than the three tenors, performing that south Pole favorite to boot, *La Traviata,* starring José Carreras as Alfredo, Placid Domingo as the disapproving father, and Luciano Pavarotti as the sweet and tender Violetta. Some lucky penguins!

Tom Crean's Rabbit: A True Story from Scott's Last Voyage, by Meredith Hooper. Illustrated by Bert Kitchen. Frances Lincoln Children's Books, 2005. (Grades 1–3)

It's very cold in Antarctica, and the *Terra Nova* is crowded with both men and animals. Tom the sailor is looking for a quiet and cozy place for his pet rabbit to have her babies. From high in the rigging to down in the hold, the crewman takes readers all through the ship while he searches for a spot where his rabbit can make her nest.

Based on the diaries of men who sailed to the South Pole on board the *Terra Nova* in 1910 with Captain Robert Falcon Scott, *Tom Crean's Rabbit* introduces the historic voyage to young readers.

Where Is Home, Little Pip?, by Karma Wilson. Illustrated by Jane Chapman. Margaret McElderry Books, 2004. (Grades K–2)

For Little Pip, the baby penguin, home is a pebbly nest on the cold Antarctic shore. Mama and Papa always remind Pip not to wander far, and she never does . . . until one day a black, glittery feather leads Pip on a chase far, far from home. As she tries to find her way back to her parents, Pip encounters some friendly animals, a mighty blue whale, a gull, and even a sled dog. But although these animals know where their home is, they do not know where Pip's home is. In her sadness, Pip begins to sing a song about home that her parents taught her, and the sound of her voice guides her parents straight to her!

THE IMPORTANT THINGS

Standards: 2, 4, 6

Margaret Wise Brown uses a simple pattern to describe many everyday things in *The Important Book* (HarperCollins, 1947).

The pattern begins with the sentence:

The important thing about _____ is _____.

This is followed by three or four details. Then the first sentence is repeated.

Use this pattern to write about a rabbit or a penguin.

The important thing about a _____ is _____

_____.

A _____ can _____

And a _____ gives_____

And sometimes a _____helps_____

and a _____ is _____.

_____.

But the most important thing about a _____is

_____

_____

_____.

From *Reading the World with Picture Books* by Nancy J. Polette.
Santa Barbara, CA: Libraries Unlimited. Copyright © 2010.

Part Seven

Australia/Oceania

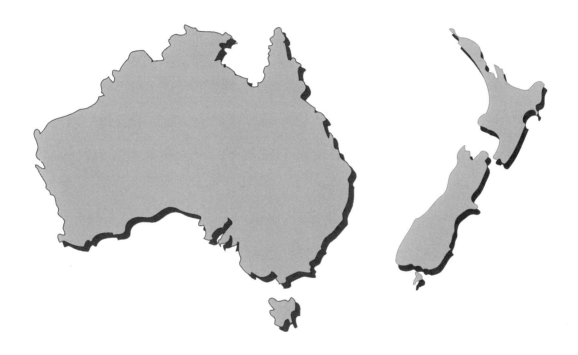

Facts about Australia/Oceania

- Australia is the only country that is also a continent.

- Australia is south of the equator and is often called Down Under.

- Australia is 2,966,153 square miles.

- There are about 18 million people living in Australia.

- The language spoken is English.

- The capital of Australia is Canberra.

- Australia has six states.

- The longest and highest mountain chain is in Australia and is called the Great Dividing Range.

COUNTRIES OF OCEANIA/AUSTRALIA

Australia	Palau
Fiji	**Papua**
Kiribati	Samoa
Marshall Islands	Solomon Islands
Micronesia	Tonga
Nauru	Tuvalu
New Guinea	Vanuatu
New Zealand	

1. Play the X Game (see page 5) using the countries of Australia/Oceania.

2. Create a word search that includes all 15 countries.

Are We There Yet?, by Alison Lester. Kane-Miller, 2005. (Grades K–2)

In a fresh approach to a travelogue, here is an Australian family who decide that the children, eight-year-old Grace and brothers Billy and Luke, will learn more in traveling about in Australia than they will in a winter term at school. So off the family goes, pulling papa's old camper trailer. Their sights and experiences include a bungee ride for mom at Surfer's Paradise. The trip is long and varied, and the tales come from the question often asked by Billy, the youngest, "Are we there yet?"

Big Rain Coming, by Katrina Germein. Illustrated by Bronwyn Bancroft. Clarion, 2000. (Grades 1–3)

Much of Australia is desert, where rain is very, very welcome. It is said that the Aborigines can predict rain, so everyone turns to Old Stephen to see when the welcome drops will fall. He does predict rain, but the showers take their time in arriving. Each day people struggle to keep cool. The kids sleep outdoors and swim in the billabong, the dogs dig shelter from the heat, and the old man sleeps in the shade. Finally, at the end of the very hot, dry week the rain falls, much to the joy of people and animals alike.

The Biggest Frog in Australia, by Susan L. Roth. Simon & Schuster, 2000. (Grades K–2)

Imagine a frog so big it could drink up an ocean! When the biggest frog in Australia woke up, he was very thirsty. Because he was a very big frog, he drank up every body of water he came to: the oceans, lakes, rivers, billabongs, puddles, and even water from the clouds. He did not leave a single drop of water for the other animals, who were thirsty, too. But there was not a single drop of water to be found.

Wise old Wombat suggests that the animals try to make the biggest frog laugh so the water will spill out of his mouth. But the frog barely hears Kookaburra's best jokes, and yawns at Kangaroo's acrobatics. Koala waddles ridiculously, but still no luck. What do you think will make the frog laugh and bring life back to Australia?

Bilby Moon, by Margaret Spurling. Illustrated by Danny Snell. Kane/Miller Book Publishers, 2001. (Grades K–2)

Bilby, a night creature, loves the moon and is upset when she sees it getting smaller and smaller each night until it disappears. She must find it! One can't be a night creature without a moon! So Bilby sets out on her search and encounters a mouse, a sand dragon, an echidna, a mole, and a frog, none of whom knows what has happened to the moon, but they assure Bilby they will help to look for it. At last Bilby meets the wise owl, who tells Bilby that the moon is not lost and that it will once again return so that all can see it.

Bossyboots, by David Cox. Crown Publishers, 1987. (Grades 1–3)

Bossyboots is a young lady who speaks her mind at all times. Long ago in Australia, when folks traveled by stagecoach, Bossyboots is a passenger in a coach on its way to Narrabri. During the journey she orders everyone around: the driver, the passengers, and even the horses. When robbers stop the coach, Bossyboots is too much for even Flash Fred, the head of the robber band, to contend with, and he ends up giving back the loot.

Bright Star, by Gary Crew. Illustrated by Anne Spudvilas. Kane/Miller Book Publishers, 1997. (Grades 2–4)

Here is a fictionalized account of a meeting between John Tebbutt (1834–1916), the Australian discoverer of "the Great Comet" of 1861 and a young girl, Alicia, who is not allowed to use her bright and inquisitive mind at school, where girls are taught needlepoint. She lives on a farm and longs for the freedom that her brothers are given. John Tebbutt is a neighbor and visits the school to talk about astronomy. He is impressed with the questions Alicia asks and invites her to visit his observatory. After he speaks to Alicia's parents, she is allowed to visit and knows that her future will be with the moon and the stars.

Diary of a Wombat, by Jackie French. Illustrated by Bruce Whatley, Houghton Mifflin, 2003. (Grades K–2)

Following her popular *Diary of a Worm,* the author has created a humorous week in the life of a wombat, a furry, cuddly, slow-moving animal of Australia. Their favorite activities are eating, sleeping, and digging holes. Here, in the words of one chatty wombat, is a day-by-day journal of a busy week: eating, sleeping, digging holes, and training its new neighbors, a family of humans, to produce treats on demand. This is a great writing model for researching and writing about the daily activities of another animal.

Ernie Dances to the Didgeridoo, by Alison Lester. Houghton Mifflin, 2000. (Grades 2–4)

Fans of Ernie will enjoy his new adventure as he goes to live for a whole year on the Aboriginal reserve of Arnhem Land in Australia's Northern Territory. As he hurries home to his classmates, he describes the new friends he has made and the varied activities that take place in Arnhem Land's six seasons.

Expedition Down Under, by Rebecca Carmi. Scholastic, 2002. (Grades 2–4)

Ms. Frizzle and the Magic School Bus crew end up on the other side of the world when they set out on a search for the cackling kookaburra. It's a wild walk-about to Australia as they race a herd of kangaroo and have a confrontation with a Tasmanian devil, all the time taking in the sights and discovering all the amazing animals of the outback.

Flood Fish, by Robyn Harbert Eversole. Illustrated by Sheldon Greenberg. Crown, 1995. (Grades 2–4)

It's a mystery! No one knows where the big fish come from, but many have ideas. For most of the year the riverbed in the desert Australian outback is dry as dust or sand. Yet when the rains come, not only does the riverbed fill with water, but the people are astonished to see big fish swimming in the water. Ideas range from the rocks growing gills to the leaves in the gum trees turning to fish when they drop. Or perhaps, as one little girl says, "the moon sows fish eggs when she cries." The mystery remains. No one knows for sure.

The Gift Stone, by Robyn Eversole. Illustrated by Allen Garns. Knopf, 1998. (Grades 2–4)

A mining town in South Australia is a lonely place to live, especially when your home is underground in the small town of Coober Pedy. Jean's father takes his family from Adelaide, where Jean's grandparents live, with him when he gets a job mining opals. Jean spends her days searching rock piles for an opal large enough to allow the family to return to civilization. She does find a beautiful opal in the wall of her aunt's underground house but saves it to give to her grandmother as a gift. Little does she know that her wish to live with her grandparents will come true when her grandmother uses money from the sale of the opal to provide the things that Jean needs.

Hunwick's Egg, by Mem Fox. Illustrated by Pamela Lofts. Harcourt, 2005. (Grades K–2)

Suppose you found an egg that really wasn't an egg at all. Hunwick is an Australian bandicoot who finds such an egg. He seeks the advice of his friends—an echidna, an emu, and a cockatoo—and takes the egg home, where he cares for it, talks to it, and becomes friends with it. When the egg doesn't hatch and his friends are concerned, Hunwick realizes that what he has cared for so lovingly is an egg-shaped stone, which he continues to talk to, care for, and love.

A Kangaroo Joey Grows Up, by Joan Hewett. Lerner, 2002. (Grades K–2)

Hop! Hop! Hop! There goes Kipper! He's a kangaroo joey, and if you watch closely you can see him grow from a tiny pink joey the size of a pea to a hopping kangaroo. Explore Kipper's world as he sleeps, eats, and goes on his first trip alone.

Koala Country: A Story of an Australian Eucalyptus Forest, by Deborah Dennard. Soundprints, 2000. (Grades 2–4)

A baby koala and his mother sit high on a branch of a red gum tree in an Australian eucalyptus forest. A hungry carpet python slithers by on the ground below. Soon baby koala will climb from the safety of his mother's back to learn to protect himself. Follow the koala and his mother through their day and observe their eating, sleeping, and interactions with the forest and other Australian animals.

Lizzie Nonsense, by Jan Ormerod. Clarion Books, 2005. (Grades 2–4)

The power of the imagination can lighten the most difficult of tasks. Lizzie lives in the Australian bush with her parents. Life is lonely and hard, especially when papa must be gone for several days to take wood into town. There is water to haul, wood to chop, food to prepare, and dozens of other tasks that mean work from dawn to dusk, but Lizzie makes the work lighter by imagining that food turns into luscious treats and a torn dress becomes a dress for a princess. Mama calls Lizzie's imaginings "Lizzie Nonsense," but Mama imagines, too, when she dresses in her Sunday best and pretends that the family is strolling to church.

My Place, by Nadia Wheatley. Illustrated by Donna Rawlins. Kane-Miller, 1994. (Grades 4–6)

Have you ever wondered about those who long ago occupied the land on which you now live? Here is a unique, intimate history of Australia, featuring colorful illustrations and maps, which starts in 1988 and works its way back 200 years to 1788, telling the history of one particular place through the generations of children who have lived there.

The Old Man Who Loved to Sing, by John Winch. Scholastic, 1993. (Grades K–2)

An old man lives in a small cottage in the Australian bush. He is lonely with only animals for company, so he winds up his gramophone and sings along with the recordings. At first the strange sound bothers the animals, but after a time they get to like the music. When the man becomes so old that he no longer sings, the animals miss the music and begin to make music of their own. The drumming sound of the kangaroos' tails, the throaty frogs' croaks, and the songs of the birds echo through the bush, and as the old man hears this music of the animals, he begins to sing once again.

Old Shell, New Shell: A Coral Reef Tale, by Helen Ward. Millbrook Press, 2002. (Grades 2–4)

When hermit crabs grow too big for their shells they must find a new home. This hermit crab travels up and down the Great Barrier Reef off Australia, and in traveling with him the reader learns much about the Reef. This particular hermit crab does find a new home, the larger shell outgrown by an even larger hermit crab.

Old Tom, Man of Mystery, by Leigh Hobbs. Peachtree Publishers, 2005. (Grades 1–3)

Angela Throgmorton lives with her mangy cat, the troublesome but lovable Old Tom. One morning an overworked Angela decides that the time has come for Old Tom to help out a bit around the house. But when Angela makes a list of chores for him, Tom suddenly becomes sick. Angela puts him to bed and tells him to rest, but Old Tom has other ideas. So while Angela is busy dusting and wiping and scrubbing and sweeping, Old Tom gets busy too . . . changing into the Man of Mystery! Angela bakes some cakes and then notices fur on her freshly scrubbed floor. Later she finds crumbs on the carpet that has just been swept. But when Angela is awakened by strange footsteps in the middle of the night, she decides it is time to investigate. Soon she is off on her own adventure, shadowing the Man of Mystery.

The Old Woman Who Loved to Read, by John Winch. Holiday House, 1997. (Grades 1–3)

This old woman thought that the quiet, peaceful farm life would give her time to do what she loved best, READ! Little did she guess all the chores that awaited her, like planting, shearing sheep, mending fences. scrubbing, cleaning, and chopping wood. Many Australian animals watch her at work and even join her in a rusty bathtub during the fall floods. But when winter comes, she finds that the work is less on the rented farm, and she knows she can do what she loves best, read her books.

The Pumpkin Runner, by Marsha Diane Arnold. Illustrated by Brad Sneed. Dial Books for Young Readers, 1998. (Grades 1–3)

An Australian sheep rancher who eats pumpkins for energy enters a race from Melbourne to Sydney, despite people laughing at his eccentricities. "Nearly all the sheep ranchers in Blue Gum Valley rode horses or drove jeeps to check on their sheep. But Joshua Summerhayes liked to run . . . with Yellow Dog trailing behind him." So it's no surprise when Joshua decides to enter a race from Melbourne to Sydney. People laugh when old Joshua shows up in his overalls and gumboots, calmly nibbling a slice of pumpkin for energy. But then he pulls into the lead, and folks are forced to sit up and take notice. Inspired by a true event (and just in time for fall's pumpkin harvest!) a talented team introduces a humble and generous hero who knows that winning isn't always the reason to run a race.

Ready to Dream, by Donna Jo Napoli and Elena Furrow. Illustrated by Bronwyn Bancroft. Bloomsbury, 2008. (Grades 1–3)

Ally loves to draw, and when she arrives in Australia she meets Pauline, an Aboriginal artist. The two soon become friends, and Ally learns that art isn't always made with paints and paper and that sometimes mistakes are the greatest discoveries. A slip of brown paint creates the brown clouds seen in a dust storm. Brown sand and gray mud make pictures glisten in the sun. A torn corner on her painting adds reality to the crocodile painting. Ally painted kangaroos on rocks and watched the kangaroo hop free as she threw the rock down a ravine. As Ally created pictures from rocks, leaves, branches, bark, sand, and feathers, crocodiles, wombats, opossums, koalas, rainbow lorikeets, goannas, and other animals came to life in ways she had never dreamed.

The Silver Horse Switch, by Alison Lester. Illustrated by Roland Harvey. Chronicle Books, 2009. (Grades 1–3)

In a rural Australian town, best friends Bonnie and Sam, who share a mutual love of horses, watch in amazement as a farm horse and a wild horse, identical in appearance, trade places. Bonnie and Sam are best friends who love horses. They befriend the ponies and horses in their Australian town except for one, Drover, who used to be wild. All she dreams about is getting back to the mountains to be free. One evening, when a wild, mountain horse who could be Drover's twin comes face to face with the cantankerous, corralled Drover, both horses get their chance at a new life.

Snap!, by Marcia Vaughan. Illustrated by Sascha Hutchinson. Scholastic, 1996. (Grades K–2)

Joey, a young kangaroo, is bored on a hot afternoon in the Australian bush, so he seeks out playmates. Sure enough, he finds various animals, who teach him interesting games like hide-and-seek, lots of knots, pick-up-quills, and pass-the-mud pies. When crocodile invites the animals to enter his big mouth to play "Snap!" they do so and are caught, until Joey invents a new game called "tickle-the tonsils," which enables all the animals to escape

Wombat Goes Walkabout, by Michael Morpurgo. Illustrated by Christian Birmingham. Candlewick Press, 2000. (Grades K–2)

Whether human or animal, all creatures have special abilities, the Australian wombat included. As the furry creature walks through the Australian bush looking for his mother, he meets other animals and a boy, who rudely ask who he is and what he can do. "I dig a lot and I think a lot," Wombat replies. Kookaburra, Wallaby, Possum, Emu, Boy, and Koala don't think digging and thinking are nearly as valuable as the things they can do, like flying, hopping, and jumping. However, when a bush fire comes, Wombat's quick thinking and digging save the day.

AROUND AUSTRALIA IN SEVEN LETTERS

Standards: 11, 13, 16, 19

Pretend that you are a world explorer planning your next trip. Using the index or gazetteer of an atlas, find a city or town in Australia that begins with each letter of your first name, then record the page number and map coordinates for each city. If your name does not have seven letters, use your first name and the first letters of your last name to equal seven letters.

Example:

P	Perth	p. 56	F4
A	Adelaide	p.106	C1
M	Melbourne	p. 58	E5

Letter	**City**	**Page No.**	**Coordinates**
_____	_____	_____	_____
_____	_____	_____	_____
_____	_____	_____	_____
_____	_____	_____	_____
_____	_____	_____	_____
_____	_____	_____	_____
_____	_____	_____	_____

Choose one city. Use the pattern that follows to name the city and one sight you would see there.

_____ is where I'll be

_____ is what I'll see.

WRITE A FACT OR FICTION BOOK

Standards: 2, 4, 6, 14, 16, 21

1. Gather interesting facts about the country.

2. Group your facts.

> Facts about people.
>
> Facts about places.
>
> Facts about products.
>
> Facts about wildlife.
>
> Other facts.

3. Choose the most interesting facts to use in your book.

4. State a fact on one page.

5. Tell on the next page whether it is fact or fiction and why.

6. Change some of the facts so that you can explain why the statement is not true.

FACT OR FICTION?

The largest crocodiles in Australia grow to a length of ten feet.

FICTION

Many crocodiles in Australia are 18 feet long or longer.

Micronesia

Micronesia is a series of more than 600 islands that cover an area of 271 square miles. Some islands were formed from volcanoes and are rich in plant life. Others are coral reefs that have emerged from the ocean and provide poor growing soil. Men are skilled in making outrigger canoes and women are weavers. The capital is Palikir on the island of Pohnpei.

Rama and Sita: A Tale from Ancient Java, by David Weitzman. David R. Godine, 2002. (Grades 2–4)

In even the most remote villages of Bali you will hear, late into the night, the shimmering metallic music of the gamelan, a collection of gongs, chimes, flutes, drums, and cymbals whose music provides the accompaniment to the surpassingly beautiful dances that serve to entertain the gods at the annual celebrations. Even the youngest children learn to dance, absorbing the delicate hand and arm movements of their parents and of the puppets, whose characters and adventures the children recognize. Among the stories learned by every child is the saga of Rama and Sita, a particularly beloved tale of intrigue, adventure, and mystery. This great Hindu epic has characters drawn from both ancient and modern shadow puppets: noble princes, terrifying giants, and menacing ogres. The entire world of gods and men is there onstage in miniature. Through deeds and words the puppets teach the children who they are, what to believe, how to behave, and their place in the universe.

MICRONESIAN MEAL

Three favorite foods in Micronesia are:

Breadfruit

_____

_____

_____

_____

_____

Taro

_____

_____

_____

_____

_____

Cassava

_____

_____

_____

_____

_____

Find out about one of these foods. What is it? What does it look like? How does it taste? On the blank lines, describe a dish that uses that food.

New Guinea and Papua New Guinea

New Guinea is an island north of Australia. It covers about 309,000 square miles. It is 1,500 miles long and 400 miles wide. The population is slightly over 5 million people. It is a beautiful island, with trees, orchids, and birds of paradise. Most people are farmers. Cash crops are coffee, tea, and rubber. The capital is Port Moresby.

A Question of Yams, by Gloria Repp. Bob Jones University Press, 1990. (Grades 1–3)

Is it possible to be punished for not praying? In New Guinea it certainly is. The Head Men of the tribal council tell the farmers that the planting of yams must always be accompanied by prayer. Kuri's father is a farmer, and he does his planting without prayer, displeasing the elders, who arrest him and decide that he must be punished. What will Kuri and his family do now?

ISLAND LIFE CHART

Standards: 10, 13, 19

New Guinea is an island. Island live can be very different from life on the mainland. Suppose you lived in New Guinea. Complete the chart, describing ways in which your life would be different.

	My Life	Island Life
Food		
Clothing		
Travel		
Work of People		
Recreation		

New Zealand

New Zealand is a Pacific Island of 103,737 square miles and a population of more than 4 million people. The Maori people first settled in New Zealand 1,200 years ago. The main crops are potatoes and fruits. Minerals that are mined include iron and gold. The capital is Wellington.

Go to Sleep, Gecko!, by Margaret Read MacDonald. Illustrated by Geraldo Valério. August House, 2003. (Grades K–2)

Gecko may be small, but he has a giant-sized problem. Every night he is awakened by the fireflies outside his window. And when Gecko doesn't get his rest, he gets a little grumpy. So he goes to Elephant, the head of the village, to complain. His request that the fireflies stop working at night sets off a comical chain of problems for everyone in the village. Through this cumulative tale from the Balinese tradition, Gecko learns that his well-being depends on that of the entire village, and he finally goes to sleep, a little wiser.

The Great White Man-Eating Shark, by Margaret Mahy. Illustrated by Jonathon Allen. Puffin, 1995. (Grades 2–4)

Norvin is an actor but unfortunately not a handsome leading man. In fact, he looks somewhat like a shark and is an excellent swimmer who "shoots through the water like a silver arrow." But Norvin has a problem. The water is too crowded with other swimmers, so he fashions what looks like a dorsal fin out of plastic and attaches it to his back. As he glides through the water, the other swimmers flee in terror at what they perceive to be a man-eating shark. Now Norvin has the swimming area all to himself . . . or does he? A lady shark shows up, and Norvin realizes that his disguise is so effective that she considers him "the shark of her dreams." What will he do now?

The Man Whose Mother Was a Pirate, by Margaret Mahy. Puffin, 1996. (Grades 1–3)

Sam is an ordinary person who wears an ordinary suit and ordinary shoes. He works in an ordinary, neat office writing down figures all day and underlining them. But Sam's mother is definitely not an ordinary woman. Sam's mother is a pirate, and she wants to sweep him away to sea. She wants to experience the pirate life again, so the little man resigns his job by putting a note in a bottle, then puts his mother in a wheelbarrow and rolls her down to the sea, where they both board a ship. He becomes the ship's cabin boy, and his mother is once again queen of the pirates.

Maui and the Big Fish, by Barbara Ker Wilson. Illustrated by Frane Lessac. Frances Lincoln Children's Books, 2004. (Grades 1–3)

This is a mythological account of the formation of the Polynesian archipelago. Long ago, when the world was new and little Maui was born, the great god Tama carried him away to the underworld to learn magic. When Maui came back to earth, his brothers made fun of him and wouldn't take him out fishing. They stole away in their boat, laughing at him and thinking he was still asleep—but Maui outwitted his brothers, caught the biggest fish in the ocean, and in the process created something amazing!

Maui and the Sun, by Gavin Bishop. North South, 1996. (Grades 1–3)

This is a Maori creation tale that explains why we have night and day. Maui is a central figure in many Maori tales, and in this tale he seeks the help of the villagers to rope the sun to slow its travel across the sky. This will allow more daylight hours for fishing. However, Maui and the villagers did not realize that more sun means the earth dries up, crops wither, and water becomes scarce. To remedy the situation, Maui and the villagers rope the moon, so that as the sun disappears, the moon appears, giving the needed balance of day and night.

Night Cat, by Margaret Beames. Orchard Books, 2003. (Grades K–2)

Oliver the cat lives in a house with a garden full of light and shadows, full of things that dance and flutter; a garden that comes to life in the moonlight and tempts the young cat to stay outside all night. And so he does. But Oliver's excitement soon turns to fear as he encounters the mysterious and scary sights and sounds of the dark garden. The garden is dark and wet and lonely—and home is safe and dry and warm. Suddenly Oliver decides that his owner might be frightened, too, and that it's his duty to go inside to comfort her. And so he does.

Punga: The Goddess of Ugly, by Deborah Nourse Lattimore. Illustrated by Lori J. McThomas. Harcourt, 1993. (Grades 2–4)

Punga, the New Zealand goddess of all things ugly, captures young Maori maidens and turns them into wooden statues. When a mischievous twin is turned into a wooden statue by Punga, Kiri finds a clever way to be freed from Punga's power. On the one night of the year when the creatures on Punga's lodge pole are allowed to dance, Kiri challenges the goddess, saying, "if any one of us is ugly, that one should be on your roof beam for all to see." Then Kiri and her friends Lizard and Mudfish perform a beautiful Maori dance and earn their freedom. When Punga reacts by sticking out her tongue, she is turned into a repulsive wooden decoration on her own lodge house.

The Sign of the Seahorse: A Tale of Greed and High Adventure in Two Acts, by Graeme Base. Puffin, 1998. (Grades 2–4)

Romance, mystery, and intrigue revolve around the Seahorse Cafe, where the beautiful Pearl Trout falls in love with Corporal Bert the Soldier crab. But Reeftown is in danger, and soon Pearl, Bert, and Pearl's brother Finneus must journey through the ocean depths to find the source of the deadly poison that is destroying the coral reef.

UNPACKING THE TOURIST BAG

Standards: 2, 4, 13, 14

List 10 items that a tourist might unpack from his or her bag after returning from New Zealand. Challenge classmates to name the country.

Example (Australia):

1. A cricket bat used in a game similar to baseball.
2. A rugby ball. Tackling is a big part of this rough game.
3. A uniform required of all schoolchildren.
4. Barbecued kangaroo, a favorite food.
5. Vegemite, a dark brown yeast spread on bread.
6. A surfboard to ride the waves of the South Pacific Ocean.
7. A program from the opera house.
8. A photograph of a wombat.
9. An emu feather.
10. A book written in Strine.

Your Turn:

1. _____
2. _____
3. _____
4. _____
5. _____
6. _____
7. _____
8. _____
9. _____
10. _____

Part Eight

Asia and the Middle East

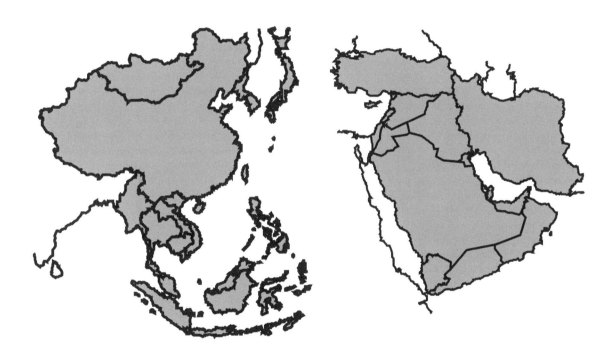

Facts about Asia and the Middle East

- At 17,176,102 square miles, Asia is the largest continent.

- Asia has the largest population, with over 3 billion people.

- The largest country in Asia by area is Russia, which is 4,845,580 square miles.

- The largest country in Asia by population is China, with more than 1 billion people.

- The longest river in Asia and the third longest river in the world is the Yangtze River in China.

- The largest desert in Asia is the Gobi desert. It is 500,005 square miles.

- The largest lake in Asia is the Caspian Sea in Asia-Europe. It is 143,244 square miles.

COUNTRIES OF ASIA

Booktalks are provided for the countries in boldface.

Armenia	**Mongolia**
Azerbaijan	Myanmar (Burma)
Bali	**Nepal**
Bangladesh	**North Korea**
Bhutan	**Pakistan** (Islamic Republic of)
Cambodia	**Philippines**
China (People's Republic of)	Singapore
Georgia	**South Korea**
India	Sri Lanka
Indonesia	Taiwan (Republic of China)
Japan	Tajikistan
Kazakhstan	**Thailand**
Kyrgyzstan	Turkmenistan
Laos	Ukraine
Malaysia	Uzbekistan
Maldives	**Vietnam**
Moldova	

COUNTRIES OF THE MIDDLE EAST

Booktalks are provided for the countries in boldface.

Afghanistan	Kuwait
Bahrain	**Lebanon**
Brunei Darussalam	Oman
Cyprus (The Republic of)	Qatar
Iran (The Islamic Republic of)	Saudi Arabia
Iraq	Turkey
Israel	United Arab Emirates
Jordan	Yemen

1. Play the X Game (see page 5) using the countries of Asia and the Middle East.

2. Create a word search using the 10 largest countries.

Afghanistan

Afghanistan lies on important trade routes in South Central Asia. It covers an area of 251,737 square miles and is home to almost 32 million people. It is a mountainous country with wolves, foxes, hyenas, and snow leopards in abundance. The tiger, which once roamed the mountains, has disappeared. Vultures and eagles are plentiful. The capital is Kabul.

Caravan, by Lawrence McKay Jr. Illustrated by Darryl Ligasan. Lee & Low, 1995. (Grades 2–4)

Young Jura is excited to be going on his first caravan with his father and the other men to take furs into the city to trade. He is in charge of three camels, and it is his task to see that no harm comes to them. The caravan travels up mountains, through fields of snow and ice. Rock falls clatter down cliffs, warning of an avalanche. The men shelter at night in a cave. At last, through the valley and moving along a winding river, the caravan arrives at the marketplace in town. Jura takes in the colorful sights of the town as bargains are struck and trades take place. The caravan returns to winter camp, and Jura is greeted by his mother and sisters, who wrap their arms around him.

ADJECTIVES

Standards: 2, 4, 6

Choose adjectives to describe (1) the marketplace as Jura sees it and (2) the refugee camp as Lina sees it.

_____ is the color of _____

It looks like_____

It sounds like _____

It tastes like _____

It smells like _____

It made (Jura/Lina) feel like _____

Armenia

Armenia covers 11,500 square miles and is home to 2,971,650 people. It is a land of many mountains. The country produces machine tools and tools for the electrical power industry. The food industry processes farm products for export. The capital is Yerevan.

A Drop of Honey: An Armenian Tale, by Djemma Bider. Illustrated by Armen Kojoyian. Simon & Schuster, 1989. (Grades 1–3)

After a quarrel with her brothers, Anayida falls asleep and dreams of a trip to market to buy the ingredients to bake a baklava: fine nuts, sweet butter, cinnamon bark, lemon peel, and most important of all, the best, sweet-scented honey. But as Anayida buys the honey, a drop spills onto the cobblestones. A bee lands on the honey, a cat chases the bee, and a dog chases the cat. Tables are knocked down and goods spilled as the villagers join the confusion, and soon the market is in an uproar, all because of a single drop of honey.

FAMILY RECIPES

Standards: 4, 11, 13, 14, 15

Ask the children if any of their parents or grandparents came from another country. Ask those who have such a contact to bring in a recipe for a typical dish from that country. Invite the parent or grandparent to come to school and tell or show how to make the dish. If a visitor is not available, find a simple recipe that the children can make. Ask each child to find one fact about the country of origin and illustrate the fact on one page, which will go into a class book about the country.

Bali

Bali is a small island off the coast of Java that has an area of 2,175 square miles and a population of more than 3 million. It is a land of many volcanoes. Its major crop is rice, and it is a popular tourist destination. The main language is Balinese. The capital is Denpasar.

Cycle of Rice, Cycle of Life: A Story of Sustainable Farming, written and photographed by Jan Reynolds. Lee & Low, 2009. (Grades 2–4)

On the island of Bali in Southeast Asia, rice farming is a way of life. The people live in tune with the natural rhythms and cycles of the water and the soil. Ingrained in their community and culture, rice farming connects them to the land and one another. Balinese farmers have planted rice using an intricate system of water sharing and crop rotation for more than a thousand years. Intertwined with their spiritual, social, and day-to-day lives, this system has made Bali a leading producer of one of the world's most important crops. And because Balinese rice farming respects the balances of nature, it serves as a remarkable example of sustainable agriculture in an increasingly industrialized world.

FIVE SENSES REPORT

Standards: 2, 6, 12

Describe the rice paddies using the pattern below.

Color: The rice paddies are _____

Sound: They sound like _____

Taste: They taste like _____

Smell: They smell like _____

Sight: The look like _____

Feeling: They make me feel like _____

Bangladesh

This is a small country (55,598 square miles), but one of the most heavily populated countries of Asia, with more than 150 million people. The land varies, with wetlands, flood plains, hills, valleys, and forests. The people grow and sell tea, wheat, tobacco, and many kinds of fruit, including mangos and bananas. The capital is Dhaka.

A Basket of Bangles, by Ginger Howard. Illustrated by Cheryl Kirk Noll. Millbrook Press, 2002. (Grades 2–4)

Sufiya is so poor that she must beg for rice and sleep on the floor of her brother's house. It is there she hears about the bank loaning money to groups to start a business. They can borrow money even if they have no goods to pledge should the money not be paid back. Sufiya and her friends must all learn to write their names and memorize the bank rules. Sufiya decides to sell bangles and the others plan to sell soap, milk, snacks, and saris. Each chooses different goods to sell, and the bank loans them the money to purchase the goods. The friends work hard to pay back their loan within one year.

Rickshaw Girl, by Mitali Perkins. Illustrated by Jamie Hogan. Charlesbridge, 2007. (Grades 2–4)

In her Bangladesh village, 10-year-old Naima excels at painting the traditional alpana patterns with which Bangladeshi women and girls decorate their homes for holiday celebrations. But she wishes she could help her father earn money, like her best friend helps his family by driving his father's rickshaw. But to do this she would have to be a boy or disguise herself as one. When Naima's rash efforts to help put the family deeper in debt, she draws on her resourceful nature to use her talents and follow the changing model of women's roles in Bangladesh.

WRITING ABOUT ART

Standards: 2, 14, 15

If the library has sets of art prints, select some that are abstract prints or patterns and display them in the classroom. Ask each child to choose one painting and to write a sentence about it that begins "This painting reminds me of . . ."

Encourage imaginative writing and stress that there are no right answers. For example, a spray of water or fog might remind a child of a genie coming out of a bottle.

When good sentences are developed they can be expanded into descriptive paragraphs and be mounted beside or under each painting.

Cambodia

Fourteen million people live in the almost 70,000 square miles of Cambodia. The land varies from low-lying plains to highland mountains. Much of Cambodia is forest, with tigers, bears, and many small animals. The capital is Phnom Penh.

Angkat: The Cambodian Cinderella, by Jewell Reinhart Coburn. Illustrated by Eddie Flotte. Shen's Books, 2001. (Grades 1–3)

In the first English retelling of this ancient Cambodian tale, our heroine goes further, survives more, and has to conquer her own mortality to regain her rightful place. Angkat—child of ashes—endures great wrongs as she seeks to rise above the distresses caused by her own family.

The Caged Birds of Phnom Penh, by Frederick J. Lipp. Illustrated by Ronald Himler. Holiday House, 2001. (Grades 1–3)

In Cambodia legend says that one who sets a bird free will have his or her fondest wish granted. Eight-year-old Ary lives in a city with air polluted by smoke, and the only birds she sees are those kept in cages and sold in the marketplace. She earns enough money to buy a bird, but when she attempts to set it free, it returns to its familiar cage. It is then that her grandfather gives her advice, which she follows. She buys a sickly bird and when she sets it free, it soars away into the sky.

Little Sap and Monsieur Rodin, by Michelle Lord. Illustrated by Felicia Hoshino. Lee & Low, 2006. (Grades 1–3)

It's 1906 and the court dancers in the Cambodian royal palace are abuzz with news of a trip to France for the Colonial Exhibition. Little Sap, a poor country girl who joined the dance troupe to give her family a better life, is apprehensive about traveling to a faraway land.

In Paris the artist Auguste Rodin is captivated by the classical beauty of Cambodian dance. He insists on sketching the dancers, especially Little Sap. As Rodin's pencil sweeps across his paper, Little Sap's worries melt away. She realizes how much she has grown as a dancer and how far she has come in fulfilling her special duty to her family.

A Song for Cambodia, by Michelle Lord. Illustrated by Shino Arihara. Lee & Low, 2009. (Grades 2–4)

In 1975 Arm was a young boy in Cambodia when his village was invaded by Khmer Rouge soldiers. Torn apart from his family, overworked and underfed, Arm had to find a way to survive. When guards asked for volunteers to play music one day, Arm bravely raised his hand, taking a chance that would change the course of his life. Arm Chon-Pond's heartfelt music created beauty in a time of darkness and turned tragedy into healing.

BOOK REPORT

Standards: 9, 12, 14

Write a five-sentence book report about one of these books. Include:

Who

_____

_____

_____

What

_____

_____

_____

When

_____

_____

_____

Where

_____

_____

_____

Why or How

_____

_____

_____

From _Reading the World with Picture Books_ by Nancy J. Polette.
Santa Barbara, CA: Libraries Unlimited. Copyright © 2010.

China (People's Republic of)

China is the largest Asian country, covering 3,705,386 square miles, and is home to 1,321,851,888 people. It is the most highly populated country in the world. It has plains, plateaus, mountains, and rivers and is noted for its Great Wall, 1,500 miles long. The paddlefish, small alligator, and giant salamander are found in China's rivers and are extinct in the rest of the world. The capital is Beijing.

Chee-lin: A Giraffe's Journey, by James Rumford. Houghton Mifflin, 2008. (Grades 1–3)

Tweega is a giraffe who lives in Africa. The chee-lin was a creature in Chinese lore that was supposed to bring good luck. When Chinese explorers landed on the coast of Africa they saw what they believed to be a chee-lin but was actually a giraffe. This is the tale of the giraffe's journey from Africa to Bengal to China and of the people he meets during the journey. Some people were kind, some were cruel, but most helped him feel at home in the new countries he visited.

Dragonsong: A Fable for the New Millennium, by Russell Young. Shen's Books, 2000. (Grades 2–4)

Chiang-An, the youngest dragon at only 224 years old, vies for the honor of being named Keeper of the Mountain, an honor bestowed by the four Imperial Dragons of China only once every thousand years. Challenged to prove themselves worthy, the dragon community must discover the perfect gift. What gifts, wonders Chiang-An, could he possibly find that would elevate him above the older dragons? Which part of China could he search that the older and more powerful dragons wouldn't get to first? Chiang-An decides he must journey where he has never gone before to search for his treasures, far from his village and far outside China. As he travels, each dragon he meets—from England, Africa, Mexico, and North America—shares with him wonderful dragon wisdoms and contributes unique gifts to Chiang-An's search. When he returns to China on New Year's Eve of the Year of the Dragon, Chiang-An carries the gift that "will be able to last a thousand years."

Goldfish and Chrysanthemums, by Andrea Cheng. Lee & Low Books, 2003. (Grades 1–3)

Young Nancy is helping Ni Ni (Grandma) in the kitchen when a letter arrives with bad news: her childhood home in China, with its beautiful garden pond filled with fish and ringed with chrysanthemums, is being torn down. Later that day at the summer fair, Nancy spots a ball-tossing game, Win a Goldfish! Aiming carefully, she wins one, and then two. Now the question is how to use them to make Ni Ni feel better.

The Greatest Power, by Demi. Margaret K. McElderry Books, 2004. (Grades 2–4)

Emperor Ping, the boy emperor known for his love of harmony, sets a challenge to the children of his kingdom: show him the greatest power in the world. "To know the greatest power in the world is to know the greatest peace," Emperor Ping announces. "Whoever knows this harmony will become the new prime minister." The children get to work right away and have many bright ideas. The greatest power must be weapons! It must be beauty! It must be money! But as a young girl named Sing reflects upon the challenge, she wonders how any of those things, which cannot last forever, could be the greatest power in the world. She is certain there is something even more powerful, and the source of this power will surprise and delight her.

The Jade Stone: A Chinese Folktale, adapted by Caryn Yacowitz. Illustrated by Ju-Hong Chen. Pelican, 2009. (Grades 2–4)

Chan Lo is a humble stone carver who is given a perfect piece of green and white jade to carve by the Great Emperor of All China. Is there a dragon in the stone, as the emperor demands? What does Chan Lo hear the stone say? What does it want to be? When Chan Lo finally succumbs to the stone's true wishes, the emperor is furious and throws him in prison. Can the spirit of the jade stone save the stone carver's life?

Jin Jin the Dragon, by Grace Chang. Illustrated by Chong Chang. Enchanted Lion Books, 2008. (Grades 1–3)

Suppose a water-breathing dragon has no idea what kind of a creature he is. This is Jin Jin's problem as he sees many creatures that have some of his characteristics, a fish with scales and a bird with claws, but he knows he is not a fish or a bird. He arrives at a village where wise Turtle and Crane reside. He plans to ask them what he is, but the village is beset by a drought. Jin Jin breathes out water and saves the crops, discovering in the process that he is a water-breathing dragon.

Lon Po Po: A Red Riding Hood Story from China, translated and illustrated by Ed Young. Philomel, 1989. (Grades K–2)

Long, long ago, a good woman lived contentedly with her three daughters, Shang, Tao, and Paotze, in the countryside of northern China. But one day she had to leave to visit their granny, so she warned the children to close the door tightly and to latch it.

Soon after, to their surprise, there was a knock at the door and a voice said it was their granny, their Po Po. What could the children do but let her in? But what a low voice she had, what thorny hands, and what a hairy face! To discover how three little girls outwit a wicked, wicked wolf, read *Lon Po Po.*

Magic Pillow, by Demi. Simon & Schuster, 2008. (Grades K–2)

This is the story of a poor boy named Ping who is stranded by a snowstorm and takes refuge on a mountain where a magician is doing his tricks. He is given a magic pillow by the magician, who tells him that sleeping on it will make all his wishes come true. Ping has one dream after another, in which he sees himself rich and powerful at times and jailed and dishonored at other times. He finally realizes that true happiness comes not from riches and power but from the love of family.

The Master Swordsman & the Magic Doorway, by Alice Provensen. Simon & Schuster Books for Young Readers, 2001. (Grades 2–4)

Little Chu wants to defend his family and protect the village from bandits. He apprentices with Master Li, the greatest teacher of the sword in all of China, and finds that having the skill means he'll never have to use it. When the Emperor sees Mu Chi's magnificent mural, he decrees that the painter's reward shall be death. After all, no one but the Emperor should own such a perfect painting. Wielding the power of art, Mu Chi is able to find a way out of his dilemma.

Panda Whispers, by Mary Beth Owens. Duotone, 2007. (Grades K–2)

Just like us, creatures throughout the world dream sweet dreams. What, then, might a panda whisper to her cub when he's settling down to sleep? "Dream of climbing." We move from treetops to ocean to plains to river to listen to the gentle murmurs of other animal parents: a dolphin, a cheetah, an otter, and many more. Alongside stunning close-up images of sleepy pairings, we see young animals' dreams of leaping, racing, sliding, swooping, and other kinds of active fun. The final image of a father tucking in his daughter with loving whispers will inspire listeners to sail off into their own dreams.

Rabbit's Gift: A Fable from China, by George Shannon. Illustrated by Laura Dronzek. Harcourt, 2007. (Grades K–2)

Winter is coming, and it is time to store food to have on hand when the snows come. Rabbit finds not one but two turnips, and knowing that one is enough for his needs, he leaves the second turnip on the doorstep of his friend, Donkey. Donkey, too, has enough food for the winter, so he takes the turnip to Goat, who takes it to Deer, who gives it to Rabbit. Since

Rabbit has more than enough food for the winter, he invites all of his animal friends to gather for a feast.

Red Butterfly: How a Princess Smuggled the Secret of Silk Out of China, by Deborah Noyes. Candlewick Press, 2007. (Grades 2–4)

A young Chinese princess is sent from her father's kingdom to marry the king of a far-off land. She must leave behind her home of splendors: sour plums and pink peach petals and—most precious and secret of all—the small silkworm. She begs her father to let her stay, but he insists that she go and fulfill her destiny as the queen of Khotan. Here is a coming-of-age tale of a brave young princess whose clever plan will go on to live in legend—and will ensure that her cherished home is with her always.

Sam and the Lucky Money, by Karen Chinn. Illustrated by Ying-Hwa Hu and Cornelius Van Wright. Lee & Low, 1997. (Grades 1–3)

Sam can hardly wait to go shopping with his mom. It's Chinese New Year's day, and his grandparents have given him the traditional gift of lucky money—red envelopes called leisees (lay-sees). This year Sam is finally old enough to spend it any way he chooses. Best of all, he gets to spend his lucky money in his favorite place, Chinatown! But when Sam realizes that his grandparents' gift is not enough to get the things he wants, his excitement turns to disappointment. Even though his mother reminds him that he should appreciate the gift, Sam is not convinced—until a surprise encounter with a stranger.

Sparrow Girl, by Sara Pennypacker. Illustrated by Yoko Tanaka. Hyperion Books, 2009. (Grades 2–4)

Ming-Li looked up and tried to imagine the sky silent, empty of birds. It was a terrible thought. Her country's leader had called sparrows the enemy of the farmers—they were eating too much grain, he said. He announced a great "Sparrow War" to banish them from China, but Ming-Li did not want to chase the birds away. As the people of her village gathered with firecrackers and gongs to scatter the sparrows, Ming-Li held her ears and watched in dismay. The birds were falling from the trees, frightened to death! Ming-Li knew she had to do something—even if she couldn't stop the noise. Quietly, she vowed to save as many sparrows as she could, one by one.

The Warlord's Alarm, by Virginia Walton Pilegard. Illustrated by Nicolas Debon. Pelican, 2004. (Grades 2–4)

In ancient China, traveling to an important feast, Chuan and his friend Jing Jing want to be the first to arrive to gain favor with the emperor. They stay overnight at an inn that has no clock and must come up with a way to awaken after four hours sleep so that they can be sure to arrive first. Chuan tells his friend about a dragon alarm clock, but they do not have all of t he materials needed to create such a clock. However, Jing Jing comes up with another clock called a "water clock," which works just as well, and the two do awaken in plenty of time to reach the emperor's palace before the others.

The Warlord's Beads, by Virginia Walton Pilegard. Illustrated by Nicolas Debon. Pelican, 2001. (Grades 2–4)

Often used by teachers of primary grades to illustrate the concept of "base ten," various types of counting frames appeared in China during the Middle Ages. *The Warlord's Beads* introduces young readers to the wonder of numbers as well as the beauty and mystery of ancient China.

The Warlord's Fish, by Virginia Walton Pilegard. Illustrated by Nicolas Debon. Pelican, 2002. (Grades 2–4)

In this story about the compass, clever Chuan is an artist's apprentice for the warlord. When some strangers feel they have been cheated in the market, Chuan serves as interpreter in the dispute, and for his trouble both he and the artist are kidnapped and, together with the strangers, are taken through the desert.

The Warlord's Messengers, by Virginia Walton Pilegard. Illustrated by Nicolas Debon. Pelican, 2005. (Grades 2–4)

The warlord's presence is requested at the emperor's banquet in two weeks, but he is 16 days away by horseback. Using their math skills, ingenuity, and the wind, Chaun and Jing Jing reach the warlord's camp and encourage him to use the sailing cart that Chuan and Jing Jing invent, a cart that sails on land, to quickly reach the warlord with an important message from the emperor.

The Warlord's Puppeteers, by Virginia Walton Pilegard. Illustrated by Nicolas Debon. Pelican, 2003. (Grades 2–4)

Young Chuan and his artist mentor are journeying across the desert to find their master, the warlord, when they meet up with a group of traveling puppeteers. When bandits attack them and steal their trunk of puppets, Chuan knows he must step in to help his new friends in order to finish the journey.

The Warlord's Puzzle, by Virginia Walton Pilegard. Illustrated by Nicolas Debon. Pelican, 2000. (Grades 2–4)

In China a beautiful ceramic tile lies shattered on the ground, and the artist who dropped it is sentenced to the land's worst punishment. The fierce warlord will execute the artist unless some wise person can put the seven pieces back together. The person will then be invited to live in the castle. Both locals and strangers from far away wait their turns for a chance to solve the warlord's puzzle.

Where the Mountain Meets the Moon, written and illustrated by Grace Lin. Little Brown, 2009. (Grades 2–4)

In the Valley of Fruitless Mountain, a young girl named Mini lives in a ramshackle hut with her parents. In the evenings her father regales her with folktales of the Old Man on the Moon, who knows all the answers to life. Inspired by these stories, Mini, accompanied by a dragon who can't fly, sets out to ask the Old Man on the Moon how they can fulfill their dreams.

Yeh-Shen: A Cinderella Story from China, retold by Ai-Ling Louie. Illustrated by Ed Young. Philomel Books, 1982. (Grades K–2)

Long ago in southern China there was a beautiful girl named Yeh-Shen. Her own mother died when she was a baby, and her father died soon afterward, leaving Yeh-Shen in the care of a stepmother who treated her very badly. Now poor Yeh-Shen was dressed in rags and made to do all the hard work in the cave where they lived. Her only friend was a fish, which her stepmother killed and ate. In her sorrow, Yeh-Shen is visited by an old man, who tells her that the fish bones are magic and will grant her any wish. So at festival time, while Stepmother and Stepsister are off dancing, Yeh-Shen makes her wish. In an instant she has beautiful clothes and golden slippers, which she is warned not to lose. But alas, at the festival, in a rush not to be seen by Stepmother, Yeh-Shen loses a slipper. Little does she know that the King has vowed never to rest until the girl who lost the slipper is found. As do all Cinderella tales, this one has a happy ending.

Yu the Great: Conquering the Flood [A Chinese Legend], by Paul D. Storrie. Illustrated by Sandy Carruthers. Lerner, 2007. (Grades 2–4)

This is the legend of Yu the Great, a Chinese hero from the twenty-first century BC. Some scholars believe Yu actually existed and that he founded the Xia dynasty, the first Chinese empire described in historical records. Some later Chinese texts describe Yu as a kind and strong emperor whose engineering projects saved China from frequent floods. But in Chinese legend, as in this book, Yu is descended from the gods and born from a golden dragon. He saves China from floods by using magical soil to plug underwater springs, with the help of a tortoise, an owl, and a dragon.

POEMS ABOUT CHINA

Standards: 2, 4, 6, 9, 14

Use these patterns to report on China. Study the examples below, then write a poem following one of the models. Be sure to include accurate information about the country you choose.

COUNTRY
Colors _____
Sounds _____
_____
Tastes _____
Smells _____
Looks _____

_____
Touch/Feeling _____
_____

Line	Five Senses Poems
1-Color	CHINA IS
2-Sound	It sounds like ____.
3-Taste	It tastes like ____.
4-Smell	It smells like ____.
5-Sight	It looks like ____.
6-Feeling	It makes me feel like ____.

Adverb Poem	
1 Adverb	Abruptly
2 Adverb	Majestically
3 Adverb	Proudly
4 Noun	The Great Wall
5 Verb	Stretches
6 Noun with description	1,500 miles
7 Any words	through China.

Phone Number Poem

Choose a phone number and put each number on a separate line. Then for each line, choose words to describe China that have the number of syllables in that line's number.

3 _____
3 _____
4 _____
8 _____
7 _____
6 _____
7 _____

India

India covers an area of 1,269,338 square miles and is home to 1,129,866,154 people, who live in 28 states. The Himalaya Mountains of India are the highest mountains in the world. Monkeys and tigers are found in the forest areas, and lions and herds of elephants are protected in national parks. India has become known for its thriving film industry. The capital is New Delhi.

Anklet for a Princess: A Cinderella Tale from India, by Lila Mehta. Illustrated by Youshan Tang. Shen's Books, 2006. (Grades 1–3)

Cinduri has a lot of work to do. Every day she walks to the lake to fetch drinking water, milks the cow, cleans the house, prepares the meals, cleans the animal pens, and sells vegetables. Her stepmother and stepsister, however, don't do any of the work. They just order Cinduri about and give her a bowl of rice and a few leftovers to eat. The lake, however, is full of magic. When Godfather Snake hears of Cinduri's troubles, he vows to make her life easier. And when the Prince comes to visit the village during the annual Navaratri Festival, Godfather Snake makes it possible for her to go, dressed in the most beautiful gold-threaded sari and sparkling diamond anklets. It is there that she wins the heart of the Prince.

Balarama: A Royal Elephant, by Ted Lewin and Betsy Lewin. Lee & Low, 2009. (Grades 1–3)

Elephants, the largest land animals on Earth, have long been a part of life throughout India. Some of these huge creatures are trained to do heavy work. Others perform in public festivals. Ted Lewin and Betsy Lewin arrive in southern India and see Drona, the Royal Elephant, who leads the glorious procession on the last day of Dasara, a festival celebrated each fall. They return for the festival the following year to find that Drona has been in an accident and a new lead elephant, the majestic Balarama, has been chosen to carry the howdah in the grand parade. All eyes will be on Balarama as he makes his debut.

Catch That Crocodile!, by Anushka Ravishankar. Illustrated by Pulak Biswas. Tara Books, 2008. (Grades K–2)

Suppose a very large crocodile slithered into the center of your small village. This would indeed be very frightening. Crocodiles have very large mouths and very sharp teeth. When a full-grown crocodile slithers into a village, who will catch that crocodile that is terrifying everyone in town? Several people in the town attempt to catch the crocodile but without success. Then a youngster has an idea. Instead of catching the crocodile, she lures it to the river with fish. Problem solved!

297

Chachaji's Cup, by Uma Krishnaswami. Illustrations by Soumya Sitaraman. Children's Book Press, 2003. (Grades 2–4)

Great Uncle Chachaji tells stories over tea to Neel about great Hindu gods and demons. But it is the tale of his great uncle's favorite teacup that teaches Neel the most, for Chachaji's cup holds far more than tea. It holds the story of the 1947 partition of India and Pakistan, when families as well as countries were divided. When people laugh at the idea of Chachaji's mother saving, of all things, a teacup, Chachaji explains that it was s symbol of a successful journey.

The Ghost Catcher, by Martha Hamilton and Mitch Weiss. Illustrated by Kristen Balouch. August House, 2000. (Grades 2–4)

A barber in Bengal is so generous to others that sometimes he has nothing left for his own family. When he comes home empty-handed once again, his wife, tired of going hungry, sends him packing until he finds a way to feed the family. As the barber rests under a banyan tree, he is terrorized by a ghost. Through his cleverness, however, he turns the frightening encounter into a solution to his problems. When he returns home to his grateful wife, their money worries are over, and the barber can continue to share with those in need.

The Happiest Tree: A Yoga Story, by Uma Krishnaswami. Illustrated by Ruth Jeyaveeran. Lee & Low, 2008. (Grades 1–3)

Meena is excited about the class play, a new and improved version of "Red Riding Hood." But when she learns that she must play one of the trees in the forest, Meena's excitement vanishes. She is just too clumsy to be a quiet, steady tree.

One day at the Indian grocery store, Meena sees a yoga class in progress, and the store owner convinces her to try the children's class. Little does Meena know she is about to find a way to grow from the inside out, just like a tree, and move beyond her feelings of clumsiness and frustration.

Heart of a Tiger, by Marsha Diane Arnold. Dial, 2009. (Grades 1–3)

As the Name Day celebration approaches, a very small and ordinary young kitten tries to deserve a noble name by following the path of the beautiful Bengal tiger. In India there is a special naming ceremony, and the kitten is determined to earn a name that will show how brave and strong he is.

Kali and the Rat Snake, by Zai Whitaker. Illustrated by by Srividya Natarajan. Kane/Miller Book Publishers, 2006. (Grades 1–3)

Kali was a good student but hated going to school, where his classmates made fun of him. He had always been proud of the fact that his father was the village snake catcher, until his classmates laughed at the idea of anyone having such an occupation. They made fun, too, of the food he brought to school for his lunch, fried termites. But one day the classroom is visited by a six-foot-long rat snake. With the children screaming and the teacher hiding under his desk, Kali knows just how to capture it and becomes the class hero.

Lily's Garden of India, by Jeremy Smith. Illustrated by Rob Hefferan. Gingham Dog Press, 2003. (Grades 1–3)

Lily, a young girl, takes a walk through the garden designed, planted, and cared for by her mother, who tells her it is a magical garden. Mother has included in the garden plants from many different countries and has grouped them together by country. As Lily strolls through the plants from India she uses her imagination to see the many ways in which the plants might be used in that country, from a chapel to the flower in a girl's hair.

The Magic Apple, by Rob Cleveland. Illustrated by Baird Hoffmire. August House, 2008. (Grades 1–3)

Three brothers embark on separate journeys to fulfill their father's dying wish that each will find happiness. In their journeys, they go to distant lands, find curious treasures, travel on a flying carpet to bring life to a dying princess, and eventually learn the true meaning of giving.

Selvakumar Knew Better, by Virginia Kroll. Illustrated by Xiaojun Li. Shen's Books, 2006. (Grades 1–3)

Here is another of the many true stories about dogs who have rescued humans from disaster. The setting of this story is a village on the coast of the Indian Ocean. The dog, Selvakumar, senses danger, and sure enough a huge tsunami wave rises up from the ocean to cover the village. The villagers head for higher ground, all except a young boy, who runs home. By pulling on the child's clothing, the dog manages to get the child to higher ground and save his life.

SUMMARIZING

Standards: 5, 11, 12, 16

Summarize one of the books from India by telling its story in three sentences.

Example: *Kali and the Rat Snake,* by Zai Whitaker.

Kali hated school, where his classmates made fun of him. They laughed because his father was the village snake catcher. When his classroom is visited by a six-foot-long rat snake. Kali captures it and becomes the class hero.

Shorten your three-sentence summary to 20 words.

Kali and the Rat Snake, by Zai Whitaker.

Kali's classmates laughed that his father was the village snake catcher. Kali captures a snake and becomes the class hero.

Title _____

Three sentences:

1. _____

_____

2. _____

_____

3. _____

_____

Twenty words:

_____ _____ _____ _____

_____ _____ _____ _____

_____ _____ _____ _____

_____ _____ _____ _____

_____ _____ _____ _____

Iran

Iran covers an area of 636,293 square miles and has a population of more than 65 million people. Iran was once known as Persia. Leopards, bears, and hyenas roam the mountain areas and shrimp, lobster, and turtles abound in the Persian Gulf. Carpet looms dot the country, for Persian rugs are famous for their beauty. Petroleum is a major export. The capital is Tehran.

Ali and the Magic Stew, by Shulamith Levey Oppenheim. Illustrated by Winslow Pels. Boyds Mills Press, 2002. (Grades 1–3)

Ali, a spoiled, selfish boy, son of a wealthy Persian merchant, treats everyone with disdain until his beloved father falls ill and he must seek help from a beggar to obtain the ingredients for a stew to relieve the suffering. However, a healing stew can only cure if its ingredients have been bought with money begged from passersby, and Ali has never begged in his life. To save his father, the boy dons the beggar's ragged cloak, enduring jeers and catcalls until he completes his mission and understands the wisdom of his mother's words, "A true Muslim gives to the poor, the crippled, the homeless, the hungry."

Ali Baba: Fooling the Forty Thieves, by Marie P. Croall. Illustrated by Clint Hilinski. Lerner, 2008. (Grades 2–4)

From the pages of *The Arabian Nights* comes an amazing tale of chance and adventure. Ali Baba, a poor man who makes his living selling wood, stumbles upon a secret cave where 40 bandits have been hiding priceless treasures. He enters the cave and decides to take some treasures for himself. Ali Baba's wife is thrilled at their newfound fortune—but when she borrows a scale to weigh the riches, Ali Baba's secret gets out. Now that the secret is revealed, will Ali Baba be able to keep his fortune? Or will the bandits get their revenge?

A Gift for the King, written and illustrated by Christopher Manson. Henry Holt, 1989. (Grades 1–3)

The king of Persia receives lavish gifts from his subjects from all over the kingdom, yet none are pleasing to him. One day on a very long walk the king needs a drink of water, but there is no water source to be found, not even a lake or stream. Then a poor shepherd boy passes by carrying a water jar, which he shares with the king. The king is so pleased with the gift of water that he gives the shepherd boy all of his other gifts.

A GIFT FOR THE KING

Standards: 2, 3, 18

Four students take the parts of four explorers, each returning from a distant part of the world with a gift for the king. Each explorer must describe the gift to the king without naming it. The king must guess what the gift is.

Each explorer will choose one gift to describe.

Desert Explorer: Rattler, vulture, cactus, sand

Arctic Explorer: blubber, walrus tusk, polar bear cub, ice

Tropical Island Explorer: coconut, palm tree, lava, pineapple

Forest Explorer: Pine tree, rabbit, wildflowers, turtle shell

From *Reading the World with Picture Books* by Nancy J. Polette.
Santa Barbara, CA: Libraries Unlimited. Copyright © 2010.

Iraq

Iraq is a Middle Eastern country of 168,753 square miles and is home to 27.5 million people. It was once known as Mesopotamia. Two-fifths of the country is desert, and wild pigs roam the marshlands. The major export is oil. The capital is Baghdad.

The Girl Who Lost Her Smile, by Karim Alrawi. Illustrated by Stefan Czernecki. Winslow Press, 2000. (Grades 1–3)

Here is the Middle Eastern version of the classic tale that attempts to get a princess to smile. When this princess loses her smile, the sun won't shine nor will the stars shine at night. The people of the kingdom are frantic. Many entertainers arrive and perform for her, but no smile is forthcoming. The ones who finally get the princess to smile are a small bird and a stranger. How they do it makes a delightful story.

The Golden Sandal, by Rebecca Hickox. Illustrated by Will Hillenbrand. Holiday House, 1998. (Grades 1–3)

Poor Maha! Her jealous stepmother makes her do all the housework, while her selfish stepsister lazes about. Since Maha's father is away fishing most of the time, there is no one to help or comfort her. All that changes when Maha finds a magical red fish. In return for sparing his life, the fish promises to help Maha whenever she calls him. On the night Maha is forbidden to attend a celebration of the coming wedding of a wealthy merchant's daughter, the fish is true to his word and a dainty golden sandal is the key to Maha's happiness.

Silent Music: A Story of Baghdad, by James Rumford. Roaring Brook Press, 2008. (Grades 2–4)

When bombs begin to fall on Baghdad in 2003, Ali drowns out the sound of war with a pen. Like other children living in Baghdad, Ali loves soccer, music, and dancing, but most of all, he loves the ancient art of calligraphy. When bombs begin to fall on his city, Ali turns to his pen, writing sweeping and gliding words to the silent music that drowns out the war all around him. Illustrations of stamps, money, and postcards reinforce the Baghdad setting along with an intricate collage of Ali huddling under a blanket next to his cat, writing. In an eloquent ending, he discovers that although the word "war" flows easily, the pen "stubbornly resists me when I make the difficult waves and slanted staff of salam—peace."

WRITE A CINDERELLA TALE
FROM THE MIDDLE EAST

Standards: 1, 4, 7, 14

The Golden Sandal is a Cinderella tale from Iraq. After reading stories from the Middle East, make a list of the common elements found in the stories.

Before writing, answer these questions:

In your tale: What is her name? _____

Where would she live? _____

What jobs would she have to do? _____

_____

What foods would she have to prepare? _____

_____

Whom would the girl want to marry? _____

What transportation is used in this time and place? _____

_____

What would be the event everyone would want to attend? _____

_____

Who would help her? How? _____

_____

What would her dress look like? _____

_____

What would she lose? How? _____

_____

Decide on a setting a city, a mosque, a marketplace, a sultan's palace, etc., and a time (past, present) for your Cinderella story. Be sure that every word you add reflects the time and place you are writing about. For some tales, research may be necessary.

Israel

Israel is a small country, established n 1948, of 8,020 square miles and a population of 6.5 million people. In addition to its coastal plain, it has highlands in the north and desert land in the south. Many highly skilled workers are found in research institutes and universities, resulting in new technologies in software and electronics. The capital is Jerusalem.

Behold the Trees, by Sue Alexander. Illustrated by Leonid Gore. Arthur Levine Books, 2001. (Grades 2–4)

Once a land called Canaan bloomed with all sorts of wonderful wild trees. Cities and towns were built, but "no new trees were planted." Then 600 years of war followed. Over the centuries, the land was fought over, conquered, and reconquered. Built up and burnt down. Exploited and neglected. Until no trees would grow and the land became barren. And then new people arrived and began to plant again and slowly made Israel bloom again, with millions of newly planted trees.

Gershon's Monster: A Story for the Jewish New Year, retold by Eric A. Kimmel. Illustrated by Jon J. Muth. Scholastic Press, 2000. (Grades 2–4)

When his sins threaten the lives of his beloved twin children, a Jewish man finally repents of his wicked ways. For years and years Gershon has committed many wicked deeds but never felt sorry about them. In fact, he swept his bad deeds into the cellar and once a year put them in a bag and tossed them in the ocean. When he becomes the father of twin boys, his children are threatened by the sea monster, so Gershon, who is sorry for his bad deeds, offers himself instead.

Harvest of Light, by Allison Ofanansky. Illustrated by Eliyahu Alpern. Kar-Ben Publishing, 2008. (Grades 2–4)

The Harvest of Light in Israel is the time of the olive harvest. Here you can see the planting and growing of the olive plants as they finally yield the delicious ripe olives. Some are collected for eating. Other olives are pressed for olive oil. The oil is then used for fuel as a family lights the candles of the menorah to celebrate Hanukkah.

Letter on the Wind: A Chanukah Tale, by Sarah Marwil Lamstein. Illustrated by Neil Waldman. Boyds Mills Press, 2007. (Grades 2–4)

When there is no oil for Chanukah, Hayim, the poorest man in the village, sends the Almighty a letter asking for help. The letter is picked up and tossed about by the wind until it floats down to come to rest in the hands of a wealthy merchant. The merchant is touched by the letter and sends not only oil for the village lamp but many other gifts as well. But many think Hayim is a thief and refuse to use the generous supplies that Hayim himself faithfully trusts are a "gift from the Almighty." A new letter questioning the situation prompts the merchant to visit the village to assure everyone of the Almighty's request for him to provide help.

Shlemiel Crooks, by Anna Olswanger. Illustrated by Paula Goodman Koz. Junebug Books, 2005. (Grades 2–4)

Here is a very different introduction to the Jewish holiday of Passover. It seems that way back in 1919 there was a tavern operated by Reb Elias Olschwanger. Very late one night two thieves pulled up at the tavern in their horse and wagon and tried to steal the wine that was stored for Passover. We then go back in time to a dispute between the pharaoh and the people over who should have wine for the celebration.

Solomon and the Trees, by Matt Biers-Ariel. Illustrated by Esti Silverberg-Kiss. UAHC Press, 2001. (Grades 1–3)

A child who is destined to be a king spends much time in the forest. He loves the growing things and the many animals he befriends. As an adult he forgets about his childhood experiences and learns a lesson all over again about the importance of taking care of the land we all share.

LISTING RESPONSE

Standards: 2, 4, 6, 8

If the school is located near a park or open area where trees are growing, take the children on a nature walk. Ask them to observe as carefully as they can the trees they see. Do they see birds, nests, insects, evidence of boring, fungus, broken limbs, moss? Which trees look young and healthy? Which trees look older? Use the pattern that follows to describe one tree.

I see a willow tree

    (Where?) In the garden, by the stream

I see a willow tree

    (describe) graceful tree, slender tree, green tree

I see a willow tree

    (doing what?) bending, swaying, shading

I see a willow tree

I see a _____ tree

    (Where?) In the _____ by the _____

I see a _____ tree

    (describe) _____ tree, _____ tree, _____ tree

I see a willow tree

    (doing what?) _____ _____ _____

I see a _____ tree

Japan

Japan covers an area of 145,882 square miles and has a population of 127,467,972 people. It consists of a string of islands that stretch for 1,500 miles. Bears, foxes, raccoon dogs, and deer inhabit the forest areas. Sea turtles, lizards, and the giant salamander are found in the coastal areas. Japan is one of the world's largest producers of motor vehicles and technology goods. The capital is Tokyo.

Amaterasu: Return of the Sun, by by Paul D. Storrie. Illustrated by Ron Randall. Lerner, 2007. (Grades 2–4)

Amaterasu's parents create the first eight islands of Japan. Amaterasu's father later puts his children in charge of parts of the natural world. Beautiful and kindly Amaterasu is made the goddess of the sun. But her brother, Susano, god of the sea and storms, is jealous of his sister's position. In fear of Susano's temper, Amaterasu hides in a cave, plunging the world into darkness. The other gods and goddesses must come up with a clever plan to lure Amaterasu from her hiding place and restore order to the world.

Basho and the River Stones, by Tim Myers. Illustrated by Oki S. Han. Marshall Cavendish, 2004. (Grades K–2)

Deceived by the clever fox, Basho trades the use of his cherry tree for three gold coins, which turn out to be washed river stones. The trickery inspires the famous poet to write a haiku, and the fox, ashamed of his actions, must devise another trick to make amends.

The Beckoning Cat, by Koko Nishizuka. Illustrated by Rosanne Litzinger. Holiday House, 2009. (Grades K–2)

A long time ago in a village by the sea, a mud-covered white cat appeared on Yohei's doorstep. Yohei was very poor, but he welcomed the stray cat and shared his dinner with her before she disappeared. Later, when Yohei's father grew ill, the boy became desperate. How could he work if he had to stay home and care for his father? But the little white cat remembered Yohei's generosity and returned, bringing help with a wave of her paw.

Butterflies for Kiri, written and illustrated by Cathryn Falwell. Lee & Low, 2008. (Grades 1–3)

Kiri loves to make things. When she receives an origami set for her birthday, she can't wait to try making a butterfly, just like the one Auntie Lu had made. Kiri chooses a bright purple paper and carefully follows the steps, but the paper tears after just four folds. Her beautiful paper is ruined! Disappointed but not discouraged, Kiri continues to practice making origami butterflies. Then one beautiful spring day in the park Kiri is inspired to make a picture of what she sees, and her creative and colorful solution turns out to be more rewarding than she could have imagined.

Erika-san, written and illustrated by Allen Say. Houghton Mifflin, 2009. (Grades 1–3)

As a child Erika was fascinated by a picture in her grandmother's house. It was a picture of a Japanese tea house with lighted windows that seemed to speak to her. Erika completes her schooling and goes to Japan to teach. Her second mission is to find the tea house of her childhood. Unable to remember her Japanese, she sees Tokyo as "a hundred cities all crammed together" and knows that she will not find her house there. After moving to and rejecting a second location (it's picture-pretty, but too noisy), she finds just the right spot in which to live and teach.

The Falling Flowers, by Jennifer B. Reed. Illustrated by Dick Cole. Shen's Books, 2005. (Grades 1–3)

What fun it is for a little girl to ride on a train. She is going to the big city of Tokyo with her grandmother, who promises her a special treat. It is not the zoo. It is not a beautiful shrine. None of the little girl's guesses are correct. Then they enter a place with hundreds of cherry trees in full bloom. What a beautiful sight! What a treat!

The Furry-legged Teapot, by Tim Myers. Illustrated by Robert McGuire. Marshall Cavendish, 2007. (Grades K–2)

Tanukis possess the ability to magically turn themselves into other things. Yoshi is excited and cannot wait to begin transforming himself. His family advises him to be patient and to practice his concentration first. Like a typical youngster, however, Yoshi disregards the advice of his elders and secretly practices changing himself. Bursting with excitement and confidence, he runs into a farmhouse and promptly changes himself into a teakettle. A problem arises when the kettle is put on the fire. The heat causes Yoshi such pain that his legs pop out (but nothing else), and poor Yoshi cannot concentrate hard enough to transform himself back.

Honda: The Boy Who Dreamed of Cars, by Mark Weston. Illustrated by Katie Yamasaki. Lee & Low, 2008. (Grades 2–4)

One day in 1914 when Soichiro Honda was seven years old, an astonishing, moving dust cloud appeared in his small Japanese town. The cause was a leaky, noisy automobile—the first the boy had ever seen. At that moment Honda fell in love with cars, and a dream took hold. He would one day make them himself. It took Honda many years to reach his goal. Along the way he became an expert mechanic and manufacturer of car parts. After World War II he developed a motorized bicycle, the forerunner of his innovative motorcycles. Eventually Honda began manufacturing cars, first race cars and then consumer cars. Constantly seeking ways to make his products better than his competitors', Honda grew into a global industry leader.

The Hungriest Boy in the World, by Lensey Namioka. Illustrated by Aki Sogabe. Holiday House, 2001. (Grades 1–3)

Jiro is a boy who has a bad habit. He will put anything in his mouth, whether it is food, rocks, or seaweed. After swallowing the Hunger Monster, Jiro begins eating everything in sight: his sister's sushi, his father's fishing nets, even his own sleeping quilt. A doctor, a priest, and a woman who speaks to spirits try to help, but to no avail, until at last his family finds a way to lure the monster out of Jiro's stomach.

If Not for the Calico Cat, by Mary Blount Christian. Illustrated by Sebastia Serra. Dutton Children's Books, 2007. (Grades K–2)

The crew of *The Jade Lotus* watches other ships disappear from sight, sure that they have slipped over the edge of the world. To save themselves from the same fate, their cabin boy, Hiro, entices a calico cat aboard. But the calico cat isn't happy; she misses her warm spot on the wharf. Roaming the ship, she runs through the flour barrel, walks over the captain's maps, causing havoc wherever she goes. Meanwhile, a mighty storm brews. Did this calico cat really bring the sailors good luck?

The Invisible Seam, by Andy William Frew. Illustrated by Jun Matsuoka. Moon Mountain Publishing, 2003. (Grades 1–3)

Michi is very good at what she does, which is sewing kimonos for her employer, Mistress Shinyo. Michi is an apprentice and has promised to do her very best in her work. However, she does such beautiful work that the other apprentices are jealous and begin to do things to make Michi's work look bad. How will she be able to keep her promise when things go from bad to worse?

Kamishibai Man, written and illustrated by Allen Say. Houghton Mifflin, 2005. (Grades 1–3)

The Kamishibai man used to ride his bicycle into town, where he would tell stories to the children and sell them candy, but gradually, fewer and fewer children came running at the sound of his clappers. They were all watching their new televisions instead. Finally, only one boy remained, and he had no money for candy. Years later the Kamishibai man and his wife make another batch of candy, and he pedals into town to tell one more story—his own. When he comes out of the reverie of his memories, he looks around to see he is surrounded by familiar faces—the children he used to entertain have returned, all grown up and more eager than ever to listen to his delightful tales.

Kogi's Mysterious Journey, by Elizabeth Partridge. Illustrated by Aki Sogabe. Dutton Children's Books, 2003. (Grades 2–4)

Kogi longs to capture the spirit of nature in his art. He draws majestic mountains, trees, waterfalls, and Lake Biwa's glimmering fish, but his paintings are always lifeless and dull—until one supernatural morning when he wades into the cool, deep, shimmering water and becomes a golden fish. There he learns firsthand the freedom within the silence that pulsates in all of life. When hunger drives him to risk the fisherman's baited hook, another miraculous transformation forces Kogi back to his life as a painter, but a painter now forever changed. Elizabeth Partridge's elegant prose and Aki Sogabe's cut-paper illustrations bring clean lines and lush color to this mysterious tale of discovery.

The Stonecutter, by Jon J. Muth. Illustrated by John Kuramoto. Feiwel and Friends, 2009. (Grades 2–4)

A lonely stonecutter spends his days chipping away at the mountain, until one day he sees a prince ride by and wishes to become a prince. He gets his wish but is soon not satisfied, for the sun seems more powerful than the prince. He asks the great spirit to let him become the sun. Soon he asks to become the rain and finally to become the mountain, which is so powerful it can withstand any force . . . except, that is, the stonecutter, who day after day chips away at its base.

TSUNAMI!, by Kimiko Kajikawa. Illustrated by Ed Young. Philomel Books, 2009. (Grades 2–4)

Ojisan, the oldest and wealthiest man in the village, doesn't join the others at the rice ceremony. Instead, he watches from his balcony. He feels something is coming, something he can't describe. When he sees the monster wave pulling away from the beach, he knows. Tsunami! But the villagers below can't see the danger. Will Ojisan risk everything he has to save them? Can he?

Wabi Sabi, by Mark Reibstein. Illustrated by Ed Young. Little, Brown, 2008. (Grades K–2)

Wabi Sabi, a cat living in the city of Kyoto, learns about the Japanese concept of beauty through simplicity as she asks various animals she meets about the meaning of her name, which is hard to explain. Wabi Sabi first asks her cat friend Snowball what it means. "It's a kind of beauty," she notes. Rascal the dog claims it is "too hard to explain to someone like you." A bird sends Wabi Sabi on a journey. The cat proceeds through the busy city to the woods. There she meets a monkey, who tries to explain, telling her, "Listen. Watch. Feel." "Simple things are beautiful." Seeing herself in her bowl of tea, Wabi Sabi seems to begin to understand. On her way home, she stops by the Silver Palace, enjoying its simple beauty. She composes three poems and at last truly begins to understand the meaning of her name.

Wink: The Ninja Who Wanted to Be Noticed, by J. C. Phillipps. Viking Children's Books, 2009. (Grades 1–3)

The happiest day of Wink's life was when he was accepted to the Summer Moon School for Young Ninjas. He is sure that he will be a great ninja. Silence is the first lesson, and everyone is very, very silent . . . except for Wink. Stealth is the second lesson, and everyone is very, very stealthy . . . except for Wink. Finally, Wink decides that he will be silent and stealthy. But no one notices! What's the point of being a great ninja if no one notices? Maybe Wink wasn't meant to be a ninja?

Yuki and the One Thousand Carriers, by Gloria Whelan. Illustrated by Yan Nascimbene. Sleeping Bear Press, 2008. (Grades 2–4)

Japanese governor must make a 300-mile trip to the capital and takes his family with him. The journey is seen through the eyes of Yuki, the governor's young daughter, who travels with her mother and small dog. Their party, with its 1,000 carriers, passes over a river, through snowy mountains, and beside the ocean, where Mt. Fuji rises in the distance. Yuki describes the sights she sees through the shuttered windows of her palanquin , as well as the food and accommodations along the way. The haikus she writes at the request of her teacher tell of her homesickness and eventual acceptance of her new life.

ACTIVITIES ABOUT JAPAN

Standards: 2, 4, 5, 21

Picture and Poetry

Collect a supply of nature magazines or Sunday magazine sections of newspapers and a supply of books of poetry. After sharing Japanese haiku, talk about how the author searched to find just the right words.. Encourage children to find a sentence or short poem they particularly love. Then they can go through the magazines to find a picture to go with the words. Each child could have just two lines accompanied by one picture. Older students who are into photography could take their own pictures, selecting exactly the scene needed to represent the chosen words. The poems do not have to be haiku.

Standards: 2, 4

Write about Japan

Find out:

1. Name

2. Two physical features

3. Three activities you can do there

4. Four things you would see

5. A descriptive phrase

Use this information to complete the pattern below.

_____

_____ _____

_____ _____ _____

_____ _____ _____ _____

_____

From *Reading the World with Picture Books* by Nancy J. Polette.
Santa Barbara, CA: Libraries Unlimited. Copyright © 2010.

Korea

There are two Koreas. North Korea covers 46,540 square miles and has slightly more than 23 million people. The capital is Pyongyang. South Korea covers 38,023 square miles and has 49 million people. The capital is Seoul.

The Firekeeper's Son, by Linda Sue Park. Illustrated by Julie Downing. Clarion Books, 2004. (Grades 2–4)

In Korea in the early 1800s, news from the countryside reached the king by means of signal fires. On one mountaintop after another, a fire was lit when all was well. If the king did not see a fire, that meant trouble, and he would send out his army. Sang-hee is the son of the village firekeeper. When his father is unable to light the fire one night, young Sang-hee must take his place. Sang-hee knows how important it is for the fire to be lit, but he wishes that he could see soldiers . . . just once. He must make a hard choice.

The Korean Cinderella, by Shirley Climo. Illustrated by Ruth Heller. HarperCollins, 1993. (Grades 1–3)

In the land of Korea, where magical creatures are as common as cabbages, lives a child named Pear Blossom. Pear Blossom is as lovely as the pear tree planted in celebration of her birth, but she is mistreated by Omoni, her jealous stepmother. Omoni forces her to rise before the sun and cook and clean until midnight, and demands that Pear Blossom complete three tasks no human could possibly do alone. She has to fill a water jar with a hole in it the size of an onion; hull and polish every grain of rice from a huge sack scattered all over the courtyard; and weed the rice paddies in less than a day, paddies that spread out before her like a great green lake. But Pear Blossom is not alone. Three magical animals assist her: a gigantic frog, a flock of sparrows and a huge black ox. It is with the help of these creatures that Pear Blossom is able to attend the festival and becomes a nobleman's wife.

The Love of Two Stars: A Korean Legend, retold and illustrated by Janie J. Park. Groundwood Books, 2005. (Grades 2–4)

Kyonu was a skilled farmer whose steers were the best in the land. Jingnyo is a master weaver whose cloth is the best in the land. They live in a kingdom in the starry sky. They fall in love the moment they meet, forgetting all about the cattle to care for and the cloth to be made. This angers the king of the starry realm, who separates them and tells them that they can meet in the Milky Way once a year, on the seventh day of the seventh month. But when the time finally arrives, Kyonu and Jingnyo cannot make it across the river of stars to be together. Their tears of sorrow cause endless rain upon the earth, until the magpies and crows think of a way to help them.

Magic Spring, by Nami Rhee. Putnam, 1993. (Grades 1–3)

An old man and his wife, longing for a child, discover a fountain of youth and benefit from its magic when they take small sips, but the water has a different effect on their greedy neighbor, who has taunted the couple because they did not have a child. The greedy neighbor drinks all of the water in large gulps and regresses to childhood, where he becomes an infant. The elderly couple adopts him.

New Clothes for New Year's Day, by Hyun-Joo Bae. Kane Miller, 2007. (Grades K–2)

New Year's Day in Korea means new clothes, and each piece of clothing has significance. As a child dresses herself she explains the meaning of her skirt, shirt, and jacket as well as her fancy socks and flowered shoes. When she is fully dressed she is ready to visit friends and wish them a happy New Year.

Sir Whong and the Golden Pig, by Han S. Oki and Stephanie Plunkett. Illustrated by Han S. Oki. Dial, 1993. (Grades 1–3)

When he manages to get a loan of 1,000 nyung by putting up a fake golden pig as collateral, a stranger thinks that he has outwitted the wise and generous Sir Whong. When Sir Whong realizes has been tricked, he must come up with a way to win back his money and his honor.

The Tiger and the Dried Persimmon, by Janie Jaehyun Park. Groundwood Books 2003. (Grades 1–3)

In this version of a classic Korean folk tale, which the author heard over and over again from her grandmother, the proud and boasting Tiger is brought low by his own vanity and foolishness. While trying to steal an ox in order to eat it, the tiger finds himself outside a small cottage in which a mother is calming a baby with an offer of a dried persimmon. The tiger, not understanding what is happening, persuades himself that a dried persimmon is the wildest and fiercest beast in the world. When in a comedy of errors a thief mistakenly jumps on the Tiger's back, the Tiger believes that this is the terrifying persimmon and panics.

Tigers, Frogs, and Rice Cakes: A Book of Korean Proverbs, by Daniel D. Holt. Illustrated by Soma Han. Shen's Books, 2008. (Grades 4–6)

Sok-dam (folk sayings) represent enduring values held throughout all strata of Korean society. Each proverb in this book focuses on a significant folk symbol or belief deeply held by Koreans. In a culture where language ability, particularly taciturnity, is highly respected, proverbs are used as a tool for expressing oneself with grace and style.

The Trip Back Home, by Janet S. Wong. Illustrated by Bo Jia. Harcourt, 2000. (Grades 1–3)

A Korean American child visits her mother's homeland. She meets her grandparents and her aunts for the first time—and discovers that family love is universal. These are the gifts brought across the ocean to Korea: leather gloves, an apron with pockets like flowers, a book with pictures and simple words. What is given in return? Simple gifts like these—and so much more.

WRITE A KOREAN TALE

Standards: 14, 15, 16, 21

Fill in the blank spaces to create a Korean tale. Use your imagination!

Title _____

Once upon a time in the capital city of Seoul lived _____. This
_____ was very _____ but
could not _____. One night this
_____ wanted to _____.

[He/she] went into the forest and _____. Suddenly a
_____ appeared and gave the
_____ a _____.
The _____ was frightened, but he/she took the
_____ and went back home as
_____ as a _____. When the
_____ arrived home, he/she _____ the
_____, which the _____ had given him/her. Immediately
the _____ turned into a _____. The
_____ was very, very happy. Now the _____
could _____.

Lebanon

Lebanon is a small middle eastern country of 4,015 square miles and is home to almost 4 million people. It is a land of rugged mountains and winding rivers. Cedar from its now depleted forests was used in shipbuilding. It is known today for its banking industry and as a trade center. The capital is Beirut.

Sami and the Time of the Troubles, by Florence Parry Heide. Clarion Books, 1992. (Grades 1–3)

On good days a 10-year-old Lebanese boy goes to school, helps his mother with chores, and plays with his friends. On bad days he lives with his family in his uncle's basement shelter while bombings occur and fighting takes place on his street. In the basement shelter there is little to do but listen to the radio or stare at the carpet. When they emerge from the shelter they see a ruined city. Sami and his friend mourn the loss of their play fort and help clean up after an attack.

FRIENDSHIP ACTIVITY

Standards: 6, 15

1. Discussion

   What is friendship?

   What things do friends share with one another?

   Is it necessary to have a lot of material things to enjoy life?

   What behaviors are associated with friendship?

2. Searching the newspaper: Find and cut out examples from the newspaper of:

   A. Two or more people who appear to be friends.

   B. A news story or picture about people who do not get along.

   C. A picture of something you would like to give to a friend.

   D. Write the word F R I E N D as an acrostic. Find and cut out words from the newspaper that begin with each letter and that describe a friend.

Malaysia

Malaysia covers an area of 127,316 square miles and is home to 24,821,286 people. Most of Malaysia is located in Southeast Asia. A large variety of animals live in the forests, including elephants, tigers, and wild pigs as well as the more scarce rhino and orangutan. The most important cash crops are palm oil and rubber. The capital is Kuala Lumpur.

Chopsticks for My Noodle Soup: Eliza's Life in Malaysia, by Susan E. Goodman. Illustrated by Michael Doolittle. Lerner, 2000. (Grades 1–3)

Five-year-old Eliza Doolittle from Connecticut narrates this photo-essay about her year in Malaysia with her scientist mother, who was studying the rain forest, and photographer father. She learns to adjust to a more primitive life where the bathroom is outside, she can spit her toothpaste out the door, clothes are washed in the river, and people sit on the floor and eat with chopsticks. Eliza also learns to speak the language. The child describes her house, the school she attends, the people she meets, the open food market, and more.

PACK YOUR BAGS GAME

Standards: 4, 5, 18

This word game will stretch one's imagination. It can be played singly or as a group. To begin, pretend that you are moving to Malaysia. What would you pack in your trunk? Name one item, then add a second item that begins with the last letter of the first item. Continue to add items until you run out of things to add. Remember, each item must begin with the last letter of the last item added; for example, jeans, socks, sweater, raincoat, etc.

Mongolia

Fewer people live in Mongolia than in any other Asian country. Nearly 3 million people live in its 604,250,000 square miles. The official language is Mongolian, although many people speak Russian or Chinese. Much of Mongolia is pasture land, so the people have large herds of livestock. Animals found in the northern part of Mongolia are elk, snow leopards, brown bears, and wolverines. The capital of Mongolia is Ulaanbaatar.

Horse Song, written and illustrated by Ted Lewin and Betsy Lewin. Lee & Low, 2008. (Grades 2–4)

"Giingooo! Giiingooooooo!" Tamir and the other young jockeys sing to their horses in wailing, high-pitched voices. They are getting ready to ride in the Naadam, the Mongolian summer festival. Tamir is one of many boys and girls who will race half-wild horses across the open desert for honor and glory.

It is these legendary child jockeys that Ted Lewin and Betsy Lewin have traveled to Mongolia to see. In the camp of the horse trainers, the Lewins marvel at the skill of the riders as they "sweat up" their horses, galloping by in swirls of dust and thundering hooves. On the day of the big race, everyone is up before sunrise, watching the riders begin their long trek to the starting line. Will Tamir be able to keep control of his horse during the 14-mile race? Who will emerge as the winner as the shimmering dust cloud of riders approaches the finish line?

RESEARCH A MONGOLIAN ANIMAL

Standards: 2, 5, 13, 15

Choose one animal found in Mongolia. Read about the animal and report your findings using this pattern.

My greatest wish is

to roam freely_____
(where?)

to grow _____
(to what size?)

to find _____ satisfy my hunger
(food)

to see my _____
(describe)

to be protected from _____
(what?)

But I didn't want

to see _____

to hear _____

to feel _____

to become one of many endangered species.

From *Reading the World with Picture Books* by Nancy J. Polette.
Santa Barbara, CA: Libraries Unlimited. Copyright © 2010.

Nepal

Located on the southern slopes of the Himalayan Mountains, Nepal covers an area of 54,363 square miles and has a population of about 29 million people. The forest areas are home to tigers, leopards, buffalo, and many deer. Legend says that the Abominable Snowman lives in the high mountains. The capital of Nepal is Kathmandu.

Kami and the Yaks, by Andrea Stenn Stryer. Illustrated by Bert Dodson. Bay Otter Press, 2007. (Grades 2–4)

Just before the start of a new trek, in the Himalaya Mountains of Nepal a Sherpa family discovers that their yaks are missing. Young Kami, anxious to help his brother and father maintain their livelihood, sets off by himself to find the wandering herd. A spunky deaf child who is unable to speak, Kami attempts to summon the yaks with his shrill whistle. Failing to rout them, he hustles up the steep mountainside to search the yaks' favorite grazing spots. On the way he encounters the rumblings of a fierce storm, which quickly becomes more threatening. Surmounting his fear of being alone in the midst of treacherous lightning and hail, Kami uses his heightened sense of observation to finally locate the yaks. Reunited with their animals, the astonished family is once again able to transport their gear and guide the mountain climbers into the majestic terrain.

PREDICTING THE WEATHER

Standards: 4, 8

Middle grade students will enjoy seeing the *Farmer's Almanac* with its annual weather predictions. Kami might have found the predictions helpful when he set out on his journey. Many meteorologists say that it is impossible to predict the weather a year in advance. Others believe the forecasts in the *Farmer's Almanac* are fairly accurate.

Keep a chart for one week to compare the *Farmer's Almanac* forecasts with the actual weather.

Date	*Farmer's Almanac* Forecast	Local Paper	Actual Weather

Pakistan

Pakistan covers an area of 310,400 square miles and is home to about 3 million people. The Himalayan Mountains cover northern Pakistan. The country is largely agricultural, with small quantities of oil and large natural gas fields. The capital is Islamabad.

Four Feet, Two Sandals, by by Karen Lynn Williams and Khadra Mohammed. Illustrated by Doug Chayka. Eerdmans Books for Young Readers, 2007. (Grades 1–3)

When relief workers bring used clothing to the refugee camp, everyone scrambles to grab whatever they can. Ten-year-old Lina is thrilled when she finds a sandal that fits her foot perfectly, until she sees that another girl has the matching shoe. Soon Lina and Feroza meet, each wearing one coveted sandal. Together as they wash clothes in the river and wait for their names to be on the list to go to America, they solve the problem of having four feet and two sandals.

Listen to the Wind, by Greg Mortenson. Illustrated by Susan L. Roth. Penguin, 2009. (Grades 2–4)

Greg Mortenson stumbled, lost and delirious, into the remote Himalayan village of Korphe after a failed climb up K2 Mountain. The villagers saved his life, and he vowed to return and build them a school. This is the story of how he kept his promise, told in the voice of Korphe's children, and shows how one person can change thousands of lives.

Ruler of the Courtyard, by Rukhsana Khan. Illustrated by R. Gregory Christie. Viking, 2003. (Grades K–2)

Is it just Saba, or do chickens scare everyone? The chickens in her yard are especially mean, chasing her and pecking at her toes. But when she sees a snake in the bathhouse, Saba realizes that chickens aren't her only problem. She has to act fast to protect herself and her grandma from the snake. Can she conquer the chickens and the snake to become the Ruler of the Courtyard? Does she really have to conquer them at all?

Silly Chicken, by Rukhsana Khan. Illustrated by Yunmee Kyong. Viking, 2005. (Grades K–2)

"Ami loves her chicken better than me. She calls her Bibi, I call her silly." Rani's mother loves Bibi the chicken more than her. At least that's what Rani thinks. That silly chicken gets all the attention, and Rani just can't stand it. Even worse, Bibi seems to know she's the favorite! But when Bibi disappears one afternoon, Rani realizes how sad her mother is. Will Rani's jealousy disappear, too? Will the egg that's left behind help?

THE STORYTELLER

Standards: 10, 11, 12

It can be fun to read a story together and to respond to the story in different ways. Before reading, each person in the group will be responsible for a different way of responding.

The Storyteller

Summarize the book or story using this form:

_____ wanted _____
     (main character)

_____

But (tell three things that happened)

1. _____
2. _____
3. _____
So _____

The Artist

Draw a picture of an important part of the story or use a Venn diagram or graphic organizer to report on the story.

The Poet

Write a poem about the main character in the story. Use the form of the cinquain.

    First Line: Who the character is (not the name)

    Second Line: Two words to describe the character

    Third Line: Three action words that tell what the character did

    Fourth Line: Four words that show how the character felt

    Fifth Line: Name of the character

Philippines

The Philippines are made up of more than 7,000 tropical islands and cover 115,830 square miles. The population is slightly more than 91 million people. Principal exports are electronic equipment, coconuts, and sugar. Much of the land area is forest, with more than 10,000 different species of plants. The capital is Manila.

Abadeha: The Philippine Cinderella, by Myrna J. de la Paz. Illustrated by Youshang Tang. Shen's Books, 2001. (Grades 1–3)

In this version of *Cinderella*, set in the Philippines, Abadeha endures abuse by her stepmother before being helped by the Spirit of the Forest. Elements of the Philippine culture are evident. Instead of white mice, there is a sarimanok, "a chicken with long flowing tail and feathers the color of the rainbow." Instead of a hearth of ashes, there is a mat torn up by a wild pig to be rewoven like new. And as in the traditional tale, she proves her worthiness to marry the chieftain by being the only maiden who can remove a ring from his finger.

Cora Cooks Pancit, by Dorina K. Lazo Gilmore. Illustrated by Kristi Valiant. Shen's Books, 2007. (Grades 1–3)

Cora loves being in the kitchen, but she always gets stuck doing the kid jobs like licking the spoon. One day, however, when her older sisters and brother head out, Cora finally gets the chance to be Mama's assistant chef. And of all the delicious Filipino dishes that dance through Cora's head, she and Mama decide to make pancit, her favorite noodle dish. With Mama's help, Cora does the grown-up jobs like shredding the chicken and soaking the noodles (perhaps Mama won't notice if she takes a nibble of chicken or sloshes a little water on the floor). Cora even gets to stir the noodles in the pot—carefully—while Mama supervises. When dinner is finally served, her siblings find out that Cora did all their grown-up tasks, and Cora waits anxiously to see what everyone thinks of her cooking.

The Mats, by Francisco Arcellana. Illustrated by Hermès Alègrè. Kane/Miller Books, 1999. (Grades 2–4)

Marcelina's father comes home from a trip to Manila with beautiful hand-made sleeping mats for each member of his large family, which includes six brothers and sisters. However, there are three additional mats left when each member of the family has received his or her mat. These mats are a memorial to the three daughters who died when they were very young.

WHEN THE SUN COMES UP PATTERN

Standards: 13, 14

What happens in (choose a country) when the sun comes up? Choose one:

In Manila, in the Philippines,

When the sun comes up

_____

_____

_____

_____

When the sun comes up

_____

_____

_____

_____

And I

_____

_____

_____

_____

From *Reading the World with Picture Books* by Nancy J. Polette.
Santa Barbara, CA: Libraries Unlimited. Copyright © 2010.

Thailand

Thailand covers an area of 198,455 square miles and has a population of 65 million people. Rice and sugar cane are its major exports. Domestic animals are elephants, horses, cattle, and mules. The capital is Bangkok.

Peek!: A Thai Hide-and-Seek, by Minfong Ho. Illustrated by Holly Meade. Candlewick Press, 2004. (Grades K–2)

A father and daughter play hide-and-seek in the midst of the animals near their house in Thailand. Papa calls on all the creatures of the jungle to help find his baby. The father repeatedly calls out, "Jut-Ay, Baby, peek-a-boo, Want to play? Where are you?" Instead of his child he is answered by a dragonfly, a rooster, a puppy, a turtle, a monkey, a hornbill, a snake, an elephant, a crocodile, and a tiger.

Tiger, Tiger, by Dee Lillegard. Illustrated by Susan Guevara. Putnam, 2002. (Grades K–2)

No one will play with Pocu, so he slouches off to amuse himself-and finds a wonderful feather. Swish. He makes the flowers bloom. Swish. He creates a great, murmuring shadow with two eyes burning bright. Pocu wants a playmate, but when the shadow follows him into the jungle and starts taking over the game, he fears he has created a monster. And it's up to him to find a way to handle his dangerous creation.

The Umbrella Queen, by Shirin Yim Bridges. Illustrated by Taeeun Yoo. Greenwillow Books, 2008. (Grades 1–3)

In a village in Thailand where everyone makes umbrellas, young Noot dreams of painting the most beautiful one and leading the annual parade as Umbrella Queen, but her unconventional designs, rather than traditional flowers and butterflies, displease her parents, who tell her she must go back to the old designs. Noot obeys, knowing that the King is coming soon to name the one who has painted the most beautiful umbrella. After all, the King would never choose a queen who breaks from tradition . . . would he be pleased to see tiny umbrellas decorated with dancing elephants?

The White Elephant, by Sid Fleischman. Illustrated by Robert McGuire. Greenwillow Books, 2006. (Grades 2–4)

How can a beautiful white elephant be a terrible curse? Run-Run, a young elephant trainer, discovers the answer when he incurs the fury of the prince. The boy's punishment? The gift of an elephant, white as a cloud. From that moment forward, the curse reveals itself. According to tradition, so rare an elephant cannot be allowed to work for its keep. It is poor Run-Run who must feed the beast the hundreds of pounds of food it eats each day, scrub it clean, brush its pom-pom of a tail, wash behind its ears, and, above all, keep it from doing any work. Oh, if only Run-Run could make the magnificent white elephant disappear! Clever as a magician, he does—but the curse has tricks of its own for Run-Run.

DECORATE AN UMBRELLA

Pretend you are looking at the top of an umbrella. Decorate it for others to look at.

THAILAND DATA BANK

Standards: 13, 16, 21

You can get information from a data bank. Make a data bank about any animal, like the one on this page about elephants.

THE AFRICAN ELEPHANT:			
EATS	LIVES	HAS	DOES
grasses	Africa	long trunk	grows 12 feet tall
leaves	tropical forests	ivory tusks	bathes in dust
495 lbs. per day	river valleys	only four teeth	pulls down trees
		wrinkled skin	lives 60–70 years

Use the information from the data bank in the blank spaces below. Sing the song to the tune of "London Bridge."

Elephants have _____ and _____

_____ and _____

_____ and _____

Elephants eat _____ and _____

And they _____

Vietnam

Vietnam covers an area of 127,243 square miles and has a population of more than 85 million people. Tigers and snow leopards are found in forest areas. Water buffalo are used in harvesting rice. Seafood is prepared for export. The capital is Hanoi.

Children of Vietnam, by Marybeth Lorbiecki. Lerner, 2007. (Grades 3–5)

Life in Vietnam is colored by a long and often violent history. One of its most recent struggles was the American War—called the Vietnam War by Americans—which ended in the mid-1970s. The war left great scars on both the land and the people, but finally Vietnam is at peace. Through words and pictures, understand what it's like to grow up in Vietnam.

Dia's Story Cloth: The Hmong People's Journey of Freedom, by Dia Cha, Chiie Thao Cha, and Nhia Thao Cha. Lee & Low, 1998. (Grades 2–4)

For centuries, needlework has been part of Hmong culture. But it has only been since the war in Vietnam and Laos, which displaced many Hmong, that the new, narrative form of "story cloths" has emerged, a bridge between past and present. Dia Cha and her family experienced this displacement. Born in Laos, Dia fled with her family to Thailand as a child, spending four years in a refugee camp before arriving in the United States. Her story is shared by many Hmong Americans. As told through the story cloth stitched by her aunt and uncle, the Hmong people's search for freedom began long ago in China. *Dia's Story Cloth* explores many aspects of the Hmong experience from peace and war in Asia to new beginnings in America.

The Lotus Seed, by Sherry Garland. Illustrated by Tatsuro Kiuchi. Harcourt Brace Jovanovich, 1993. (Grades 2–4)

A young Vietnamese girl who is forced to leave Vietnam saves a lotus seed and carries it with her everywhere to remember a brave emperor she saw cry on the day of his abdication. The sight of the weeping emperor in the palace gardens touches her, so she takes a lotus seed in remembrance. She keeps the seed with her always, until one summer a grandson steals it and plants it in a mud pool near the family's American home. The following spring a lotus grows from the mud puddle, and in time the elderly woman gives a seed to each of her grandchildren, reserving one for herself.

Why Ducks Sleep on One Leg, by Sherry Garland. Illustrated by Jean Tseng and Mousien Tseng. Scholastic, 1993. (Grades 1–3)

Long ago in Vietnam, three ducks received only one leg each. Made fun of by the other animals, and unable to paddle well enough to catch fish or to move quickly on land, the ducks are very unhappy. With the help of a rooster and a goose, they send a written plea to the Jade Emperor and appeal to the village guardian to deliver it. However, the guardian solves the problem for the ducks by giving them extra golden legs from an incense burner. When he warns the ducks that they must guard their new legs carefully, the three start a new duck habit of tucking their golden legs up under their wings at night, safely out of sight.

ACROSTIC

Standards: 2, 4, 6, 14, 16, 21

Choose one of these countries from Asia: Japan, Korea, Vietnam, Thailand, or Nepal. Follow the pattern to include interesting facts about the country. Each phrase or sentence must begin with the first letter of the country's name.

Example:

C   hina contains Mount Everest, the highest mountain in the world.

H   istory of China goes back 4,000 years.

I   nvention of paper took place in China in AD 105.

N   ew Year's celebrations in China feature parades with dragons.

A   Great Wall in China took 1,700 years to complete.

Index

About the Author

NANCY POLETTE is an educator with over 40 years' experience. She has authored more than 150 professional books. She lives and works in Missouri, where she is a professor at Lindenwood University.